Credit Unions in the South Pacific

Studies in Finance

General Editor: Dr Neil Runcie, School of Economics, The University of New South Wales, Kensington, Sydney, Australia

1.* The Economics of Instalment Credit
SBN 340 09595 4
by Neil Runcie

2.* Credit Unions in the South Pacific—Australia, Fiji, New Zealand, Papua and New Guinea
SBN 340 09596 2
Edited by Neil Runcie

3.* The Management of Instalment Credit—The Australian Experience
SBN 340 09594 6
Edited by Neil Runcie

Other titles in preparation

* Conjoint titles in the series, *Australian Studies in Economics*, published by University of London Press Ltd

Credit Unions in the South Pacific—Australia, Fiji, New Zealand, Papua and New Guinea

Edited by Neil Runcie,
The University of New South Wales

UNIVERSITY OF LONDON PRESS LTD

SBN 340 09596 2

University of London Press Ltd
St Paul's House, Warwick Lane, London EC4

Printed and bound in England by
C. Tinling and Co. Ltd, Liverpool, London and Prescot

The Authors

G. A. Arbuckle, S.M., M.A. (Cantab.), Ph.D., Mt. St. Mary's Seminary, New Zealand

S. F. Arneil, President, Association of Credit Union Leagues of the South Pacific and President, Australian Federation of Credit Union Leagues

P. S. Ferguson, Registrar of Savings and Loans Societies, Papua and New Guinea

T. P. Fitzgerald, President, South Australian Credit Union League

D. G. Flynn, B. Com. (N.S.W.), Department of Education, N.S.W.

A. C. K. Lo, S.J., B.A. (Melb.), School of Economics, The University of New South Wales

M. J. Phillips, Asst. Manager, Papua & New Guinea Division, Reserve Bank of Australia

N. Runcie, B.Ec. (Syd.), Ph.D. (Lond.), School of Economics, The University of New South Wales

J. Ryan, Director, A.C.T. Credit Union League

C. Smith, Managing Director, New Zealand Credit Union League

R. G. Smith, Former Secretary, Western Australian Credit Union League

J. Stanford, B.Ec. (Syd.), School of Economics, University of Queensland

Preamble

'Credit unions teach people about money.'

Marion Ganey, S.J.

Our text is an insight into credit union objectives and achievements in the South Pacific by a great teacher of credit unions. This book is a first study of regional credit union development, a study of pioneering efforts to establish a social movement and a progress report.

Part I examines the nature of credit unions in the context of the South Pacific. S. F. Arneil's paper is an historic document in Australian credit union development. It is followed by a more general study of the economics of credit unions.

Part II comprises the regional studies which report variety in approach and experience. In this aspect of the work the help and collaboration of credit union leaders and government workers are gratefully acknowledged. It is an unfinished story.

Part III gives views on the prospects for growth. In particular the final chapter attempts some appraisal of the actual objectives and achievements.

Contents

A*

Part I The Nature of Credit Unions

1

The Place and Problems of Credit Unions in Instalment Credit Expansion*

by S. F. Arneil

1. The Nature of Credit Unions

A short while ago a bank manager confided in one of my friends that credit unions must fail because they had no stability, and must run out of both depositors and borrowers. He was quite sincere in his belief. Another of my friends, the director of a credit union, lunched with a public relations officer employed by one of the major finance companies. The publicity expert was unable to understand the reason for the enthusiasm of volunteer workers in what he considered to be an area of finance similar to that of a finance company. It was obvious that he had little or no knowledge of the credit union movement and of its philosopy. Recently, I read what I would call a rather vicious attack on credit unions, and on the credit union movement, in a periodical devoted to coal, steel, and the waterfront. I might say that in this latter article the new banking policy put forward with regard to advances on unsecured terms was also viciously attacked. It seems clear that although most people in Australia have at least now heard of credit unions, few, as yet, understand them.

What is a Credit Union?

A credit union is a group of people bound by some intangible bond of association, perhaps the bond of the same employer, the same religion, the same politics, the same trade, profession, hobby or the same type of misfortune (e.g. parents of sub-normal children have a credit union). The people who are bound by this invisible bond pledge themselves to save together, and lend their savings to one another at the lowest possible rates.

* Prepared for the First National Instalment Credit Conference, The University of New South Wales, May 1964 (revised 1967).

That is all really that there is in a credit union. It is not committed to any creed, politics or race. Credit unions are an idealistic movement, based on the co-operation principle of self-help. Although the movement is idealistic, it is also realistic in its approach and conscious of its responsibilities. Let me take you through the steps required to form a credit union and manage it; say a credit union in a factory employing 200 employees.

There is the Credit Union League in New South Wales whose function is to foster credit unions. First we approach *one* person in the factory, preferably a leader and not necessarily on the office side. We talk to him of credit unions. Once he is convinced of the advantage of the movement we ask him to interest three or four others and request that they study the subject from literature supplied to them by the League. Alternatively the approach to the League might have come from an employee or staff social club.

Our next step is to approach management and sell management the fact that a good credit union will result in better staff morale all round with resultant advantages to the business as a whole. The more forward-thinking managements agree to provide the facility of pay-roll deductions, and some a niche in an office where the credit union filing cabinet may be kept. The management having been persuaded that a credit union would be an advantage to both staff and management, our next task is to call a meeting of all staff, and talk to them. After the staff have expressed a desire for a credit union they are requested at the meeting to elect a 'rules committee' of say seven or eight people. It may be suggested to them to elect to the rules committee those of the staff whom they would like eventually to elect as directors. The rules committee will work hard on the rules with an officer or a director of the Credit Union League, until they are thoroughly conversant with the rules, and reasons for them. Model rules are available from the Registrar of Co-operative Societies, or the League, and require alteration only in those particular aspects which are peculiar to the new credit union (e.g. name, address, bond of association, which provides exact definition of eligibility either to be a member or a borrower). The next step is the calling of a formation meeting at which the business is the reading of a statement outlining the reasons which have indicated that the credit union would be successful, the adoption of rules, the election of the first board of directors, and the members of the first supervisory committee.

It will be explained to the meeting that membership will require the completion of an application form, the payment of a small entrance fee, usually 50 cents, and payment of, for example, \$10 share capital which will rank for dividend from profits made. It should be noted that the $10 share capital may be paid by instalments over a period to suit the member. The minimum share capital holding may be as low as $2. At the formation meeting the members may be advised that a rate of interest not exceeding 5 per cent per annum will be paid on all monies deposited with the credit union in excess of the $10 share capital. The official documents, as signed at the meeting, will then be sent to the Registrar, and registration is normally made within a fortnight. Upon registration of the credit union, it is open for business, and the education of members in the three main planks of the credit union begins:

Save Regularly
Borrow Wisely
Repay Promptly.

Saving precedes lending. When the first savings are sufficient, the first loans can be made. As the loans are repaid in regular instalments, further loans can be made to members. The new credit union is in business.

The board will work hard examining applications and granting loans and, with the experience of the League behind them, the directors must succeed. The members of the board do their credit union work in their own time, during lunch hour or other hours. They will be unpaid in the early years of the credit union but in later years may receive a small honorarium. This description should be sufficient to illustrate the elementary steps of forming and establishing a credit union. The ultimate success of a credit union will come only with a loyal pursuance of the philosophical ideals laid down by the early pioneers of this self-help movement.

Objects of Credit Unions

Credit unions obtain most of their money for lending from the savings of members. This is the prime purpose of a credit union—to teach thrift. People save in a credit union, not only for a rainy day, but to pay their bills and accounts which will accrue whether they save for them or not. For example, a householder must pay rates on his house, a car owner must pay insurance and registration. The credit union movement teaches that if the member does not adequately and regularly save for these items, he is living beyond his means. Thus, in the first place, the credit union movement attempts to teach people to save for the items for which they are bound to save. Secondly, we teach them to save for a rainy day, and to save for the things which they would like to have, such as a car or a new room on the house, or new furniture, or a deposit on a block of land and so on. This is where the money comes from and a prudent and careful credit union movement realises that people must be compensated in a material way by the payment of a rate of interest on the money which they save. We could not expect people to save without receiving some remuneration or at least the same remuneration as they would receive in a savings bank.

Early History

Credit unions were born out of misery, usury, famine and unemployment. In 1849, the crops failed in a little town in Bavaria and the farmers, as usual, pledged themselves to the usurers for their goods, their household equipment, their farm tools, and their future crops. A succession of crop failures had placed the farmers in the position where most of them were ready to walk off their farms and see the fruits of years of labour lost to them for ever. The mayor of the town, Wilhelm Raiffeisen, conceived a plan whereby the rich of the parish would pool their money and lend to the poor. However, the rich soon became tired of lending to the poor as the rates of repayment were so slow, and the scheme was abandoned. The mayor then called the farmers together and suggested to them that although they had little, they should pool what little they had for the common good. It was a good plan, and it worked and it was from this little village in Bavaria that credit unions sprang. The farmers pooled their savings and lent them to one another at the very lowest possible rates of interest, and this philosophy has remained to this day.

Raiffeisen was a Protestant and his movement spread from his village throughout Germany to Canada where it was embraced by Desjardins, a French-Canadian Catholic. Desjardins was a parliamentary reporter who was for ever distressed at the misery in Canada, but particularly in the Province of Quebec at that time, and at the inability of the poorer classes either to obtain cheap finance or to rid themselves of the yoke of heavy interest repayments with which most of them were continuously burdened. In 1901, Desjardins began a credit union in Levis, in Quebec, and from this beginning they have spread throughout Canada to such an extent that in some areas of Canada, even the banking system takes second place to the credit unions. Desjardins also formed the first credit union at New Hampshire in America in 1909. The American movement grew and was fostered by Filene, a millionaire and a Jew. He spent one million dollars in the early years of the movement to foster credit unions in America. His enthusiasm inspired followers of this new movement and credit unions spread throughout America. Credit unions in America really began to march with the foundation of the Credit Union Extension Bureau in 1921. It was financed entirely by Edward A. Filene, and a great American, Roy F. Bergengren, was hired to head the Bureau. In 1934, the Credit Union National Association was organised and this is the association with which almost all the credit union leagues in the world are now federated. The generosity of Filene may be better understood if one reviews the conversion of a million dollars in 1909 to comparable value in today's currency. It would convert to many millions of dollars.

Types of Credit Unions

(a) *Community credit unions.* Community credit unions are those whose bond of association embraces members of a particular community. The community credit union is the ultimate ideal in credit unions for the fostering of a strong community spirit. It has not been found practicable in this country to establish and commence a community credit union in itself. Rather they are more easily built up from the local parish credit union. Community credit unions cover all members of the community irrespective of calling or creed.

(b) *Parish credit unions.* These credit unions embrace within their bond of association members of a particular church living within the limitation of the parish boundaries. Parish credit unions have been found to be one of the most inspired types of credit union, wherein the office bearers work unceasingly without remuneration for the benefit of members. Parish credit unions in N.S.W. have a very successful record and generally speaking maintain a first-class service to members. Three former parish credit unions own their own buildings and have full-time salaried staff to look after the members. Parish credit unions exist in N.S.W. attached to a variety of churches of different denominations.

(c) *Industrial credit unions.* Industrial credit unions may be divided into two groups: the first, and at one time the most numerous, being those credit unions which have been formed within public service departments or instrumentalities, and the other being those which have been formed in free enterprise industry. Public service credit unions do not usually attain the ideal of service usually rendered by other credit unions. There appears to be, in many cases, a hesitancy in directing the credit unions to expand their service by payment of full-time staff, provision of offices, and similar implications of restrained growth. It has been found that the 'public service' type of credit union does not interest itself as much as others in actual promotion of the movement to members, the emphasis being more on the borrowing and investing benefits, rather than the saving benefits. Industrial credit unions in private enterprise, on the other hand, appear to be extremely successful in this country. There has grown up a tremendous spirit of service in this latter type of credit union, with an eagerness to exploit the functions of publicity and service to the greatest degree. The hesitancy of credit unions in public service organisations to lend to members who are not 'permanent' does not apply to the industrial credit unions in private enterprise where the members, generally speaking, have no lien on a job and may be dismissed, put off, or retrenched at any time. This potential loss of employment has *not* deterred the advance of this type of credit union, and as yet there have been no significant problems with regard to delinquent loans. Another type of industrial credit union is that based on a trade union.

(d) *Other types of credit union.* There appears to be no limit to the types of credit union which can be formed in Australia. There is a credit union in the Royal Blind Institute of N.S.W. where the information and material are recorded in Braille. We have credit unions amongst national groups (e.g. the Russian community of Sydney) and in professional groups such as architects. The limit will only be reached when all people in Australia have availed themselves of their benefit.

Credit Union National Association

There are sixty-seven Leagues in 'CUNA' which is the focal point of the training and education of credit unions and credit union personnel throughout the world, and for the preparation and supply of material used in the credit union movement. The Credit Union National Association, which has many departments, includes the World Extension Department which functions primarily as a means of extending the movement to peoples throughout the world. CUNA, as it is called, is financed entirely by dues from credit unions throughout the world.

In Australia, the rate of dues payable to the Leagues is approximately 65 cents per member per year, of which 9 U.S. cents per member is paid to CUNA. The latter dues are set by the Annual General Meeting of CUNA which delegates attend from all over the world. The credit union ideal recently caught the attention of UNESCO which adopted it as an easy and satisfactory method of assisting countries where there were under-developed peoples. The United States Government, pressed by the fear of communism in South America, also recognised the movement as one which, by the teaching of self-help and the automatic raising of living standards, would be a prime weapon against the spread of communism. Accordingly, the United States Government makes grants to CUNA which are used by CUNA to assist the people of South America and the West Indies. The programmes, particularly in South America, have been most spectacular. In Peru, where in great areas the people were little better, and at times worse off, than the poorest of peasants, they now walk in dignity, and with freedom from want, as a result of credit union activities. Credit unions and their ideals have taught these people that they are quite capable of managing their own affairs. Credit unions serve all types of people. I shall indicate below some of the more unusual groups of people outside Australia who have benefited from the use of credit unions.

All Types of People may be served by Credit Unions

In Canada, the Dhukabors have gained a notoriety which is often the despair of the Canadian people and, particularly, the Canadian Government. You may well recall some of the more peculiar problems associated with this race of ex-Russians. One of their more light-hearted gestures is occasionally to burn everything in their villages, including the clothes they are wearing, and, clad only in their birthday suits, start life afresh. I personally saw one of their villages in Canada, which, for no apparent reason, had been completely razed to the ground. The North West Mounted Police had been called but had been too late to stop the destruction. If left to themselves, the Dhukabors could possibly remain, by our standards, completely anti-social, but, believe it or not, there are now credit unions among some of the Dhukabors and the change in outlook has been remarkable. They now accept the responsibility of looking after their own money and have some very successful credit unions.

In the south of Texas and on the border of Mexico there are many very poor people, who have lost their self-respect; they were, and are, despised by people of means and those more fortunate in the community. The poor people I mention make up the illiterate section of the community and have little to offer other than their hands. Through the weight of usury over a very long time, and lack of intervention by governments or other institutions to raise their living standards, many continue to be impoverished. These people are mostly transitory workers, fruit pickers and the like, people perhaps in whom one would not once have placed a great deal of trust. This area was investigated by CUNA representatives and, after a long period, the first of what we now call 'low income' group credit unions was started with spectacular results in its benefits to members. The people in the credit unions have been completely revitalised; they now have a sense of purpose and have become good citizens with a stake in the country.

In Alabama, I personally saw the black and the white problem and it is a problem upon which I would not dare to offer an opinion. However, I can say something. It was an instalment credit economy for many negroes I met in Alabama. It was the natural thing for the high-pressure salesmen to sell a new car to the negro. It was natural that the negro be offered a car, refrigerator, television set, etc. on practically no down payment and easy terms, and that he would accept this offer to increase his living standards. The rate of repossession of these articles was unbelievable to me, but it was patiently explained by some of the salesmen that quick repossession and a quick resale was the only way in which they could make a proper living. The coloured people I saw on this matter accepted it as a matter of fact that the expensive and better articles which they could buy would only be theirs for short periods. This was their life. In one store for coloured people, I found interest rates for goods on instalment credit being charged at usurers' rates. It was quite obvious that it was to the disadvantage of the stores to sell the goods for cash. It is into this field of frightful usury that credit unions in Alabama have moved under the direction of the Alabama Credit Union League, a League previously composed of white credit unions. The results have been a revelation. White people working solidly with black people for the common good have done, and will do, much to break down racial intolerance and, at the same time, the raising of living standards for these people has been recognised as a goal for all of Alabama.

Finally, let me mention Fiji. Here the credit union movement was fostered by a Jesuit priest who was invited to the country by the Governor, Sir Ronald Garvey. Sir Ronald had previously seen the work of this Jesuit in British Honduras. Whereas the Fijian was once considered to be a man of little worldliness with no grasp of financial matters, he is now lifting himself to a better world by the use of the credit union movement and perhaps even more important is financing a school for the training in Fiji of credit union leaders from islands surrounding Fiji.

2. Management of the Credit Union

The management of the credit union is vested in directors, normally no more than nine, who are elected by the members on a system of one vote per member. The directors usually hold office for two years retiring by rotation each alternate year, being eligible to stand again for office if they so desire. The directors have full power to manage the affairs of the credit union, but provision is also made for a quota of the members to call an extraordinary general meeting of the credit union, if it is suspected that the directors are not performing their duties in accordance with the law and in the best interest of members. Payment of directors' fees is discouraged for the first years of the credit union's existence and this has the advantage of attracting only those persons inspired with the credit union philosophy of helping others.

The new Credit Union Act will include many clauses regarding directors and their obligations, all of which are designed to ensure that the credit union is run without bias and without profit to the directors (e.g. a clause will be inserted that directors who are more than two months in arrears on loans must vacate their directorships). The reason for this is obvious: a director who is in arrears in his loan repayments would be loath to press for strong action against any member who is similarly placed. Again, to ensure that directors attend their meetings, the Act already provides that the absence of a director from three successive meetings without leave automatically dismisses him from the board.

Rates of Interest on Savings

In the early years of the credit union movement in New South Wales, many credit unions were in public service departments, where the work of the credit union was somewhat limited, and expenses were correspondingly very low. As a result of this, and the mistaken impression that taxation was not payable on profits, there was little appreciation of the need to provide for contingencies. The 'deposit' system at this time had not been introduced and the profits were distributed almost entirely by way of dividends on shares. To reduce taxation on credit unions (after it began to be levied) the system of 'deposits' earning a set rate of interest was introduced which thereby reduced profits and therefore taxation. For this reason a high rate of interest on deposits was struck, leaving, in many cases, little or nothing for administrative expenses, promotions and reserves.

Rates of interest on deposits were in some cases as high as 8 per cent but the majority of credit unions adopted the rate of 6 per cent per annum on the minimum monthly balance. The introduction of such a rate attracted not only people interested in the credit union movement, but also the investor looking for high rates of return, coupled with a virtual 'at call' advantage. Here again, many credit unions made the mistake of accepting extremely large deposits without encouraging the regular depositors in the lower income group. The large investment virtually placed many small credit unions on a razor's edge, inasmuch as a large withdrawal often meant a curtailment of the lending of money until sufficient loan repayments and further deposits had been received to restore the liquidity of the credit union.

A big disadvantage of the high interest rates previously adopted, and in some cases still adhered to, is that they have become the master and not the servant of the directors of some credit unions. Although the growth of the credit unions requires more service for members with consequent increase in administrative expenses, some directors are actually too timid to reduce interest rates on deposits for fear of incurring a loss of confidence of the members, with subsequent withdrawal of savings. This attitude is in marked contrast to the recent action of the Permanent Building Societies which reduced interest on deposits to 5½ per cent per annum without any noticeable increase in withdrawals of deposits resulting. However, once the dangers inherent in high interest rates on deposits became apparent, the New South Wales Credit Union League made recommendations to the credit unions to reduce interest rates. In many cases the interest rates were reduced and at the same time the League, which comprises the majority of the credit unions in New South Wales, has recommended to new credit unions a maximum deposit interest of 5 per cent. This is the same rate as the dividend usually payable on shares.

Rates of Interest on Loans

In the early movement in New South Wales, and probably in most other states, there was great diversity in the method of calculating interest on loans. Many credit unions adopted the system of a 'flat' rate of interest whereby the total amount of interest was added to the loan at the outset and the whole of the loan plus interest was repaid by equal instalments. A disadvantage, and perhaps the biggest of all for credit unions which have not the facility of payroll deductions, is that *losses of interest begin to accrue under this system immediately the loan repayments fall into arrears*. This fact is well recognised by all lending institutions and penalty provisions are often applied by them to counteract it. In credit unions, penalties in the form of fines at a daily rate of, say, 2 cents a day, were often quoted as a deterrent to late repayments, irrespective of amounts.

However, as a workable measure the calculation of penalties and fines is a task which is sometimes difficult in credit unions, particularly when the office bearers are volunteers. Again, the imposition of fines, which are usually far in excess of the true rate of interest, does not prove a deterrent to a delinquent borrower and the imposition of fines *has not been found* to encourage people to pay promptly. It has been found on the other hand to be a source of ill-will to the credit union by the delinquent borrower.

The answer to these inadequacies as now recommended by the New South Wales Credit Union League is to follow the system adopted by the Credit Union National Association and most credit unions throughout the world. It is the calculation of interest on the *outstanding balance of loan*, for the period. The simplicity of this method is particularly suited to the credit union movement and directors of credit unions are now able to ascertain, as required, the actual amount of earned interest. Although this system provides for the correct 'payment' of interest by the borrower, he still repays his loan and interest by equal instalments as before.

The instalments are calculated by the method previously used, that is, taking a 'flat' rate of say 5½ per cent interest, adding it to the principal and dividing the whole by the estimated number of repayments. The small degree of error in this calculation is adjusted on the last instalment. It is perhaps in the method of calculating interest on the monthly 'outstanding balance' that the credit union movement holds an advantage over most private lending institutions operating in instalment financing in Australia.

Calculation of Earned and Unearned Interest

One of the most unsatisfactory aspects of credit union accounting in the earlier years of the movement was the loose method of assessing earned and unearned income. During this period the 'flat' rate system of interest was popular and under this system repayments were calculated by adding to the amount of the loan the total interest for the period and dividing the whole by the number of instalments. Accurate calculations of *earned* interest became a problem immediately the period of the loan extended into a second financial year and this became even more of a problem as the loan limits were raised and the period of repayment extended.

Volunteer secretaries and directors made hard work of the problem, but the difficulties were not confined to the smaller credit unions and it was found that few credit unions were correctly calculating the earned interest. At one time the biggest credit union in Australia was simply apportioning the total interest in equal instalments over the period of the loan. Again, another large credit union which made it a practice to assist borrowers by consolidating the balance of a loan with a further loan found the calculation of earned income such a trial that, as a matter of administration only, it did not allow rebates of interest on consolidations and the borrower therefore paid heavily for the privilege of consolidating one loan with another. The adoption of the 'outstanding balance' system of charging interest has solved the problem of calculating unearned interest, as under this system the interest earned is known at the end of each month. The advantage to the board of directors for budgeting purposes is obvious and better management of the credit union is the direct result.

Audit and Supervision

In New South Wales, credit unions must employ a registered public accountant, one who is not a member of the credit union, to act as auditor. The Registrar of Co-operative Societies has inspectors who also inspect the books and look for discrepancies in them. The Credit Union Advisory Committee is so conscious of this matter that it has recommended that the new Act make it obligatory for the Registrar of Co-operative Societies to render an annual inspection of each credit union's books and that, in the event of the Registrar having insufficient inspectors to perform this task, outside auditors be commissioned or employed by his department to do so. In addition to these precautions, however, the Credit Union League strongly advocates the setting up of a supervisory committee by members of each credit union, completely independent of the board of directors and answerable direct to the members of the credit union. Again, the Credit Union Advisory Committee has recommended that the new Act contain a stipulation that an annual report of the credit union be sent to every member, so that they may take such action as they think fit, if the reports disclose deficiencies.

Securities

It is said, and it is true, that a man's character is the most important security he can give when applying for a credit union loan. This security has been tried and *not* found wanting. However, the credit union as a whole must protect itself from undue risks, particularly against contingencies beyond the control of the member, such as loss of a job. A limit of $800 has been prescribed by the N.S.W. Registrar of Co-operative Societies as the ceiling of an unsecured loan, this ceiling having been granted on an application by the Credit Union League. The prescribing of such a ceiling, however, does not automatically entitle the borrower to such an amount, and credit unions will carefully consider whether security in hand, or by personal guarantee or indemnity, should be taken. In addition it is not unusual to insist that credit union savings of the member be temporarily 'frozen' as additional security. Securities for amounts above $800 must be other than personal, and registered Bills of Sale are quite usual and in cases of large loans a second mortgage may be accepted.

Reserves

The stability of the credit union movement and its ultimate success and ability to ride over bad times, such as recessions, may be assured by building up and maintaining adequate reserves. Lessons which have been learnt by the failure of many financial institutions in Australia since World War Two guide the leaders of this new movement and the Registrar of Co-operative Societies. The Co-operation Act, as it now stands, provides for a transfer of 5 per cent of the net profit to a statutory reserve and ensures that the transfer is converted into trust funds or prescribed securities. However, since the introduction of the deposit system as a straight-out method of reducing tax, the credit unions have, to some extent, lost sight of the importance of reserves in their efforts to keep payments of taxation to a minimum.

The directors of the League have now made it a policy that the Act should be interpreted to mean that the *mere fixing of a rate of interest payable on deposits is not sufficient reason to postpone or prevent the transfer of an adequate percentage of profit to statutory reserves.* It follows that, were the rate of interest on deposits to be placed high enough to ensure that there were no profits left after all the direct expenses had been paid, then, as a simple consequence, there would be nothing left to place to reserves. The League board interprets the deposit system with relation to reserves to mean that not only is a transfer to be made of 5 per cent of the disclosed net profit, but that perhaps 5 per cent of the amount of interest payable on deposits should also be transferred (i.e. that the high rate of interest on deposits is not to be considered solely as an item of expense necessary to attain the income). It appears from annual reports that credit unions are now becoming a little more reserve conscious, and a minimum goal of 7½ per cent of gross assets is the current objective. It has been pointed out by the League that, where the reserves are made up from profits, then any income from the reserves is clear profit to the credit union, because there is no interest payable to a member, the reserves belonging to the credit union as a whole.

Bad Debts and the Credit Union

It is a conviction of the credit union movement that most people are honest and delinquent loans are, it seems, few. In almost every case, the directors of the credit union will know the borrower, will know of his needs and of his capacity to repay. This tends to reduce the possibility of bad debts arising. However, the credit unions are cautious enough, and have sufficient sense of responsibility to their members, to take all adequate precautions to protect their members against bad debts. Guarantees and indemnities are usual for amounts up to $800, whilst security other than personal is required for loans above that amount. Statistics regarding bad debts in credit unions in Australia are not yet available but, from what little we know of this subject, it would appear that they are extremely small. The Credit Union National Association's latest statistics on bad debts give a figure of less than half of 1 per cent of total loans for the movement.

3. The League and Its Services

New South Wales Credit Union League

The N.S.W. Credit Union League was founded in 1956 with representatives of twelve credit unions. For the first few years it led a fairly precarious existence. It has now reached a stage where it exercises a sizable influence on the lives of over 100,000 members and their families, and to a lesser extent on the economy of this state. In 1963, delegates from seventy credit unions attended the annual convention at which plans were laid for a more rapid expansion of the movement. In 1967, over 180 credit unions were affiliated with the N.S.W. League.

The League forms the majority of credit unions now being registered in N.S.W. and this is likely to continue. It is unfortunate that the League is hampered by such scarcity of funds, but it will continue to grow. The League is a focal point of the credit union movement in N.S.W.; it maintains its own supply department, provides expert advice, will attend board meetings, chapter meetings, education sessions, and so on, for any credit union in the League. It manages the loan protection service and the newly created Central Division. The President of the League is a member of the Credit Union Advisory Committee and the League is particularly active in seeking legislative change. In the defence of its principles and in the extension of the movement, the League has demonstrated its efficiency via television, radio and newspaper publicity. The League maintains the best library of credit union films in Australia and, as far as is known, has the biggest library of credit union literature in Australia.

Life Savings

Investigation is proceeding by the N.S.W. Credit Union League into the possibility of providing 'life savings insurance' for credit union members. To introduce 'life savings' it will be necessary for the League to negotiate a policy of this special type of insurance with an established company in Australia or, if this fails, to establish its own insurance company. Life savings is a service under which the credit union pays to the next of kin of a deceased member a sum up to twice the amount standing to the credit of his or her shares and deposit account, depending on the amount standing to the credit of the deposit account and the age of the member. The provision of life savings overseas has been found to create a great incentive to save, and has been of great assistance to next of kin on the death of a member. A particular application of this kind of insurance, in North America, is the use of it for the purpose of building an estate for a deceased member. For example, a member, in that area, may borrow $2,000 for the express purpose of placing it in his deposit account. On his death, his loan is cancelled under the loan protection policy and his savings of $2,000 are doubled and become payable to his or her beneficiaries. The 'life savings' provision is one of the normal services to credit union members overseas and is considered to be a desirable feature for members in Australia.

Loan Protection—Die and the Debt Dies with You

Credit unions, being non-profit 'service' organisations, regard 'loan protection' or the principle of the 'debt dies with the debtor' as one of their best achievements. Under a comprehensive insurance policy administered by the Credit Union League, most credit unions insure against the death of the borrower. Under the principle of *no hidden charges* the cost of premiums is paid by the credit unions and *not* by the member, so that next of kin and the credit union stand to gain by this service. The next of kin gain by being relieved of a debt at a time when the borrower (usually the breadwinner) has died, and the credit union is spared the harrowing, and often unpleasant, task of attempting to recover monies outstanding on the death of the borrower. It is interesting to note that a similar protection for home owners is being introduced into the Commonwealth Legislation under the title of 'mortgage protection'. The credit unions in the N.S.W. Credit Union League have had this protection for their members for some years.

League—The Central Division

Temporary surpluses of savings or shortages of loan monies are problems which will always remain with individual credit unions. It is only by a bonding together of these surpluses that this problem may be overcome, and, following overseas practice, the Credit Union League has established a Central Division to which most credit unions will eventually belong. The Central Division is, in fact, a clearing-house for surplus monies and a bank or source of supply from which credit unions requiring money may draw. There is no doubt that the Central will eventually have assets running into millions of dollars which will grow with the movement. As a prerequisite to joining the Central Division, member credit unions are required to lodge with the Central 2 per cent of their gross assets, growing to a minimum of 5 per cent of their gross assets within twelve months, and on this money they will receive interest at 5 per cent per annum. This 5 per cent lodgment must be maintained within three months of the issue of each subsequent audited balance sheet. Provision has been made for negotiation with individual credit unions where the initial share capital of 5 per cent of gross assets could cause hardship.

All monies surplus to the 5 per cent lodgment will bear a rate of interest not more than $\frac{1}{4}$ per cent per annum of that which would be paid for a similar deposit in a 'fixed deposit' in a savings bank. This does not appear to be a great incentive, but we believe it will be enough, and we believe that the credit unions will see that we are trying to be realistic in our approach to a problem which is universal in financial institutions. Provided that the appropriate authority is placed in the rules of the credit union, it may borrow from the Central, at any time, amounts in excess of $2,000 and up to an amount not exceeding 25 per cent of its assets. Credit unions are already authorised to borrow up to $2,000 under the Act. The rate of interest at present on loans from the Central has been fixed at 7 per cent per annum which, although it may sound high, has been fixed for the purpose of deterring credit unions from using the Central as a permanent source of cheap money. Credit unions borrowing from the Central will be required to give a charge over the whole of their assets.

4. Legislation and Government Influence

Legislation

Special legislation governing credit unions in Australia is almost non-existent and the movement is governed by various Acts which were designed basically to cover consumer co-operatives and building societies. In 1960 the N.S.W. Government appointed a Credit Union Advisory Committee to advise the Government on matters concerning credit unions with particular reference to legislation. This committee, which consisted of then four and now five members under the chairmanship of the Registrar of Co-operative Societies, has worked steadily towards the framing of improved legislation for credit unions. At the annual general meeting of the N.S.W. Credit Union League in 1961, it was unanimously resolved that the Government be pressed for a separate Credit Union Act in order that the infant movement might be both fostered and protected. The resolution, which was endorsed by the Credit Union Advisory Committee, was accepted by Mr Landa, the Minister for Co-operative Societies. To assist in the preparation of an Act to cover Australian conditions, every credit union act in the world was examined and their best points were studied by the Credit Union Advisory Committee. The work has now been completed and the proposals will be presented to the Government for incorporation into a Bill for Credit Unions. A list of the Acts under which credit unions in Australia are governed is as follows:

New South Wales—Co-operation Act 1923–1963
Victoria—Co-operation Act 1961
Queensland—Co-operative Societies Act 1946–1962[1]
South Australia—Industrial and Provident Societies Act 1923–1954 (as amended)
Western Australia—Co-operative and Provident Societies Act 1903–1961
Tasmania—Co-operative Industrial Societies Act 1928 and amendments
Australian Capital Territory—Co-operative Societies Ordinance 1939–1963.

Government Interest

(a) *New South Wales.* The N.S.W. Government showed only an academic interest in credit unions until two incidents sparked off an interest which has resulted in the fostering of the credit union movement becoming a part of official government policy. The first interest began with the acceptance by the Honourable A. Landa, Minister for Housing and Co-operative Societies, of an invitation to attend a credit union dinner given for promotional purposes. The dinner was for the members of the Australian Broadcasting Commission Staff Association Credit Union and,

[1] New co-operative legislation specifically recognising credit unions was introduced in 1968. *Ed.*

at the dinner, credit union films were screened. Mr Landa was quick to see the limitless potential for good in the movement. He acted quickly with encouragement on every side including a recommendation for a small subsidy to the N.S.W. Credit Union League, the setting up of the Credit Union Advisory Committee and, by his advocacy, an adoption by the Government of an atmosphere of support for the movement. The second incident, which completed the chain necessary for the complete fulfilment of the new government policy of sponsorship of the credit union movement, was the occurrence of a visit to Canada (including Novia Scotia) and the U.S.A. by the Registrar of Co-operative Societies, Mr A. R. Crosky. Mr Crosky was not overseas on credit union matters but on an investigation of certain aspects of the building society movement. It was in North America that he came face to face with the credit union movement and its obvious potential: for raising the real value of money for the wage earner by the teaching of thrift, and with the second advantage of availability of ready finance to honest but 'unsecured' workers. Mr Crosky, like Mr Landa, adopted the movement as his own and threw himself into the task of doing everything possible on a departmental level for the promotion of the movement and the protection of the members' savings. It is perhaps not usual for a new venture to be adopted so vigorously by a Minister and his Departmental Head but the credit union philosophy does this to people.

(b) *Queensland.* The Premier of Queensland, Mr Nicklin, has expressed interest in the movement after attending a credit union dinner as did Mr Landa. However, the movement in Queensland is so much in its infancy that it cannot give the necessary follow-up to any public interest displayed and it could be some time before the movement really finds its feet.

(c) *Other States.* There has been little government interest displayed so far.

(d) *Commonwealth Government.* The Commonwealth Government has as yet given no indication of official interest in the movement, although the N.S.W. Government has made approaches to it through Mr Landa to inspire Commonwealth interest in the promotion of credit unions on a national level. One obstacle perhaps could be the fact that each state has an Act of some sort governing credit unions on a state level. However, in the U.S.A. there is a Federal Credit Union Act which allows credit unions to be chartered under its provisions even though there may be a credit union act in that particular state. The constitutional position in that country, however, is rather different from ours and we must find our own way towards the development of any Australia-wide organisation.

Government Supervision

Oversight of credit unions by the Registrar of Co-operative Societies is provided for under the Co-operation Act. The Act contains adequate machinery for the protection of the members' savings, but the New South Wales Credit Union League considers that the provisions of the Act are insufficient in themselves unless the appropriate government department, i.e. the Registry of Co-operative Societies, conducts regular examinations of all credit unions, especially in these early years of the movement and of a credit union's existence.

This protection, or perhaps paternalism, is essential to a movement in which the accounts are kept by people who are not always skilled in accountancy. This may appear to be a disadvantage, but perhaps, if we consider the losses of millions of pounds of the public's money in company crashes since World War Two, we could venture the opinion that people with little experience in money management do not have a monopoly on the problem of money 'mismanagement'. However, in recognising the fact that credit union treasurers may not have a great deal of skill in accounting for monies received and disbursed and in financial management, the prescribed accounts required to be kept by credit unions have been made as simple as possible without reducing their effectiveness.

Inspectors from the Registry of Co-operative Societies are trained to act as advisors to the credit unions in addition to their normal duties of examination of the accounts as a measure of safeguard to the members. It is unfortunate that with the rapid growth of the movement the number of inspectors were at one stage insufficient to carry out the number of inspections considered desirable. The Credit Union Advisory Committee noted this problem and made recommendations to the Minister to assist with the examination of credit unions. Fidelity guarantees for directors, treasurers and staff handling monies are required under the Act as a further protection for members' funds.

It might be as well to illustrate certain requirements under the Act with regard to credit unions. In examining them it can be seen that they have been framed specifically to meet the requirements of a movement which, in the main, is conducted by unpaid directors and by people who may not normally understand the rigid provisions laid down under Acts framed to control business undertakings.

Disregarding legal terminology, the following circumstances in which the Registrar may wind up a credit union may be of interest:

(a) When the number of members is reduced to less than seven or in the case of an association or union of associations to less than two.
(b) When the society has not commenced business within a year of registration or has suspended business for a period of more than six months.
(c) When the society has wilfully, and after notice from the Registrar, violated the provisions of this Act or of the regulations or of the rules of the society.
(d) When the society has not made and transmitted to the Registrar the alterations, if any, in its rules as required by the Act.
(e) When there are, and have been for a period of one month immediately before the date of the registrar's certificate, *insufficient directors of the society to constitute a quorum* as provided by the rules of the society.
(f) Following an inquiry pursuant to the provisions of the Act into the affairs of a society or the working and financial condition of a society, that in the interests of members or creditors of the society, the society should be wound up.

Division 2 of Part 6 of the Act sets out a number of offences against the Act and any proceedings instituted for the purpose of punishment for a breach of the provisions of the Act could be instituted by the Registrar who has the obligation to police the provisions of the Act. The Sections of the Act covering offences are Sections 101–113 and cover such offences as:

(a) refusing to furnish information lawfully required by the Registrar or by any other person under the Act;
(b) contravention of the restrictions imposed by the Act;
(c) carrying on business with too few members;
(d) using a name other than the society's registered name;
(e) taking money in consideration of allotment of shares before a society is registered;
(f) handing out false copies of rules;
(g) falsification of balance sheets, etc.;
(h) misappropriation of a society's property; and,
(i) failure to comply with any requirements of the Act generally.

Part 8 of the Act which commences at Section 115 makes provision for the administration of the Act. The Registrar, or inspectors appointed by the governor, may inspect personally, or through such inspectors, any minutes or books, or any report into the affairs of the society, obtain from any bank in which the funds of the society are deposited, or invested, a statement of the amount of such deposit or investment, and any other particulars required by him to be furnished. Section 118 provides that the Registrar *shall* on the application of a majority of the board, or of not less than one third of the members, call a special meeting of the society or hold an enquiry into the affairs of the society. Section 121 provides that the Registrar, and any inspector appointed by the Governor, may, for the purpose of any enquiry or inspection, administer an oath or give notice in writing requiring attendance of any person at the enquiry for the production of relevant books or documents, or require a director or other officer of the society to furnish information relating to the affairs of the society. Any such person failing to comply shall be guilty of an offence and liable to a penalty not exceeding $600 or imprisonment for a period not exceeding six months or to both. There is, of course, always an appeal from the decision of the Registrar to the courts. Under Section 123 the Registrar must make a yearly report of his proceedings and of the principal matters transacted by him during the preceding year, which is laid before Parliament.

Published Statistics by Government Departments

It is unfortunate that published statistics by state government departments, other than New South Wales and Victoria, are of little use for compilation of accurate aggregate figures. Recommendations will be made to the various state governments to correct this.

5. The Problems of the Credit Union in Australia

The Credit Union in Australia

It was as far back as 1924 that the New South Wales Government wrote to the new Credit Union Extension Bureau, asking for information on credit unions. It was probably as a result of the information supplied that provision for urban credit societies was included in the Co-operation Act, as amended just prior to World War Two. After the War, the first credit union was founded in Sydney by Kevin Yates, a man who had served in the R.A.A.F. in Canada, and who had come into contact with, and who had been impressed by, the credit union ideal. The first credit union was called the Universal Credit Union and was designed to serve Catholics in Sydney.[2]

[2] On earlier credit union formation in New South Wales and Victoria see chapters 7 and 8 below. *Ed.*

It is still functioning and is a successful credit union with its own building and paid officers.

There are now credit unions in all states and statistics are given later. Now what type of people in Australia are served by credit unions? Are they poor people or wealthy people, idealists or just ordinary people? We have found that all types and classes of people belong to and manage successful credit unions. We have university professors in the University of New South Wales, bonded together in a credit union which embraces all staff in the University, from the lowest paid to the highest. We have 'white collar workers' in their own credit union, 'blue collar workers', a credit union for clergymen, credit unions for various religious groups, for racial groups, for professional groups, for people with similar misfortunes, for example, parents of subnormal children. There seems to be no end to the types of people or areas which can be embraced by credit unions.

Education of Directors in Methods and in Philosophy

The problems which have become evident in the new movement have arisen mainly from one aspect—lack of education of directors in the methods and philosophy of the credit union movement. The difficulties were not unexpected and have occurred in other countries but the regrettable fact is that we have not benefited as much as we should have done from mistakes made, and since corrected over a period of many years, in other countries where the movement is flourishing. In an economy such as ours, private enterprise continually holds up the rate of profit as a measure of success and we are conditioned to accept this criterion. Little thought has perhaps been given to the fact that a high rate of interest, say on finance company debentures, can only be paid to lenders *if a high rate of interest is charged to borrowers*. 'Co-operative thinking' is incompatible with one individual reaping extensive gains from others' misfortunes but rather aims at 'just' recompense for work performed and money invested. The realisation of this objective and others to be mentioned is one of the problems of the new movement.

Geographical Problems and the Lack of Leaders

The lack of leaders in a new movement coupled with the size of our continent, present difficulties which realistically constitute a barrier to rapid expansion. The answer may be in the more widespread adoption of the movement, and support from churches, trade unions, governments and employers. Were adequate support forthcoming, the training of potential leaders could be done more readily on an area basis, and thus enable the establishment of credit unions in new areas. If, for example, the Hospital Employees' Association of N.S.W. were to support the movement, whole areas or electorates could be covered by bringing together interested members from each hospital of any size in the area, and training the groups of potential leaders together. In this way, five or six credit unions might be established simultaneously. The problem of distance may be illustrated by a recent visit to Broken Hill by the Manager of the Credit Union League, an officer of the Registry of Co-operative Societies, and myself. Advance publicity of the visit was highly successful. Our three-day visit was made up of a series of meetings with various employers, local government officials, and as many representative groups as possible. A public meeting was also held and the imprimatur of the Barrier Industrial Council for the introduction of the movement, if requested by the workers, was obtained.

The city of Broken Hill is what we would consider to be a perfect city in which to establish credit unions, and we estimated the turnover in savings and loans in Broken Hill could reach $3,000,000 per annum. We had the nucleus of three or four credit unions established, prior to our leaving the city. There are as yet *no* credit unions in Broken Hill. With our departure the enthusiasm faded or there was a reluctance to establish a credit union without the backing or support of competent leaders on the spot. Opportunities to establish credit unions in areas remote from Sydney will be limited until more leaders are trained to promote them.

Management and the Credit Union

Management has found that a good credit union is good for its own business. Employees who are managing their own money and are eligible for cheap money when required are better workers than those who may be worried with financial troubles. Experience has shown that an investigation of eight thousand credit unions in the manufacturing industries in the U.S.A. brought out four major benefits from credit unions. These were:

(a) fewer worker money problems;
(b) higher worker morale;
(c) greater productivity; and,
(d) better leadership development.

One administrative problem, that of coping with garnishees or wage attachments, is lessened when a credit union is available to the employees. It also induces greater sense of responsibility, leadership and loyalty. With credit unions working so well in the interests of management, there is a possibility that management may wish to participate in running them. Any attempt to gain entry (by making subsidies for example) should be discouraged. Participation could involve attempts to control its lending policies through nominees on the board, and, if this happens, the credit union is in danger of failing; credit unions are democracy in action and management has found them not a tool but an ally.

Management Control of the Credit Union

The credit union which accepts a management nominee on the board of directors, either officially or unofficially, has negated one of the first principles of the credit union, i.e. that each member has one vote and that directors are elected by the members. How naïve would be he who would say that the management nominee would exert no pressure on the credit union. His very presence at a board meeting could be an inhibiting factor when decisions are made regarding loans to members. For example, a member applying for a loan is required to make a statutory declaration giving all sources of income, including, if he is married, the income of his wife. Sources of income will include income earned outside the company's employ. There are good reasons for requiring this information. It will assist the board to assess the ability of the borrower to repay his loan and without this information many a loan application would be refused.

Now, we come to the position where the company nominee has learned that one of the employees has sources of income outside his salary or wages from the company. This knowledge could be detrimental to the borrower in his opportunities for promotion within the company. Again, were the company nominee to take this information outside the board of directors of the credit union, and he must be under some obligation to do so, another precept of the credit union, the rule of confidential dealings with members, would be broken. Again, a member in need of ready finance, but knowing that a management nominee would learn of his additional source of income, contrary to company policy, may prefer not to use the credit union at all. Here the credit union has unconsciously denied a member a service which is his due.

It can be said, of course, in defence of management nominees on the board that, it being so provided in the rules and agreed to at the formation meeting, the members have democratically agreed to the point. However, the same members have the power to alter the rules at any time, although who would be the first member to give notice of motion of a change in the rules to debar management nominees? Most members would be reluctant to do so. The implication is obvious: the credit union should avoid the position of having a management nominee in the first place. Credit unions which have management-nominated boards of directors may be well run and well managed but they do not come into the concept of credit unions as envisaged by the N.S.W. Credit Union League nor of the Credit Union National Association.

Subsidisation of Credit Unions by the Employer

One of the quickest methods of destroying the objectives of a credit union is extreme subsidisation by the employer. By 'extreme' we mean subsidisation to such an extent that the credit union becomes completely dependent on the subsidy to maintain its operations.

Take the case of an industrial credit union, and I have one or two in mind, where the secretary-treasurer is an employee of the company. In addition, all the accounts are posted on the company's book-keeping machines by the company operators without cost to the credit union. This organisation, though masquerading as a credit union, is really a welfare department of the company and the very benevolence of the company has had the following effects on the credit unions concerned:

(a) Directors are relieved of the responsibility of 'balancing' a budget and of building a credit union to the stage where it can transfer from hand postings to machine ledgers, from volunteer secretary to part-time staff and later to the employment of full-time staff. This initial period is the training period in which good credit union directors are made.

(b) Limiting of certain expenditure which may normally be considered necessary. Credit unions spend a lot of money in promotional work in order to increase membership and service to members. Credit unions aim to bring to their members the realisation that the credit union movement must be brought to as many people as possible outside the precincts of the particular credit union.

Expenditure associated with this type of promotion, no matter how modest, appears to be restricted, probably because of the unvoiced feeling that the company would be displeased to see *any* expenditure not *directly* associated with its own particular credit union. This attitude is likely to extend to such fields as membership of the Credit Union League, the service organisation which is maintained by dues from the credit unions.

Recessions and the Credit Union

During the Great Depression there were no credit unions in New South

Wales. For experience we must look once again to the U.S.A. where it was found that credit unions were actually strengthened during the period 1929–39. Liquidations of credit unions were few and most of those that occurred were the result of poor management. Some liquidations were, of course, inevitable as plants closed, but credit unions usually were able to pay off more than one hundred cents on the dollar. Most credit unions reported that they wrote off no more bad debts than they do today. The Credit Union League encourages a systematic building of reserves to cope with all contingencies, including recessions, and, in addition, plans a separate stabilisation fund for the assistance of credit unions which fall into financial difficulties. During the 'credit squeeze' in Australia in 1959–60 credit unions reported a systematic increase in both members and savings with no increase in bad debts. Thus credit unions possess a high measure of financial stability.

Savings Banks: Friend or Foe?

The present relationship between the credit unions and the savings banks is friendly. Savings banks have co-operated fully with credit unions and in many cases have provided overdraft accommodation to enable credit unions to give greater service to members. However, future relationship and competition between the savings banks and the credit unions is something of which a great deal of conjecture has been made. So far no firm policies appear to have been made but for the sake of the record let me place before you the credit union feeling on this matter.

Firstly, we feel that we have first place and will always remain ahead in the field of assistance to members on 'unsecured' loans. By the very nature of the movement competition cannot even make an impression on the credit unions in this field. You will recall that the Commonwealth Banking Corporation, followed, I think, by the Bank of New South Wales, made a 'great thing' of the introduction of a new policy for unsecured loans. From personal observations and discussions with bank managers it would appear to me that the anticipated business from this service *did not come up to public expectations.* Various conditions laid down (quite rightly so from the bank's point of view) debarred many borrowers from making application for relief. The biggest disadvantage, we believe, from the bank manager's point of view, is that only rarely would he be in a position to have the same appreciation of the applicant's character and of his complete financial problems as the credit union director working alongside the applicant.

In the matter of savings we believe that savings of the wage earners in the credit unions will increase by millions of dollars with apparently no foreseeable limit. We are of the opinion that most of this money would *not* have been saved in the savings banks anyway. We know from our experience that the credit union teaches people to save who do not normally save or who have perhaps never saved. Education of credit unionists in the advantage to themselves of regular savings, plus an understanding of the philosophy of the movement, plus the convenience of 'on the spot' saving when the wage earner receives his pay packet, are the keys to this growth. We believe that the fact that credit unions pay higher than bank interest is not the most important reason which makes credit unionists good savers: convenience of saving, participation in profit and the knowledge that members are in a 'self-help' movment, attract members to the credit union.

In the U.S.A. the banking institutes are making a united and concentrated effort through the American Bankers' Association to curb the growth of the credit union movement in the U.S.A. Restrictive legislation is being introduced into almost every state in the U.S.A. but as yet little of it has been accepted as law. In support of our contention that credit unions cater for a field rather different from, and not in competition with, savings banks, we note that the largest credit union in Australia, with over $2 million in savings, is situated within the Commonwealth Banking Corporation's staff.[3]

There is one field allied to the private savings banks, however, with which we are in direct competition, and that is the private finance companies, including those whose shareholding includes investment from the private banks. The credit union movement is not so naïve as to wish to eliminate private finance companies, nor would it be desirable to do so. We do believe, however, that increased competition will eventually force the rates of interest charged by some of them down to a more reasonable level.

6. The Place of the Credit Union in Instalment Credit Expansion in Australia

The Credit Union and Real Income

The real value of the income of the wage or salary earner is the value of goods or services he can exchange for his income. In return for his work, the income received enables him to acquire goods and services the quantity

[3] At 30 June 1968, after 14 years of operations, this credit union held over $6 million of members' savings. *Ed.*

of which will vary according to the price he must pay. The price he must pay in many cases is one which includes high interest rates and extraneous charges; the average wage earner has not the ready cash to bargain for certain types of consumer goods and this makes the effective price higher.

The credit union movement changes this pattern completely. In the first case the worker can borrow ready cash at a lower rate of interest than he would have to pay if he bought on terms and secondly he pays no 'hidden charges'. Here is the first instance where the wage earner increases the real value of his wages: he pays less interest. Perhaps a greater advantage, however, is his ability to buy cheaper for cash. This does not mean that he should by-pass the usual outlets of distribution and attempt to 'buy wholesale'; this is not part of credit union thinking. However, ready cash is miraculous in its ability to make prices tumble and in this instance the real income of the wage earner increases considerably. He is able to buy more consumer goods for a given income as a result of discounts for cash, or a greater bargaining ability.

The flexibility of the credit union facilities has opened other avenues to the wage earner which have hitherto been closed to him. Take the case of a family man who has purchased three items on hire purchase. This is not unusual. He has probably purchased the items at different times and would owe a different amount on each. A disadvantage to him is the fact that he must make three separate repayments, one for each item purchased. He may be unable to reduce the repayments where he finds the commitment too burdensome. Here is an avenue of relief which is particularly suitable to the credit union. The member may consolidate all his outstanding loans into one loan from the credit union with a much reduced rate of repayment. A simple example may be given as follows:

TABLE 1

PURCHASE	ORIGINAL AMOUNT	BALANCE OWING	PERIOD OF REPAYMENT	FORTNIGHTLY INSTALMENTS
1 television set	$312	$208	3 years	$4·00
Floor coverings in 1 room	$164	$58	2 years	$3·15
Vacuum cleaner	$80	$20	80 weeks	$1·00
	$556	$286		$8.15

The above items, for the purpose of simplicity, are exclusive of interest and other charges. The member, by consolidating his outstanding balances, a facility not available under normal circumstances, can take a new loan of

$286 at fortnightly repayments of $3·67 over a period of three years. The reduction in payment of $4·48 per fortnight represents relief for the wage earner of a most practicable kind. If we exclude interest rate differences, it could be argued in this instance that the borrower has not really saved money on the consolidation in that the higher repayments would be spread over a shorter period, but this may not be what is required by the borrower who needs more 'take home' money.

With regard to the 'cost' of interest payments, the borrower from the credit union receives real benefit compared with the borrower who has to rely on the usual lending authorities financing the purchase of consumer goods. To illustrate this point the following comparison is taken from an actual hire purchase agreement and compared with a hypothetical credit union loan for a similar amount. It will be understood that the amount shown as 'deposits' would not normally be paid by the borrower from the credit union, as he would normally borrow the total amount he required.

TABLE 2

	CREDIT UNION (hypothetical case but actual interest rate charges)	FINANCE COMPANY (actual example)
Cash price of article	$230.97	$230.97
Less deposit	$30.97	$30.97
	$200.00	$200.00
Add interest charges (2 year term)	$21.60	$39.50
Total amount repayable	$221.60	$239.50

The borrower from the credit union saves the sum of $17.90 in interest charges on the modest loan of $200. An added advantage to the borrower from the credit union is that his loan is automatically insured against his death.

The Credit Union and Housing Finance

One of the greatest contributions the credit union movement can make in Australia is to housing. Provision of finance for alterations to houses, balance of purchase price and the construction of additional rooms is an important application for this kind of finance. More spectacularly, the field of second mortgage finance is one which cannot be used too much to assist homeseekers in Australia. The experience of building societies has revealed that most people buying or building houses require second mortgage finance. Rates of interest for second mortgage finance in comparison with first mortgage are so exorbitant, and in some cases include so many hidden charges and pitfalls for young people, that we would be so bold as to suggest that the whole system of interest calculations used by private lending institutions should be examined.

Not the least of these unfortunates have been returned soldiers who availed themselves, and are still doing so, of bridging finance during the period from which their War Service Loans have been granted to the time the money becomes available. In such cases there is absolutely no risk to the lending institution. Let me add that the lawful limits of interest which may be charged by finance companies is accepted by most people as something which is here to stay and being within the law must be accepted with resignation. It is a similar attitude to that adopted by millions of people who are perpetually hungry and by millions of people who live and die under the weight of that usury. If it is lawful to charge such heavy rates of interest that home seekers must suffer severely in the disbursement of their income, then it is desirable that home seekers use equally lawful means to ease their burden. The credit union can be used for amounts up to $2,000 whilst the credit union and/or the permanent building society is the answer for amounts required in excess of $2,000.

Let me give you an example of what happened to a young married couple who were presumptious enough to borrow money to put a roof over their heads. I can support my comments with documentary evidence and I have personally spoken to the credit manager of the finance company concerned. I have been astounded by the latter's quite obvious belief that this was a normal case. I would hasten to add that this is not an isolated case. Briefly, this young couple borrowed $6,400 repayable with interest over twelve years, as the balance of the purchase price on an old house. After thirty months during which twenty-eight payments were made at the rate of approximately $92 per month, a total of $2,576 had been paid to the finance company. The payments were heavy and they found it such a strain that they discussed with me methods by which they could procure finance with perhaps less burdensome payments. The payments of $2,576 had reduced the debt of $6,400 by $68!

Comparable tables are attached to show what the position would have been had the couple borrowed the maximum allowed under the Act from a credit union, to wit, $2,000 with the balance of $4,400 from a permanent building society. Repayments have been made at the same rate (i.e. approximately $92) and have been calculated as having been received by both the credit union and permanent building society on the same dates as they were received by the finance company.

TABLE 3

	FINANCE COMPANY (12 years)	CREDIT UNION (5 years)	PERMANENT BUILDING SOCIETY (12 years)	TOTAL OF CREDIT UNION AND PERMANENT BUILDING SOCIETY
This is what they borrowed	$6,400	$2,000	$4,400	$6,400
This is what they repaid	$2,576	$1,120	$1,456	$2,576
This is what they finally owed	$6,332	$1,266	$1,682	$4,548
This means				
They paid in interest	$2,508	$386	$738	$1,124
They reduced their loan by	$68	$734	$718	$1,452

Note: Amounts are approximate to the nearest dollar. In the case of the permanent building society, management fees of approximately $52 should have been charged but against this a dividend on shares of $54 would have been earned by the borrower so both amounts have been disregarded.

Schools Savings Credit Unions

The profit value of school bank accounts is recognised and competed for vigorously by both government and free enterprise banks. There is, of course, a profit to be made on savings, and by introducing children to a particular bank there is a greater chance of gaining their eventual adult custom. It is equally obvious that the profit will *not* be returned directly to the children nor to their parents. In areas outside of Australia, for example in British Columbia, the introduction of credit union teaching and credit unions in schools has been an outstanding success. However, it would be impracticable at this stage of the credit union development in Australia to introduce school credit unions in areas where there was not already established a parent credit union in the community which could act as a receiver for the monies collected. Perhaps the new Central Division of the Credit Union League could be one avenue into which credit union funds saved by schoolchildren could be deposited in those areas where there was not already established a community or parish credit union. The teaching of credit union philosophy in the schools has apparently been accepted by the present Minister for Education, and this is a big step forward in the development of this philosophy. It is important at this stage in the teaching of this movement that the philosophy be accentuated more than any other aspect of it. Credit unions are organisations which in the first place teach thrift and secondly help other people. It is essential that this basic teaching be included in plans for schoolchildren.

Australia and the Colombo Plan

The influence that Australia could make on Asia through the teaching of the credit union movement is limitless and we have many precedents to support this belief. The credit union movement has been adopted by UNESCO as one of the greatest and most practicable methods of teaching underdeveloped countries to help themselves. As already mentioned the U.S. Government in its tremendous Aid Programme has commissioned the Credit Union National Association, by contract, to introduce the movement into vast areas of South America. Credit unions in Peru, Argentina and Brazil, and also in the West Indies, have been introduced by this method and are completely changing the living standards of the native peoples. In Australia, we have not yet availed ourselves of the opportunity to teach students under the Colombo and Afro-Asian Schemes this method of self-help in order that they may pass on the methods and philosophy in their own countries.

It is interesting to note that the Reserve Bank of Australia, in association with the Australian banks operating in Papua and New Guinea, has accepted responsibility for the introduction and promotion of credit unions in that Territory under the title 'savings and loan societies'. The first step in this experiment is to form a club and teach the natives to save. This is not an easy task but is fulfilling the first object of a credit union, the teaching of thrift. Once the natives have been taught to save they may form a society. They are taught to borrow wisely and to repay regularly. The societies operate for a probationary period, which continues until the organisers are satisfied that the natives are capable of and willing to conduct the society efficiently. At this stage the society is officially registered as a savings and loan society. At 30 April 1963 there were nineteen registered savings and loan societies in operation covering a membership of almost 1,000 Papuans and New Guineans with total savings of $36,000. In addition there were ninety-six savings clubs operating within their probationary period. These probationary societies had a membership of about 5,000 members who had accumulated savings of $50,000. The indigenous members are running these clubs and societies themselves with initial training and continuing assistance, where required, from officers of the banks.

The vast geographic areas represented by African and Asian students are a source of great potential recruitment for the movement; the availabliity of credit for rural areas is already recognised by some of the countries represented as essential for their progress. The few talks we have given to some of these students have met with enthusiasm, and we are hoping to run a short series of classes for a selected group shortly. Unfortunately, these are all arranged on a non-governmental level and are only a fraction of what might be done.

7. Summary and Conclusion

This paper has outlined briefly the place and problems of credit unions in the Australian economy and their potential influence for good for our near neighbours. The main features of this movement, in Australia, at the present time are:

(a) The lack of knowledge of the movement and its methods by the Australian community.

(b) The lack of leaders in a movement which demands self-sacrifice and idealism as against the more general materialism and profit seeking.

(c) The problems of replacing suspicion and material thinking with a philosophical ideal in the minds of those who will benefit the most.

(d) In all states other than N.S.W. a lack of government interest coupled with inadequate legislation.

When these main problems are overcome the co-operative ideal will have done more than stabilise the finances of the wage earner, it will have delivered to him a control of his money and a subsequent independence which has hitherto been, generally speaking, beyond his ability to attain. The challenge of teaching 'self-help' to people in underdeveloped countries close to Australia is an exciting prospect which could bring great credit to Australia and lasting benefits to the countries assisted.

The United Nations, which is financing development of credit unions in South America, has found that as the people raise their standards of living and increase their self-respect by the use of the credit union movement, so the growth of communism tends to decrease or disappear. Whilst the first result is the main objective, the second is one which may give us food for thought.

STRUCTURE OF A CREDIT UNION

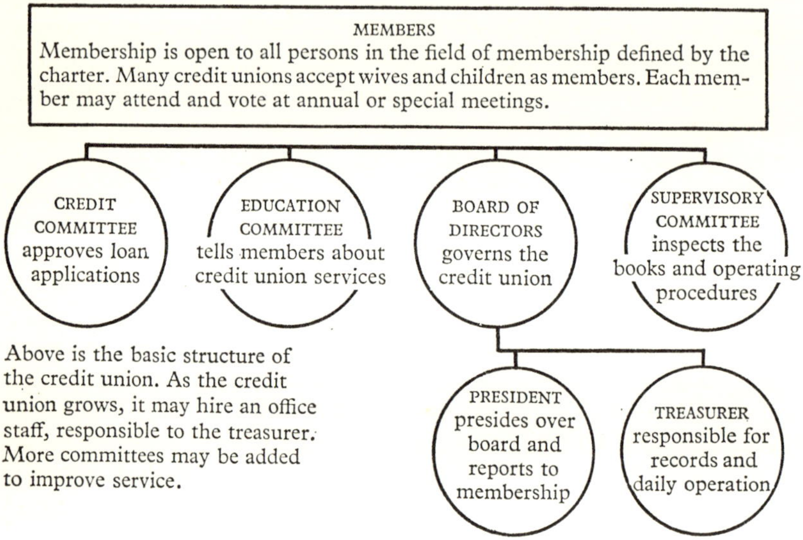

To sum up this paper I would like to quote an extract from one of the last speeches of Roy F. Bergengren, a credit union pioneer and advocate who died on 11 November 1955:

> 'Man is his brother's keeper. We believe that. We don't talk about it. We do it.
>
> We believe in democracy. We don't talk about institutions of, for and by the people. We make institutions that are literally of, for and by the people.
>
> We believe in the integrity of the human race. We know that, if the average man wasn't honest, there could be no credit unions.
>
> And, therefore, it seems to me that we are enlisted in a cause that is very great, that has the possibility of international spread which will carry forward, consistently with the purpose of God, the great ideal of human progress.'

STRUCTURE OF THE CREDIT UNION MOVEMENT

CUNA SUPPLY CO-OPERATIVE

Governed by board of directors elected by member leagues. Self-supporting by sale of materials to leagues and credit unions.

CHAPTERS

Formed by credit unions to provide helpful programs within their own area.

CUNA

Governed by international directors elected by member leagues. Supported by dues from leagues, and from credit unions in non-league areas.

LEAGUES

Governed by directors elected by member credit unions. Supported by dues from credit unions.

The diagram below outlines the service structure which credit unions have evolved to answer their growing needs.

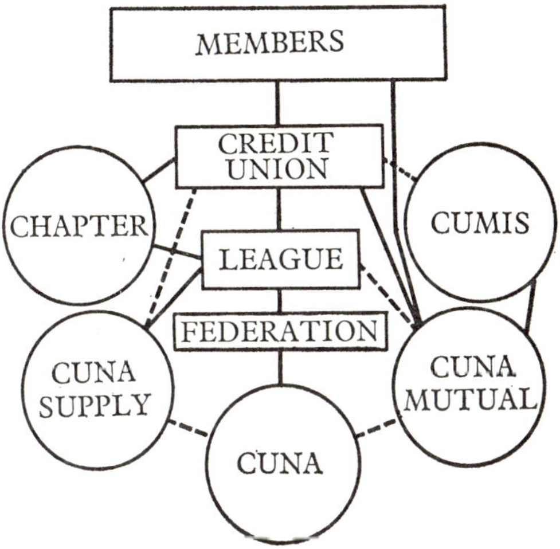

Comment on 'The Place and Problems of Credit Unions in Instalment Credit Expansion'*

by Neil Runcie

We have heard an inspired address from Mr Arneil about the development of the credit union movement in Australia and in the world at large. The credit union movement, at the present stage in Australia, is comparatively small. In spite of the very rapid expansion of credit unions, notably in the United States and Canada where they have been the most rapidly growing financial institution both in terms of their number and in terms of their total debt in the post-war period, the movement is only just starting to gather force within the Australian economy. Now how do we explain this slow development here in view of the very rapid expansion of instalment credit which has occurred and very high level of indebtedness which has been achieved in the Australian economy? Firstly, even within New South Wales where the main growth has taken place, the legislation has only gradually facilitated the expansion of this movement. It is only recently that the maximum amount of a loan which credit unions can make has been raised to $2,000. The position in the other states is not as satisfactory and I think that the Minister (Mr Landa) and Mr Arneil would both agree that the basic legislation and the regulations governing credit unions in the State are in need of streamlining in order to facilitate the formation of credit unions.

I am wearing several hats in commenting on Mr Arneil's paper, because as well as being an academic economist I am Chairman of the University of New South Wales Staff Credit Union Ltd, which was established nine

* Address opening the discussion on Mr Arneil's paper, First National Instalment Credit Conference, May 1964.

months ago and has grown very rapidly by credit union standards.[1] After nine months we had 500 members, or approximately one quarter of the staff of the university as members. After ten months we will have made two hundred thousand dollars of loans. The formation committee of the credit union took nine months in order to work through the provisions of the Act and the regulations under it and to draw up its own rules. This was a considerable period of time and there were all sorts of difficulties which we encountered in interpreting the legislation and the regulations under it. There is an urgent need for separate credit union legislation. For example, in New South Wales the rules with regard to all co-operatives are also the model rules which are provided for credit unions; and they require significant modification in order to form a credit union.

Mr Arneil has mentioned that the Credit Union League and the Registrar of Co-operatives are involved in providing services of various kinds. At the present stage of development in Australia these services are comparatively rudimentary. There is, for example, no manual of procedures for committees (i.e. the sorts of manual which the finance companies and credit retailers have for their departments). There is not, as yet, a standardised model set of forms. Our formation committee debated, at great length, for example, the range of possible questions which we might ask loan applicants. After nine months of operation we decided that we will need to extend the range of questions in order to appraise the credit standing of our applicants who are all university staff! We needed to investigate not only the problem of design of forms and the sorts of legal instruments that could be used but, in addition, we needed to consider the possible features of our growth that would occur in the first and subsequent years, particularly the financial features. Throughout our short existence we have drawn up funds and profits budgets. I have not the slightest doubt that this represents a more sophisticated approach than is found in most other credit unions. The same difficulties are there in other credit unions, even if they are not always tackled with the best tools available.

The second main point is that one of the chief limitations on the growth of credit unions in Australia is the supply of qualified leaders. People who accept responsibility on the boards of credit unions are accepting the same responsibilities as a person on a board of directors in a public company. There are, in fact, some additional obligations of the kind that Mr Arneil mentioned. Thus there is a need for this movement, if it is going to grow

[1] See Neil Runcie, 'Credit Unions on the Campus—II', *Vestes*, The Australian Universities Review, Vol. XI, 1968.

rapidly in Australia, to put a certain amount of 'investment effort' into an education programme and into the design of a manual of procedures for the various types of credit union. Problems will differ according to the type of credit union. The parish credit union raises a different set of problems to the employer-based credit union.

There are a number of controversial observations which Mr Arneil has made about credit union management. He has expressed League policy on a number of points but we should be aware that there are inevitably some points of difference regarding that policy. For example, the question whether credit union directors should be paid raises a number of issues. My own views have not yet reached the stage of maturation on this point but it seems that there may well be a case for some sort of payment in order to impress responsibility within the board of directors. Not all people have the same enthusiasm as Mr Arneil and this variation in dedication is one of the problems in the credit union board. You will always have some people on the board of directors who will not be pulling their weight.

In the structure of a credit union, as shown in Mr Arneil's diagram, there are some points with which I would quarrel. For example, unquestionably it is the board of directors which is primarily responsible to members and underneath the board of directors should come your credit committee, and your education committee or, as we call it within the University Credit Union, the promotion committee. I would also add to that structure a finance committee, because the problem of funds management is important in policy formation. Credit unions operate on fine margins given their average scale of operations. In general, they cannot afford to build up large excess funds. The procedure which we have adopted has been to set limits on deposits: a maximum amount of deposit has been specified and this has been progressively raised from $2,000 up to its present level of $7,000 from any one person. We have also made a condition that people cannot withdraw funds from the credit union, except by arrangement, at a rate higher than $1,000 per month. In addition we have proceeded to make arrangements for a bank line of credit, initially on a stand-by basis, and subsequently on a come-and-go basis.

While I greatly admire the initiative involved in the formation of the 'Central' this is, at present, a controversial feature of credit union development. The Central is lending at 7 per cent and the banking system can provide a cheaper source of funds at present. In fact, we want to be able to maintain unused credit lines at the cheapest possible rate. I do not think that the Central quite achieves that at the present time. Now there are a number of other features of credit union development which perhaps will present problems in the near future. I was very interested in Mr Arneil's remark about the life savings plan. Further, it would probably help credit unions significantly if they could insure against their bad debts. In fact their bad debts experience is extremely low and it seems that some sort of co-operative arrangement might be considered by the movement. Now it is not wholly true to say that the movement is entirely divorced from discount stores. Credit unions are approached by discount stores and they have sought the attention of the members of credit unions for obvious reasons: they encourage 'cash' purchases with credit union loans.

With regard to the relationship of instalment credit debt to income, it is very difficult to assess a particular level of indebtedness and to suggest that it has reached a saturation point or a level at which it provides a very heavy burden on the community. It is true that some members of the community will always get into difficulties. This problem of advice to the borrower on his commitments calls for greater effort on the counselling side of the credit union movement (and of other credit financiers).

Further, the funds which the credit unions are mobilising do not represent only new savings in the community. A significant portion of the funds flowing into the credit union movement, and a portion of the funds which will facilitate its expansion in the future, will come from transfers of deposits. This follows, in part, from the rate of interest which is being paid: 5 to 6 per cent on deposits. This rate of interest would appear very attractive to many people who hold deposits elsewhere. The credit union movement should accept this money for it is competing with other financial institutions for growth, and in order to provide expanded services for members.

2

The Economics of Credit Unions

by Neil Runcie

1. Introduction

The economic analysis of credit unions deals with only one aspect of a complex social movement. The credit union movement was originally conceived in the nineteenth century as an attack on poverty[1] and was run, on a self-help basis, by earnest amateurs. Today, although it is run more and more by professionals, who have improved its services, the main aim is still the same. Thus there has been great growth both in underdeveloped countries, and in developed economies where there are pockets of poverty. More recently in the latter economies, credit unions have become a vehicle of co-operation in instalment credit finance for a much wider section of the community.

The main drive to the expansion of the movement appears to be humanitarian; indeed, the international spread of credit unions is one of the most exciting social phenomena connected with human betterment in the free world. With the prompting of CUNA International and its affiliates,[2] credit unions have grown in numerous underdeveloped countries such as Tanzania, Fiji and the Territories of Papua and New Guinea. Other organisations have also assisted, such as U.S. Government agencies, government departments in some of the territories concerned and other bodies, such as credit union leagues in neighbouring territories. Even in the more developed economies the leaders of the movement are still philanthropic social activists, in the tradition of nineteenth century philanthropy which, inter alia, stimulated the growth of co-operatives and the people's bank movement. The movement retains organisational features (e.g. in the extensive committee system) which reflects this earlier origin. Nevertheless, in the advanced countries, the professional group has been having considerable impact in the

[1] G. Boyle, *The Poor Man's Prayer*, Helicon, Baltimore, 1962.
[2] The World Extension Department of CUNA was established in 1954.

development of managerial attitudes within the movement (partly in the sense of James Burnham's vested class in the managerial revolution and partly in the sense of improved operational technique). In Canada and the U.S.A. credit unions are extensively developed while in Australia, though small and inhibited, the credit union movement is growing.[3] And even in the United Kingdom, where the co-operative movement has traditionally shunned credit unions, several have recently been established, notably among West Indian immigrants.

2. The Economic Nature of Credit Unions

A credit union is a group of people with a common bond who associate together to pool a portion of their savings and wealth for lending within the group. It is a distinct part of the co-operative movement and is usually subject to detailed state regulation and supervision. The bond of association should enable the credit union to expand within its defined 'potential' market with minimum costs; the nature of the bond exercises a considerable influence on these costs. The bond of association may be based, for example, on employment with a particular employer, or membership of a particular trade union, or a particular religious group in the community, or the people living together in a particular suburb; these are the main types. The bond of association facilitates the administration of the credit union; it provides the sense of purpose essential to a venture of this kind, which has traditionally relied on a great deal of voluntary effort on the part of some of its members to organise its activities.[4]

The credit union encourages its members to save regularly and to make deposits into a common pool from which loans are made to members for a wide range of consumer and sometimes producer purposes. The credit union's facilities may be extended to cover the saving and even the borrowing needs of the member's household; and in community and parish credit unions this is the normal pattern. Regular instalment repayment is a feature of all lending. The credit union movement encourages self-help and financial independence of the members by:

[3] S. F. Arneil, 'The Place and Problems of Credit Unions in Instalment Credit Expansion', *Paper to First National Instalment Credit Conference*, The University of New South Wales, May 1964. It was estimated that the 179 N.S.W. credit unions, out of 325 credit unions in Australia at May 1964, accounted for 70 per cent of the credit union outstanding debt. A slightly revised version appears as chapter 1 in this volume.

[4] For a discussion of the nature of a credit union see John T. Croteau, *The Economics of the Credit Union* (especially chapter 1), Wayne State U.P., 1963.

(a) encouraging people to save for their commitments and generally for a specific purpose;
(b) financial assistance from the common pool;
(c) life insurance cover on all loans made (and a recent development of life cover for deposits has been undertaken in some cases); and,
(d) financial advice and counselling and a limited amount of consumer education.

3. Instalment Credit and the Growth of Credit Unions

Credit union statistics are seriously incomplete in most countries other than the United States and Canada. Eight main tests are applied by CUNA International to determine which co-operative credit organisations should be included in its world-wide credit union statistics:[5]

(a) The main function of the organisation is to collect savings from its members and to make loans to its members.
(b) Members exercise democratic control on the basis of one vote for each member.
(c) Capital is derived mainly from the savings of the members.
(d) Loans are made only to members, for provident and productive purposes at reasonable rates of interest.
(e) The organisations are non-profit.
(f) The organisations are not considered direct sub-divisions of government financial institutions.
(g) Members have limited liability.
(h) No discrimination is made on the basis of race or political or religious beliefs.

Tables 1A and 1B indicate the international geographic spread of credit unions 'officially recognised' by CUNA but are not a reliable guide to their growth. For example, in 1964 CUNA made official contacts with 2,400 *caisses de credit mutuel* in France and 12,500 non-agricultural credit societies in India (with capital of R.S.1 Lakh and over): statistics for the latter groups are included in the world coverage of officially recognised credit unions for the first time in that year, but in subsequent years the aggregates for these countries have been adjusted downwards without earlier revision. Those familiar with the history and development of credit union ideas will regard it as anomalous that the German Raiffeisen

[5] CUNA International Inc., *International Credit Union Yearbook*, 1965, p. 64.

TABLE 1A WORLD SUMMARY OF CREDIT UNION OPERATIONS, 1963–1966

Country or Region	End of 1963		End of 1964		End of 1965		End of 1966	
	Credit Unions	Members	Credit Unions	Members	Credit Unions	Members	Credit Unions	Members
	No.	No. '000	No.	No. '000	No.	No. '000	No.	No. '000
North America	25,985	17,746	26,547	19,031	26,777	20,955	27,568	22,534
Latin America	1,853	382	2,396	559	3,461	2,158	3,809	2,282
All Other Countries	4,246	943	18,154	6,110	17,214	5,956	17,464	4,678
Total	32,084	19,071	47,097	25,700	47,452	29,069	48,841	29,494

Source: International Credit Yearbook, 1965 and *1967*.

TABLE 1B WORLD SUMMARY OF CREDIT UNION OPERATIONS, 1965

Country *a*	Active Credit Unions	Members	Shares and Deposits	Loans Out-standing	Assets
	No.	No.	U.S.$'000	U.S.$'000	U.S.$'000
North America					
Canada	4,658	4,202,334	2,300,315	1,706,704	2,570,232
U.S.A.	22,119	16,753,106	9,248,865	8,095,444	10,552,125
West Indies					
Jamaica	129	32,952	6,515	6,254	7,203
Grenada	18	1,540	58	49	63
Netherlands Antilles	65	13,314	692	593	n.a.
Dominican Republic	82	9,563	319	238	n.a.
Central America					
Mexico	525	40,967	1,423	1,353	1,624
Costa Rica	102	18,100	1,505	1,377	1,652
British Honduras	44	14,325	1,259	661	1,425
South America					
Bolivia	156	37,693	1,927	1,990	2,388
Brazil	104	43,400	643	581	698
Colombia	444	73,042	2,154	2,022	2,426
Ecuador	188	23,869	709	604	724
Peru	532	214,164	21,501	20,475	24,570
Europe					
Italy	1	1,880	1,836	1,678	2,132
Ireland	126	41,800	3,337	2,730	n.a.
Asia					
Philippines	737	66,716	6,376	2,813	6,748
Malaysia Federation	413	150,587	29,308	17,940	33,427
Thailand	77	112,222	10,176	9,396	n.a.
Australia b					
New South Wales	216	74,607	15,249	14,801	16,735
Queensland	24	2,013	1,241	n.a.	n.a.
South Australia	7	2,945	1,062	1,567	1,675
Victoria	105	12,841	2,450	2,252	2,570

Notes: n.a. Not available.

a The list of countries is not comprehensive; it excludes, for example, credit unions in Fiji and New Zealand; compilation dates not specified.

b For a more complete summary of Australian statistics see chapter 14, tables 1 and 2.

Source: International Credit Union Yearbook, 1967, pp. 34–6.

TABLE 2 THE GROWTH OF CREDIT UNIONS IN THE U.S.A.

Year	Active Credit Unions	Members	Shares and Deposits	Loans Outstanding to Members	Reserves	Assets
	No.	No. '000	U.S. $m	U.S. $m	U.S. $m	U.S. $m
1909	1	n.a.	n.a.	n.a.	n.a.	n.a.
1921	190	72	n.a.	n.a.	n.a.	n.a.
1925	419	108	n.a.	n.a.	n.a.	n.a.
1929	974	265	n.a.	n.a.	n.a.	n.a.
1932	1,612	301	n.a.	n.a.	n.a.	31
1934	2,489	427	n.a.	n.a.	n.a.	40
1935	3,372	642	n.a.	n.a.	n.a.	50
1936	5,241	1,170	n.a.	n.a.	n.a.	83
1937	6,105	1,538	n.a.	n.a.	n.a.	116
1938	7,059	1,868	n.a.	n.a.	n.a.	147
1939	7,964	2,309	n.a.	149	n.a.	194
1940	9,023	2,826	n.a.	190	n.a.	253
1941	9,891	3,304	n.a.	220	n.a.	322
1942	9,767	3,145	n.a.	149	n.a.	340
1943	9,223	3,024	n.a.	122	n.a.	355
1944	8,808	2,934	339	121	22	398
1945	8,683	2,843	369	128	24	435
1946	8,764	3,020	429	190	27	495
1947	9,000	3,340	510	284	31	591
1948	9,338	3,749	605	398	35	701
1949	9,924	4,091	703	516	43	827
1950	10,591	4,610	850	680	52	1,005
1951	11,283	5,196	1,040*a*	747	59	1,198
1952	12,291	5,888	1,356	985	67	1,516
1953	13,703	6,636	1,688	1,308	75	1,895
1954	15,073	7,356	2,039	1,552	91	2,270
1955	16,201	8,154	2,447	1,934	110	2,743
1956	17,256	9,061	2,914	2,326	137	3,271
1957	18,203	9,819	3,382	2,778	165	3,813
1958	18,838	10,432	3,870	3,078	198	4,346
1959	19,452	11,263	4,436	3,708	232	5,024
1960	20,047	12,038	4,975	4,377	272	5,653
1961	20,615	12,883	5,636	4,818	326	6,383
1962	20,951	13,762	6,331	5,477	381	7,186
1963	21,369	14,587	7,166	6,171	441	8,131
1964	21,807	15,619	8,242	7,046	510	9,361
1965	22,119	16,753	9,249	8,095	590	10,552
1966	22,692	17,897	10,106	9,094	769	11,609
1967	23,207	19,070	11,143	9,910		12,749

Notes: n.a. Not available.

a No statistics on deposits in State Chartered Credit Unions are available before 1952.

Source: International Credit Union Yearbook, 1967, p. 37. Compiled from official sources: Bureau of Labor Statistics, Bureau of Federal Credit Unions, State Supervisory Agencies.

societies[6] and other co-operative groups (e.g. in Indonesia) are left out of the count.

In North America, since the end of World War Two, credit unions have been the most rapidly expanding institutions connected with the financing of instalment credit. In both the United States and Canada, the movement has reached substantial proportions and it continues to make steady progress in the face of severe competition from the banking system, from sales finance companies and from consumer (personal loan) finance companies. Table 2 analyses the absolute growth of credit unions in the U.S.A. and table 3 analyses the relative growth of U.S. credit unions compared with other institutions financing 'instalment credit' debt.

These tables demand a measure of comment. First, the continued growth of credit unions in the U.S.A. during post-war recessions, and even earlier in the Great Depression, is outstanding. There are, however, fluctuations in the rate of growth which warrant further examination. Such examination may reveal that the rate of credit union formation, deposits, new loans granted and collections are functions (sometimes lagged) of changes in personal disposable income. Secondly, instalment credit debt connected with the retail sale of goods and services and short-term and medium-term personal instalment loans (i.e. excluding housing but including home improvement loans) are the most important components of the total loans outstanding to U.S. credit union members: the comparison of outstanding debt in tables 2 and 3 shows that over 90 per cent of outstanding debt is instalment credit debt. Thirdly, table 3 shows that the share of credit unions in the total instalment credit debt quadrupled in the post-war period to 1966 and nearly doubled from 1956 to 1966. Fourthly, credit unions hold less than 15 per cent of the total instalment credit outstanding, and thus are a small, but growing, part of the total range of institutions financing the community's instalment credit debt. Fifthly, table 3 records the enormous expansion of instalment credit in the U.S. economy in the post-war period.

In the advanced western economies the scope for the expansion of credit unions as financial institutions is intimately connected with the boom in the demand for instalment credit facilities. Table 3 shows the results of competition with other financial institutions, and with the retail outlets. This competition for the consumers' 'instalment credit dollar' has a number of interesting aspects. Taking a longer period than that shown in the table,

[6] The CUNA tests are rigidly applied to exclude co-operatives that deal in goods. On the early Raiffeisen experiments see F. Braumann, *A Man Conquers Poverty*, CUNA, 1963.

TABLE 3 CREDIT UNION SHARE OF U.S. INSTALMENT CREDIT DEBT

Year	Total Instalment Credit Debt	Amount Held by: All Financial Institutions	Commercial Banks	Sales Finance Companies	Consumer Finance Companies	Credit Unions	Other Financial Institutions	Retail Outlets	Credit Union Share of All Financial Institutions	Credit Union Share of All Debt
	U.S. $m	U.S. $m	U.S. $m	U.S. $m	U.S. $m	U.S. $m	U.S. $m	U.S. $m	%	%
1939	4,503	3,065	1,079	1,197	n.a.	132	657	1,438	4·3	2·9
::										
1941	6,085	4,480	1,726	1,797	n.a.	198	759	1,605	4·4	3·3
::										
1945	2,642	1,776	745	300	n.a.	102	629	686	5·7	3·9
::										
1955	28,906	24,398	10,601	8,447	2,623	1,678	1,049	4,508	6·9	5·8
1956	31,720	26,977	11,777	9,117	2,940	2,014	1,129	4,743	7·5	6·3
1957	33,868	29,200	12,843	9,609	3,124	2,429	1,195	4,668	8·3	7·2
1958	33,642	28,659	12,780	8,844	3,085	2,668	1,282	4,983	9·3	7·9
1959	39,246	33,570	15,227	10,319	3,337	3,280	1,407	5,576	9·8	8·4
1960	42,832	37,218	16,672	11,472	3,670	3,923	1,481	5,615	10·5	9·2
1961	43,527	37,935	17,008	11,273	3,799	4,330	1,525	5,595	11·4	9·9
1962	48,034	41,782	19,005	12,194	4,131	4,902	1,550	6,252	11·7	10·2
1963	54,158	47,405	22,023	13,523	4,590	5,622	1,647	6,753	11·9	10·4
1964	60,548	53,141	25,094	14,762	5,078	6,458	1,749	7,407	12·2	10·7
1965	68,565	60,273	29,173	16,138	5,606	7,512	1,844	8,292	12·5	11·0
1966	74,656	65,565	32,155	16,936	6,014	8,549	1,911	9,091	13·0	11·5
1967	77,946	68,273	33,992	16,851	6,294	9,169	1,967	9,673	13·4	11·8

Note: n.a. Not available.
Source: International Credit Union Yearbook, 1967, p. 38.

we may advance a three-stage theory of instalment credit growth. In the first stage the retailers are the dominant institutions connected with the financing of instalment credit. Instalment credit is a means of sales promotion: it widens the total market for the products being financed by bringing into the market those persons who could not afford the goods before, and it acts as an aid in inter-firm competition. The consumer finance of furniture, pianos, and sewing machines was undertaken in the later stages of the nineteenth century. But it was the advent of the motor car and other consumer durables (e.g. refrigerators, T.V. sets, radiograms) which has broadened this market enormously. Manufacturers sometimes financed directly the sales of their products at retail to achieve this mass market for their production.

In the second stage of development the familiar pattern of institutional specialisation with the growth of the market occurred. The sales finance company became the dominant institution connected with the financing of instalment credit. The retail sale of motor vehicles is a notoriously under-capitalised business in most countries and sales financing of motor vehicles, both at the wholesale and at the retail level, has been an important aspect of the growth pattern in these markets.

In the third stage of development the largest institutions in the capital market come into the picture: thus the commercial banks become the dominant holders of instalment credit debt. The commercial banks have an advantage over other institutions in the capital market. By keeping customers' accounts and providing chequing facilities they provide the most convenient means of payment in modern societies. As the banks are the administrators of the community's payments mechanism they hold the transactions balances and a good deal of the idle funds of economic units in the community. These funds are held, in part, at zero rates of interest to the banks who may even charge for activity in customers' accounts. Thus, commercial bank entry into new finance areas may be at highly competitive interest rates and in the United States they are the 'low raters' in many areas. The banks tend to impose tighter terms than other lenders and, partly in consequence, attract the high-quality borrowers.

Although credit unions have been described as 'private banks' and as 'small co-operative banks', because they offer deposit and borrowing facilities to members, they do not generally provide chequing facilities. This is an important difference compared with the commercial banks, and in particular in the source and in the cost of their funds. For this reason the credit unions are unlikely to grow to a point at which they occupy the

TABLE 4 THE GROWTH OF CREDIT UNIONS IN CANADA

Year	Credit Unions	Members	Shares and Deposits	Loans Outstanding to Members	Reserves	Assets
	No.	No. '000	U.S. $m	U.S. $m	U.S. $m	U.S. $m
1921	100	33	n.a.	n.a.	n.a.	n.a.
1922	108	32	n.a.	n.a.	n.a.	n.a.
1923	111	32	n.a.	n.a.	n.a.	n.a.
1924	119	31	n.a.	n.a.	n.a.	n.a.
1925	122	33	n.a.	n.a.	n.a.	n.a.
1926	154	36	n.a.	n.a.	n.a.	n.a.
1927	159	41	n.a.	n.a.	n.a.	11
1928	168	41	n.a.	n.a.	n.a.	11
1929	178	45	n.a.	n.a.	n.a.	12
1930	179	46	n.a.	n.a.	n.a.	11
1931	174	44	n.a.	n.a.	n.a.	12
1932	168	41	n.a.	n.a.	n.a.	10
1933	162	36	n.a.	n.a.	n.a.	9
1935	277	52	n.a.	n.a.	n.a.	10
1937	441	77	n.a.	n.a.	n.a.	14
1939	844	152	n.a.	n.a.	n.a.	21
1940	1,167	201	n.a.	n.a.	n.a.	25
1941	1,314	238	n.a.	n.a.	n.a.	31
1942	1,486	296	n.a.	n.a.	n.a.	44
1943	1,780	374	n.a.	n.a.	n.a.	69
1944	2,051	479	n.a.	n.a.	n.a.	93
1945	2,219	591	139	n.a.	n.a.	146
1946	2,422	689	179	n.a.	n.a.	188
1947	2,516	779	209	n.a.	n.a.	221
1948	2,608	851	239	n.a.	n.a.	254
1949	2,819	940	264	n.a.	n.a.	282
1950	2,965	1,036	289	n.a.	n.a.	312
1951	3,121	1,138	334	n.a.	n.a.	359
1955	4,100	1,731	603	373	31	653
1956	4,258	1,870	701	489	28	761
1957	4,349	2,060	787	500	40	846
1958	4,485	2,187	935	596	47	1,009
1959	4,570	2,360	1,060	731	50	1,158
1960	4,608	2,554	1,207	822	55	1,314
1961	4,592	2,751	1,387	948	59	1,508
1962	4,621	2,914	1,544	1,075	71	1,698
1963	4,607	3,559	1,732	1,251	96	1,932
1964	4,684	3,859	1,998	1,473	107	2,255
1965	4,658	4,202	2,300	1,707	109	2,570
1966	4,772	4,527	2,617	1,951	135	2,923
1967	4,760	4,763	3,016	2,245	149	3,367

Note: n.a. Not available.
Source: International Credit Union Yearbook, 1967.

TABLE 5 CANADIAN CREDIT UNIONS: COMBINED BALANCE SHEETS OF LOCALS (31 December 1961)

Sources and Uses of Funds	CAISSES POPULAIRES		CREDIT UNIONS	
	C. $m	%	C. $m	%
Assets				
Cash: Deposits at Centrals	111·0	13·2	33·4	5·1
Other Cash	29·0	3·4	20·4	3·1
Shares of Central	6·5	0·8	23·0	3·5
Other Investments	246·5	29·4	49·8	7·6
Personal Loans	56·8	6·8	429·7	65·4
Mortgage Loans	346·5	41·3	83·5	12·7
Other Assets	43·4	5·2	16·9	2·6
	839·8	100·0	656·6	100·0
Liabilities				
Borrowings and Other Liabilities	2·7	0·3	29·7	4·5
Deposits	734·8	87·5	78·9	12·0
Shares	56·7	6·8	499·8	76·1
Reserves	38·1	4·5	25·4	3·9
Undivided Earnings	7·6	0·9	23·0	3·5

Source: Canadian Royal Commission on Banking and Finance, *Report*, Ottawa, 1964, p. 158.

dominant role in the fourth stage in the evolution of instalment credit institutions (unless, of course, they are able to modify their activities to provide a more complete range of banking services). However, this view does not mean that there is not considerable scope for credit union expansion within the existing institutional pattern (but at the expense of some other instalment credit financiers).

In two other important respects credit unions are like commercial banks (and other financial institutions). First, they encourage the flow of savings in the community and they attempt to mobilise idle balances: this increases their capacity to make advances or investments. In consequence their activities also increase the velocity of circulation of money. Secondly, credit unions, like banks and other financial intermediaries, may create credit. The ability of credit unions to create credit is far more restricted than in the case of the banks because their cash return flow arising from advances is significantly less. However, in so far as credit unions can attract deposits as a result of making advances, they are increasing their lending powers. Thus, although the movement places considerable emphasis on the importance of regular savings by members, the flow of funds into advances may represent new savings only in part. Hence credit unions are competing in the general market for deposits and must offer sufficiently attractive rates of interest to attract the funds required for their expansion.

In Canada credit unions are relatively more important even than in the United States. Credit union membership in Canada in 1966 represented 22·4 per cent of the total population compared with 9·0 per cent in the U.S.A.[7] In spite of this higher degree of market penetration, and the entry of the Canadian commercial banks into active instalment credit financing since 1959, the Canadian credit unions appear to have been able to maintain a high growth rate as shown in table 4. The dependence on credit unions as financial institutions in Quebec Province, where they are known as the *caisses populaires*, is greater than elsewhere in the Dominion. The statistics of sources and uses of funds in table 5 suggest that the *caisses populaires* have evolved more along the lines of people's banks than elsewhere.

4. The Financial Stability of Credit Unions

The stability of any undertaking and especially of a financial institution has an important influence on its rate of growth through its ability to attract and retain funds. Credit unions, like other co-operatives, are 'non-profit' institutions and, perhaps a little paradoxically, this feature may restrict their growth. First, the 'non-profit' feature does not mean that credit unions do not make profits, but that the surplus belongs to members; this surplus may be returned as an interest rebate to borrowers, a dividend on share capital, an interest bonus to lenders (rare) and/or it may be used to promote the short- and long-run interests of members through the growth of the credit union and its activities. However, 'non-profit' also means that the main aim is not to maximise profits but to provide the service as cheaply as possible to lenders whilst encouraging an adequate flow of savings by paying a sufficiently high rate of interest and by other means. The 'non-profit' feature may also mean that credit union workers are not paid or are only partly paid. This latter feature restricts the growth of credit unions through dependence on voluntary effort; it may even affect their financial stability through insufficient attention to financial management including the recovery of potential bad debts.

The inability to apply the 'profit' test in isolation means that other criteria must be developed to judge the success of credit union operations.

[7] *International Credit Union Yearbook, 1967*, p. 10.

Dr John B. Hawley in a study of Michigan credit unions has suggested four ratios which he found convenient for operational investigations: (a) the ratio of actual to potential members; (b) the ratio of borrowers to members; (c) the ratio of expenses to income, and (d) net earnings to shares outstanding.[8] These ratios are all capable of being readily established, but other less easy to measure indices may be significant. For example, the ratio of instalment credit debt due from members to the credit union, to total instalment credit debt of (a) the members, and (b) the potential membership of the credit union, provides two measures of the market penetration being achieved. Again, the success in fund raising might be measured by the delays in making funds available for approved loans or in the credit standards being applied. Some borrowers will judge the efficiency of a credit union by the time involved in processing loan applications. Some directors may consider that absolute growth is a test of efficiency in any voluntary organisation; indeed the boards of many public and private companies project this test to shareholders!

For the United States, Dr Walker Polner (Director of the Research and Economics Department of CUNA International Inc.) has undertaken some very interesting development of financial ratio analysis for credit unions: no less than sixty-seven ratios based on standardised financial reporting of credit union operations have been developed.[9] Moreover, these ratios are available for sub groups by (a) type of credit union; (b) credit union asset size; (c) region; (d) number of full-time employees of the credit union; (e) number of part-time employees of the credit union; (f) dividend rate; (g) availability of payroll tax deduction. Management improvement by financial ratio analysis has been extensively employed in some other industries in some countries but credit union operations appear to be particularly suitable for investigation and management improvement by this means.

In a separate study of dividends paid by credit unions, Dr Polner revealed for a U.S. sample group in 1963[10] that:

(a) there was a tendency for credit union dividend rates to rise in the 1960s;

[8] J. B. Hawley, *A Study of Member Credit Unions of the Michigan Credit Union League relating Participation, Cohesiveness, Uniformity of Opinions and Attitudes, and Other Factors to Credit Union Success*, Unpublished Ph.D. thesis, University of Michigan, 1956.

[9] W. Polner, *Operating Ratios, 1963*, CUNA International Inc., 1965.

[10] W. Polner, *Dividends Paid by Credit Unions in the United States and Canada at the End of 1963*, CUNA International Inc., 1964.

(b) 81 per cent of credit unions were paying 4 per cent or more as dividends;
(c) 50 per cent were paying 4½ per cent or more;
(d) 32 per cent were paying 5 per cent or more; and,
(e) rates up to 9 per cent were reported.

Dr Polner goes on to report that 'credit unions were paying higher dividends than most other financial corporations in the United States'. In this surprising statement Dr Polner appears to be comparing the dividend rate of credit unions and other financial co-operatives with the deposit rate of private financial corporations. This may be a fair comparison but the choice of language is confusing.

However, another significant test of management efficiency is bad debt experience. The accounting definition of a bad debt as a non-recoverable debt begs the question, from management's point of view, of the time involved in recovery, and of the costs of recovery, as well as the difficulty of establishing the bad debts in advance. The usual accounting procedure is to adopt a statistical convention and to vary this, if necessary on management's assessment, depending on the quality of the paper in the financier's portfolio. Research into the probability pattern of bad debts over time is sadly lacking in the management accounting of all instalment credit financiers. Tardy recognition of bad debts is a criminal deficiency in financial reporting.

This does not mean that any level of bad debts is a reflection on management. No, or few, bad debts may mean that the credit union is not taking risks and is failing to serve the people who need help most. There are various ways of controlling the quality of the contracts accepted: for example, by ensuring that the borrower has a substantial equity in a motor vehicle, or insisting on a minimum period of residence or minimum period of employment. Bad debts are substantially controllable by developing tests of this kind. The provision for bad debts is the cost to be built into the pricing structure for carrying some contracts which are risky. Credit unions are multipurpose lenders and, surprisingly, generally charge a single rate for all risks.[11] The main reason for this is the difficulty of discrimination in a group in which there is a bond of association. However, multiple rates are a means of resolving a conflict between the interests of the low risk and of the high risk borrowers in the management of the credit union. When this conflict is unresolved, it may lead to a more restrictive policy than would otherwise be necessary. Nevertheless, the unique rate principle has strong

[11] The single rate principle is part of the Code of Ethics of the N.S.W. Credit Union League.

support within the movement and discrimination against costly small amount borrowers is rarely applied.

The bad debt test has been especially significant for credit union management in Australia: (a) in their first and second year of operation when reserves are small, and (b) because of a trend towards undercapitalisation as a result of the decision to tax credit unions on their surplus in the late 1950s.

Connected with the bad debts provision is, of course, the provision for unearned income. Some deficiencies in credit union practice where flat rate charging has been employed are known: practice has varied from the 3-2-1 formula, to 'even spread', and to the rule of 78.[12] No Australian credit union appears to use a set of actuarial factors.[13] Where credit unions use a monthly charge on the outstanding balance (e.g. 1 per cent or $\frac{3}{4}$ per cent per month), I would agree that the need to provide for income spread is obviated subject to one qualification: provision must be made in the accounts either under the heading of bad debts or of some future contingencies reserve for costs which are not spread over the contract life in proportion to the funds invested.

Although it has been suggested that all financial institutions should maintain cash or liquidity ratios, credit unions have been able to operate successfully on very low liquidity and to minimise the costs otherwise involved. High built-in liquidity in credit unions arises from:

(a) contractual repayments;
(b) contractual savings plans which frequently are effected by salary and wages deductions;
(c) stand-by or come-and-go credit arrangements with banks; and,
(d) ability to raise funds from members (either as shares or deposits) and to raise deposits from non-members.

To these facilities must be added the credit union Central (a regional 'central bank' for credit unions) or a stabilisation fund which exists either

[12] Where the total finance charge is calculated on the original amount of the loan the charges are spread over the contract life: in the 3–2–1 formula by dividing the period into three equal parts, spreading the charges available in the ratio shown between the parts and then spreading the charges evenly within these parts; an even spread means equal amounts of charges to each month; and the rule of 78 involves an allocation of the charges roughly in proportion to the funds invested in each month. See N. Runcie, 'The Measurement of Unearned Income: a General Theory', *Australian Economic Papers*, Vol. III, Nos. 1 and 2, June–December 1964.

[13] However, this was partly due to the absence of suitable tables. Now see M. F. Desmarchelier, B. J. Hill, C. C. Ringstad, G. L. Robinson and N. Runcie, *Income Conversion Tables: Instalment Finance*, Law Book Company, Sydney, 1964.

formally or informally to ensure that all credit unions which are members of a league may meet their commitments.

The concern of the authorities about the financial stability of credit unions, however, has mainly sprung from the character of management. The directors of credit unions are, in general, part-time amateurs of diverse background and frequently not well equipped for corporate responsibility.[14] In consequence, the enabling legislation has generally imposed on credit unions a high degree of supervision which is, in some respects, more detailed than for other co-operatives. Detailed annual inspections by officers of the State or Provincial or Federal regulatory authority have been the aim; in case of difficulty more frequent inspections are undertaken. These official investigations are imposed on top of the normal functions of an auditor.

The credit unions have responded to this challenge in two main ways: first, by undertaking a vigorous educational campaign for directors and, second, by encouraging the members of each credit union to set up an independent supervisory committee which is empowered to protect member interests by internal audit. Some brief comments on this response are necessary. The organisation of groups of credit unions into chapters for educational purposes and the educational schools and conferences organised by regional leagues are commendable. Moreover, the efforts of CUNA International Inc. to train credit union leaders from overseas are particularly praiseworthy. These training efforts might well be extended to the members of supervisory committees who too frequently view their main task as account checking rather than as an operational audit of activities; the supervisory committees rarely develop their own criteria for judging the success of the credit union. In Canada, the Porter Commission even suggested that the local credit unions must come to bear much of the cost of official inspection—perhaps through leagues, centrals, mutual aid or stabilisation funds.[15] Self-policing by the movement is regarded as both inevitable and desirable; the trend is apparent although the institutional means of carrying out this suggestion can be expected to evolve only slowly.

[14] The international symbol of the credit union movement was until May 1967 the little man under the credit union umbrella. One severe critic has commented that credit union directors are frequently 'little men' trying to be 'big men'!

[15] For an excellent account of credit unions in Canada see the Porter Commission, *Report of the Royal Commission on Banking and Finance*, chapter 9, Queen's Printer, Ottawa, 1964; and Gilles Mercure, *Credit Unions and Caisses Populaires* (Working Paper prepared for the Royal Commission on Banking and Finance), Queen's Printer, Ottawa, 1962.

5. Credit Unions and Monetary Policy

The operations of credit unions have not been a major source of concern to the monetary authorities in the main western economies as have the operations of other instalment credit financiers. Even in Canada the Porter Commission only recommended that the centrals should be subject to meaningful cash reserve requirements and uniform supervision by the federal monetary authority. However, in those countries where instalment credit terms control is imposed, the credit unions should expect to be subject to the same terms as all other instalment credit financiers: minimum down payments and maximum repayment periods for various classes of sales financing may be required.

The main reason for the comparative lack of interest of the monetary authorities is the atomistic structure of the credit union movement and its comparative smallness as an instalment credit financier compared with the other institutions.

In the Australian case, the total instalment credit debt outstanding rose from $A11·2 m. in June 1945 to around $A2,000 m. in June 1965. The credit union share at the latter date may have been about 2 per cent. In view of the high level of instalment credit indebtedness in Australia this comparatively low credit union share is surprising and appears to be due to four main factors:[16]

(a) some deficiencies in the enabling legislation and lack of uniform legislation throughout the Australian states;
(b) the scarcity of trained credit union leaders;
(c) some official restraints on the growth of credit unions; and,
(d) the highly competitive nature of Australian instalment credit financing.

Deficiencies in the enabling legislation include lack of uniformity between the states, limits on the maximum amount of a loan and lack of suitable model rules. As elsewhere, and particularly outside North America, the lack of trained leaders is the most serious deficiency. But the highly competitive nature of the Australian instalment credit market has inhibited some credit union growth. Not only are Australian terms easy by international standards, but the charges from finance companies are highly competitive for some classes of borrower. Nevertheless, on the basis of

[16] For an early study of the Australian scene see N. Runcie, 'The Concept and Growth of Credit Unions in Australia', *Paper to Second National Credit Convention* University of Melbourne, May 1965.

oversea trends, there would appear to be an enormous scope for the expansion of credit unions in Australia. Not only may the credit unions fill some obvious deficiencies in the capital market (e.g. second mortgage financing) but they may help to eliminate some retailer and finance company bad debts! The personal loans tier in the Australian instalment credit structure remains comparatively underdeveloped and this deficiency provides considerable scope for credit union expansion so long as banks and finance companies remain reluctant to enter the personal loan field in a significant way.

Credit union development in the Territories of Papua and of New Guinea is being promoted by the Reserve Bank of Australia as a means of monetising the economy and of developing sound attitudes towards financial management among the indigenous people. A two-stage development plan was implemented in 1962. The first stage involves the formation of savings clubs which are subsequently promoted to the status of savings and loan societies if they prove successful. At June 1965 there were 254 savings clubs and 62 societies in operation.[17]

However, credit union development in the United States and Canada continues to provide the main guidelines for credit union growth. In this connection the Porter Commission in its sympathetic study of the movement in Canada concluded:[18]

'The credit unions and *caisses* will no doubt continue to evolve and change, to become larger in size and more professional in operation, and to be more and more subject to market forces as a result of growing competition and narrowing earnings spreads. Yet we feel their emphasis will always be coloured by their wider social objectives of encouraging thrift, rehabilitating the financially improvident through the sound use of credit, and giving priority to the smaller borrower who cannot turn elsewhere at reasonable rates. While naturally anxious to see the interests of the whole community safeguarded, we have been no less concerned to ensure that the *caisses populaires* and credit unions are as free as possible to continue serving the local and special needs of their members in the spirit of co-operation and self-help which has been so largely responsible for their development.'

Thus the social impetus of the movement depends on its environment while its economic growth depends on its comparative efficiency as an

[17] Reserve Bank of Australia *Annual Report*, 1965, p. 28. For a detailed discussion see chapter 4 below.

[18] op. cit., pp. 170–1.

instalment credit financier and the stage of development of the instalment credit market. A small movement may still have considerable social impact and may force other financiers and the legislature to consider social implications in framing their policies[19] on instalment credit development.

[19] A sophisticated approach to the problems of debt recovery in the United States is involved in the development, in the 1960s, of the Consumer Credit Counselling Service sponsored by the National Foundation for Consumer Credit and other bodies.

Part II The Regional Studies

3

Savings Clubs and Savings and Loan Societies in Papua and New Guinea

by M. J. Phillips and P. S. Ferguson

1. Introduction

An essential condition for the economic growth of any country is the establishment and development of a workable monetary and financial system. In Papua and New Guinea, whilst the pace of development on all fronts has been accelerating over recent years, the institutional framework of the financial and credit system still remains fragmentary.

The requirements for a suitable financial system can best be examined against the particular needs of the Territories and their people. Their level and pace of advancement, together with their emerging attitudes, will largely determine the timing and the shape of the institutions set up.

Papua and New Guinea had at 30 June 1966 a population of about 2·2 million broken up into a large number of discrete tribal groups speaking more than 700 languages and dialects. The country is extremely rugged, and subsistence agriculture is still the main occupation of most of the population. In pre-European times most of the traditional societies were non-monetary in the western sense, and even today many tribal groups have yet to reach the stage of direct involvement with the monetary economy. Daily needs of these people are simple and can be obtained by their own individual efforts or by a system of barter or exchange.

Contact with European culture has, however, been responsible for a general widening in awarenesses, and has hastened more and more of the population towards some kind of monetary involvement. A great increase in cash-cropping—the production of copra, coffee, cocoa and other tropical crops for export—has raised indigenous money incomes five fold over the last ten years, and also has provided a major stimulus to development. Some groups, like those in the Gazelle Peninsula of New Britain or along sections of the Papuan coast, have been in contact with European influence since before the turn of the century and have a relatively long experience of the monetary economy. For many, however, it is a relatively new experience; often it has been individuals selling their labour for money—men leaving their villages to work on plantations or in the towns, and later returning home bringing with them wealth in the form of consumer goods of European manufacture—who have provided the initial connection. Among most groups, particularly those reasonably close to the centres of European influence, the 'demonstration' effect has been considerable. Demand for European-type goods has led to a demand for European-type purchasing power—money, coupled with an embryo demand for economic advancement. In some cases, however, particularly in areas where outlets for cash spending have been lacking, one of the attributes of money—that it can be stored—has led to hoarding with little economic use of the money.

Thus, present development is characterised by the juxtaposition of non-monetary societies with those just feeling their way into the periphery of the monetary system, and others with more sophisticated ideas and concepts.

The overall direction of movement is clear, but the process of change has brought many problems. At all levels, economic advancement and the accompanying cash nexus are having profound effects on social values, reciprocal obligations, status levels and the like. Sometimes, for example, there is conflict between new leaders who have been successful in the field of economic development, and traditionalists trying to maintain prestige. Each society operates within a different physical, cultural, political and economic environment, which makes the problem more intractable and the adoption of a uniform approach difficult.

The process of monetary involvement has been fraught with many misunderstandings about money and its uses. There have been attempts to absorb the new thing, money, into the environment against a background of traditional behaviour and belief patterns which are mostly inapposite. For a large part, money—its why and wherefore—remains a mystery, and the range of its uses remains unfathomed. Here is a gulf which needs to be bridged. In addition, the rapid rate of growth of political institutions and awareness which is now taking place makes a hastening of the level of understanding of monetary and financial matters a necessity. Responsible political decision-making demands an understanding of the economic environment within which the decisions must be made and the economic consequences which might follow.

2. The Clubs and Societies

To meet this problem it becomes necessary to improve the financial and monetary content of education syllabuses, to provide practical experience for the people in financial management and decision-making, and to develop a financial system suited specifically to the Territories' needs. Savings and loan societies represent one step in the achievement of these ends.

Savings and loan societies are the standard credit society of limited liability, based on capital contributed solely by members,[1] with limited powers to borrow from outside sources, and with loans restricted to members only. In operation, they differ in only minor degree from the credit unions of Australia or from similar groups in many other developed and underdeveloped countries. Their main differences lie in their genesis and in the concept of their role in the financial system.

Savings and loan societies were started on the initiative of the Reserve Bank of Australia,[2] Australia's central bank, with the co-operation and support of the commercial banks. The Reserve Bank has accepted responsibility for promoting and assisting societies until the movement is strong enough to handle these tasks itself. Savings and loan societies are, in essence, very small-scale co-operatively-run banks. They form an integral part of the general banking and financial system.

Legislation and Organisation

The first savings and loan society commenced operations in the Territories in May 1962. Preceding this, however, had been a fairly intensive period of detailed preparation. During 1959 and 1960 the Australian central bank had conducted studies[3] of the use of money and the need for credit by the indigenous people of Papua and New Guinea. These were followed by a study of the information available on the effectiveness of various types of credit agencies and savings mobilisation agencies in other countries, and an on-the-spot investigation into the credit union movement in Fiji.[4] As a

[1] Shares are the main funds, in contrast to Australia where deposits predominate.

[2] All of the Reserve Bank's responsibilities relating to Papua and New Guinea are handled by the Bank's Papua and New Guinea Division.

[3] J. R. Thomas and D. Ryan, *The Use of Money and Need for Credit by the Indigenous People of the Territory of Papua and New Guinea*, Commonwealth Bank of Australia, July 1959; and P. W. E. Curtin, M. J. Phillips and E. V. Fleming, *Report on Visit to Papua and New Guinea*, Reserve Bank of Australia, January 1961.

[4] P. W. E. Curtin and M. J. Phillips, *Credit Unions in Fiji; their relevance to Papua and New Guinea*, Reserve Bank of Australia, March 1961.

result, and because of its conception of the role such a system of societies could play in the financial system, the Bank decided that efforts should be made to establish credit union type activity in Papua and New Guinea.

The Savings and Loan Societies Ordinance[5] was passed by the then Legislative Council of Papua and New Guinea on 28 September 1961, the Assistant Administrator (Economic Affairs) saying, 'the (banking) system needs supplementing on the lower levels of savings and credit. As we see it, an essential supplement to the banking system, and one of special value in our present stage of development, is the type of pre-banking system, in the form of savings and loan societies, outlined in this bill.'[6]

From the outset, then, savings and loan societies have operated within the framework of legislation designed specifically and exclusively to cover them. The Savings and Loan Societies Ordinance sets forth the powers and the general constitution of societies. They are corporate bodies with limited liability; they have power to hold property, enter into contracts and institute legal proceedings; each society is run by a board of directors elected by members, with a loans committee to consider applications for loans, and a supervisory committee responsible for auditing the society's books and generally supervising its operations. Often, the loans committee will have some directors among its members, but a director or a member of the loans committee may not also be on the supervisory committee. Both the loans committee and the supervisory committee are elected by the members at the annual meeting when elections are held also for the board of directors.

A Registrar of Savings and Loan Societies, appointed by the Administrator of the Territories, is empowered to administer generally the Ordinance. His tasks are to explain to interested groups what these societies are and how they can be helpful to them; to help to set them up; to assist in the training of their officers, and generally to watch their progress. The Reserve Bank of Australia has agreed to maintain and staff the Registry and the Registrar is an officer of the Reserve Bank.

Since inception of the movement, a two-tier approach to the commencement of new groups has been adopted. Only a group which can demonstrate viability and effective management as well as willingness and eagerness to work together can become registered under the Ordinance as a savings and loan society. It must first complete a probationary period as a savings club, during which time the major emphasis is on the accumulation of savings.

[5] *Ordinance No. 46* of 1961.
[6] *Papua and New Guinea: Legislative Council Debates*, Vol. VI, No. 3, p. 192.

Clubs do not grant loans to their members, and usually operate in excess of a year before applying for registration as a savings and loan society.

Provisions of the Savings and Loan Societies Ordinance do not extend to savings clubs. Clubs are essentially a device to test the viability of a group which has thoughts of establishing a savings and loan society. During the 'trial' period as a savings club, officials from the Registry visit the group on several occasions to observe its progress, to explain in more detail the way a society works, and to ensure that an adequate record is being kept of the club's funds. Registry officials stress that, although they are available at all times to give help and advice, nevertheless during the club stage the onus is on members themselves to demonstrate to the Registrar that the group can work together satisfactorily. Not all savings clubs ultimately become registered; some 20 per cent of all clubs commenced between May 1962 and June 1967 discontinued their operations prior to formation as societies. Sometimes this was due to internal friction or factional struggles within the group, at other times to a general lack of interest by members. Normally, clubs are commenced upon request from groups themselves; care is taken to avoid any suggestion of dragooning groups into club formation.

To obtain registration as a society, a minimum of 20 members must be able to demonstrate some form of common bond. In the main, clubs and societies have been formed by people living in rural areas although, particularly over the last two years, an increase in urban groups has been apparent also. There are two main nuclei around which groups have tended to form:

(a) *geographical*, where the common bond is based on residence within a certain area, for example, the same village or a close group of hamlets, and

(b) *kinship*, where the common bond is membership of the same clan or extended family.

Some groups have also been formed where a common employer has been the bond, and others where membership of the same mission has been the predominant factor. In more than two-thirds of all groups the common bonding appears to have been residence in the same village. Mission-based groups account for approximately 10 per cent of the total, and employer-based groups for only about 3 per cent. For urban-based societies, it has been most usual for membership to have been drawn from members of the same tribal group living in the one town. Several groups have been formed with multi-racial membership.

Each society is run by its members acting in an honorary capacity.

Although the rules provide that payment may be made to the secretary and treasurer for their services, in practice such payments are little more than nominal. It has thus been possible for societies to keep their operating expenses to a minimum.

Growth

As can be seen from tables 1 and 2, progress of both societies and clubs has been rapid.

TABLE 1 PAPUA AND NEW GUINEA: GROWTH OF SAVINGS CLUBS, 1962–8

30 June	Number of Clubs	Total Membership	Total Funds ($A)
1962	1	40	100
1963	52	2,273	18,274
1964	111	5,156	57,712
1965	254	11,138	138,186
1966	346	14,783	224,787
1967	340	14,004	259,347
1968	298	12,142	298,263

Source: For all tables in this chapter the data is from the Registry of Savings and Loans Societies.

TABLE 2 PAPUA AND NEW GUINEA: GROWTH OF SAVINGS AND LOAN SOCIETIES, 1962–8

30 June	Number of Societies	Total Membership	Total Funds ($A)
1962	1	80	592
1963	4	209	6,256
1964	23	1,161	48,058
1965	62	3,426	163,422
1966	139	7,523	392,507
1967	189	10,038	580,824
1968	208	10,781	695,978

In the early stages, field work was concentrated in the Gazelle Peninsula where the local Tolai inhabitants already had well-developed cocoa and copra holdings and where money had been used concurrently with an indigenous shell currency for many years. Demand soon spread to other areas, and at the end of June 1967 some 529 clubs and societies with a total membership of over 24,000 persons were operating. The average membership of each society was 53 persons and of each club 41 persons.

The regional distribution of groups is set out in table 3, and at 30 June 1967 clubs and societies were operating in 15 of the Territories' 17 Districts.

TABLE 3 PAPUA AND NEW GUINEA: REGIONAL DISTRIBUTION (at 30 June 1967)

DISTRICT	SAVINGS CLUBS		SAVINGS AND LOAN SOCIETIES	
	No.	Funds ($A)	No.	Funds ($A)
P.N.G. Coastal				
Central	16	11,664	7	17,770
East Sepik	19	14,892	3	8,280
Gulf	1	674	1	1,993
Madang	9	2,224	—	—
Milne Bay	2	497	1	1,287
Morobe	73	54,458	25	54,205
Northern	24	20,686	5	10,706
New Guinea Islands				
Bougainville	26	11,109	8	16,359
East New Britain	74	77,154	118	429,900
New Ireland	18	14,758	—	—
Manus	5	2,137	1	3,312
West New Britain	10	9,664	—	—
Highlands				
Chimbu	2	1,073	1	1,559
Eastern Highlands	44	29,695	13	26,588
Western Highlands	17	8,642	6	8,865
TOTAL	340	259,347	189	580,824

Funds mobilised by clubs and societies have been substantial. As tables 1 and 2 demonstrate, in the five years since 1962 savings by members have risen at an average annual rate of almost 250 per cent to reach a level of $840,000 at 30 June 1967. This represented an average holding of $57.90 for each society member and $18.50 for a club member. About two-thirds of all funds were held in societies.

Members' savings have come from a variety of sources. Most commonly, they have represented part of income earned from cash-cropping activities—on the coast mainly copra and cocoa, and in the Highlands coffee. In urban areas, most members are in wage employment and their savings have come from wage earnings. Some groups organise special functions to raise extra money which is then apportioned and contributed on an individual basis. Where proper safeguards are taken, some groups also accept 'village funds'—money which belongs to the group jointly and which has been collected usually from some previously organised group activity, for example, a jointly-owned coconut plantation. Some money contributed to societies by richer members is earned from small businesses run by them—e.g. trucks, trade stores.

Society funds are contributed by members in the form of shares which can, in most cases, be withdrawn upon demand. The rules also provide for deposits to be accepted from members but, to date, all contributions have taken the form of shares. Dividends are payable to members on the basis of shares held (i.e. the extent of their saving with the society), with a maximum rate of 7 per cent laid down by the Ordinance. Societies are at present exempt from paying income tax.

As may be seen from an examination of the aggregate balance sheets set out in table 4, funds are used by societies in three ways: held in a savings bank account, loaned to members, or invested in 'approved' securities. During the earlier years of society operations, members tended to place emphasis on building up aggregate savings to adequate levels, and

TABLE 4 PAPUA AND NEW GUINEA: SAVINGS AND LOAN SOCIETIES AGGREGATE BALANCE SHEETS (at 30 June)

	ASSETS ($)				
Classification	1963	1964	1965	1966	1967
Cash at Bank (including General Reserve Fund)	2,556	33,884	89,280	203,135	303,613
Loans: Granted cum. fig.	670	4,700	51,336	189,495	310,798
less Repaid cum. fig.		346	9,614	46,443	102,807
Outstanding	670	4,354	41,722	143,052	207,991
Investments	3,030	9,820	32,420	46,320	69,220
TOTAL	6,256	48,058	163,422	392,507	580,824
	LIABILITIES ($)				
Classification	1963	1964	1965	1966	1967
Shares Issued *e*	6,037	45,225	152,608	364,907	528,185
General Reserve Fund *e*	129	1,757	5,877	13,921	24,840
Accumulated Surplus *e*	90	1,076	4,937	13,679	27,799
TOTAL	6,256	48,058	163,422	392,507	580,824

Notes: cum. fig. Cumulative figures.
e Estimated.

demands for credit were only slowly forthcoming. The last three years have seen a change, however, and at 30 June 1967 outstanding loans to members stood at $208,000 or 36 per cent of societies' total funds. Over 3,000 of the 10,000 society members had received loans.

The responsibility for approving loans rests with the loans committee of each society subject to any policy determined by the board of directors. The range of purposes for which loans may be made is very wide, the main limitation being that the loan should in some way contribute to the individual borrower's general advancement or to that of his family. In fact, as table 5 shows, loans have been requested by individual members mainly for productive purposes or to effect domestic improvements. Up to 30 June 1967, $84,000 of credit had been extended to members for the purchase of motor vehicles (mostly trucks), $71,000 for purchase of building materials to construct or improve members' houses, $47,000 to assist with the purchase of goods for stocking trade stores, and approximately $39,000 for other trading purposes. A further $44,000 had been lent for agricultural purposes—to purchase fencing wire and agricultural equipment, to erect copra driers, to purchase land, and to hire farm labour.

The Savings and Loan Societies Ordinance sets the maximum interest rates which may be charged on loans by societies. These are:

(a) 1 per cent per month on the unpaid balance of the loan; or

TABLE 5 PAPUA AND NEW GUINEA: LOANS GRANTED BY SOCIETIES, 1962–7

Purpose	Loans No.	Amount Granted ($A)
Building Materials	758	70,961
Trading	492	38,812
Trade Store Goods	422	47,010
Purchase of Motor Vehicles	288	84,430
Hiring of Labour	266	13,962
Purchase of Fencing Wire	108	6,649
Purchase of Sewing Machine	92	6,098
Agricultural Tools & Crop Processing Equipment	86	5,682
Purchase of Land	83	7,354
Erection of Copra Drier	76	10,300
Purchase of Radios & Refrigerators	64	3,229
Education Expenses	28	1,436
Builders' Tools	15	567
Miscellaneous	287	14,308
TOTAL	3,065	310,798

(b) a flat rate of 6 per cent per annum on the full amount of the loan over the full period for which it is granted.

However, the Ordinance also provides for a minimum permissible interest charge of 10 cents a month. In practice, most societies charge interest on a 'flat rate' basis at the maximum of 1 cent a month for each $2.00 lent. Interest is debited to accounts once each month.

With the close bonding between members, board of directors and loans committee, physical security usually is not required for loans. In the majority of cases, loans are made on the basis of the personal standing of the borrower, though additional personal guarantees are often sought from other members of good standing as supporting security.

The period for which a loan is made depends upon the amount and purpose. Most, however, are repayable within two years.

Funds surplus to the immediate, or short-term projected, needs of a society may be invested 'in securities of or guaranteed by the Commonwealth or in such other securities as are prescribed'.[7] At 30 June 1967 societies had investments of $69,000, approximately $366 per society, almost entirely in Premium Securities issued by the Papua and New Guinea Administration. These securities are redeemable at short notice. For many members, 'investment' is an entirely new concept, and Registry officials have placed considerable stress on explaining what is involved and the general relationship between interest rates and risk.

Members of most societies have placed a great deal of emphasis on the building up of reserves to put their society in a strong financial position. The Ordinance lays down that one-fifth of a society's net earnings in each year must be paid into a General Reserve Fund, until the balance of the Fund reaches a minimum of one-tenth of total deposits plus issued capital. Beyond this, however, many societies have preferred to retain profits in the first few years rather than pay dividends. Others have paid dividends from the first year of operations.

Federation and Leagues

Prior to March 1966 all societies were individual entities linked only through their connection with the Registry. However, it had always been hoped that, as the movement grew and the education of members increased, responsibility would move increasingly from the Registry to societies themselves. In response to the expressed demands of societies, a Federation

[7] *Ordinance*, Section 16 (c).

of Savings and Loan Societies was formed in March 1966 on a Territories-wide basis to promote co-operation amongst them and to act for their common benefit. An important function of the Federation since its inception has been to conduct a contributory fund to be used to pay the outstanding balance of any loan due from a deceased borrower to a member society. Societies pay into a central fund a small fee based on the level of their outstanding loans, and from this pooled fund a deceased member's loan is repaid to his society. The Federation also acts as supplier of stationery items to member societies, a function previously carried out by the Registry, and generally acts to consider matters of common interest to all societies. A board of directors elected on the basis of regional representation meets at regular intervals.

In addition to the Territories-wide Federation, there has been a move to form District Leagues of societies. The first of these was formed in March 1966 in the Gazelle Peninsula of New Britain where savings and loan activity has been strongest; and a further League commenced in the Eastern Highlands District in August 1967. The services provided by these two Leagues vary somewhat because of the differing needs of societies in their areas. Generally, however, they assist member societies with their book-keeping and management problems, and also provide an advisory service on loans for members. The Gazelle League, for example, employs an experienced New Guinean carpenter who is available to advise society members on all aspects of home building. In the Eastern Highlands, where there is a general shortage of members capable of maintaining society records, the League conducts a central book-keeping service for societies wishing to make use of it.

Both the Federation and the Leagues employ their own staff and meet their operating costs from member societies' contributions.

As at June 1967 it had not been necessary for any society to have recourse to borrowed funds. Each group had generated sufficient savings to meet credit demands by its members. This may not always remain the case. The Federation and Leagues may be able to promote a more effective use of societies' funds, channelling surpluses from societies with excess liquidity to societies whose funds are temporarily insufficient to meet their members' demands for loans. They might also have a significant role to play as intermediaries in bringing borrowed funds into the movement from external sources such as, for example, the Papua and New Guinea Development Bank.

3. Impact on the Economy

Even after a relatively short period of operation, savings and loan societies are beginning to have an impact on former patterns of saving and capital formation in the areas where they have been established.

Their general effect on patterns of saving and spending has been to divert money, mainly current earnings, from current consumption or from some alternative form of saving (individual bank account or hoarding). In societies where wage earnings are the main source of funds, there is little doubt that in the absence of such activity, the bulk of money saved would have gone into current consumption and little into individual bank accounts.

The effect on the savings patterns of individual society members varies in general according to their age and location. Younger members—especially in groups formed in or relatively close to an urban centre—usually have a higher propensity to consume, and societies appear to have made a greater change in their expenditure patterns than is the case with older members.

Clubs and societies are tailored, perhaps better than any other existing institution, to attract funds from hoardings into the orthodox financial system. The evidence suggests that a fair measure of success has been achieved, especially in the Highlands, and that better results will be achieved as confidence of the older men in the scheme grows. Certainly clubs and societies have been successful in diverting to the banking system some of the current earnings which would otherwise have found their way into hoards.

The savings and loan society movement in Papua and New Guinea is not without its problems. The educational level of most members and many office bearers; the lack of familiarity with money and its usage; communications problems; all create difficulties. Some problems have begun to emerge in the repayment of loans, and special action has been taken by the Registry and the District Leagues to intensify member education on the responsibilities which go with borrowing. Generally, however, these problems are a necessary consequence of monetisation, an expression of the process of financial evolution, and all are capable of solution.

On the credit side, societies are helping to satisfy a need for small-scale credit at the village level. In doing this, they are indirectly working to prevent the introduction of private money lending and usury[8] on any

[8] Usury has yet to be a problem in Papua and New Guinea. This contrasts, for example, with Fiji and a number of Asian countries, where credit unions have been fostered partly to provide an alternative to private moneylenders.

widespread scale. They are providing an introduction for indigenous people to more sophisticated credit channels, and over the longer term will also assist existing financial institutions to acquire progressively a more indigenous character.

As a general medium of education to improve understanding about money and its uses, and also by serving to heighten local appreciation of banking and western accounting concepts, societies can be considered a valuable addition to the economic structure. They are providing an insight for the indigenous people into aspects of investment, and are giving experience in general organisation (conduct of meetings, etc.) and financial decision-making—all this helping to bridge the gap between the modern money economy and the different socio-economic concepts of traditional societies.

As existing societies grow and societies commence in new areas, a more significant impact on the overall economy of Papua and New Guinea can be expected. In the final analysis, changes in attitudes and behaviour patterns wrought by grass-roots institutions, including savings and loan societies, will be profoundly significant to the process of economic development in Papua and New Guinea reflecting the adjustment of the people to the transition to a money economy.

4

Economic and Social Development in the Fiji Islands through Credit Unions*

by G. A. Arbuckle, S.M.

1. Introduction

It is common today to insist that education is the key to development. This stems from the increasing awareness that human factors are ultimately the principal conditions in economic and social expansion. The insistence on education is to be commended. But too few seem to attempt to define in precise terms what form education should take, its principles, purpose, and the role of the instructor. As far as possible, any vagueness of purpose and method must be removed if long-term success of investment in human resources is to be guaranteed.

Credit unions in the Fiji Islands[1] have become widely successful as an educational programme for social and economic development. The 288 credit unions are run entirely by the people themselves and without government assistance.[2]

* This chapter is an abridgement of an article which appeared in *Journal de la Société des Océanistes* in 1968.

[1] The total area of Fiji, of which the two main islands comprise 87 per cent, is 7,055 square miles, scattered over some 90,000 square miles of sea. The great part of the major islands is high, steep, broken country, deeply dissected by water courses. Credit unions are mainly confined to the chief island, Viti Levu. At the end of 1964 the total population of the Colony was estimated to be 456,000. The indigenous Fijians (predominantly of Melanesian stock with an admixture of Polynesian) numbered 41.5 per cent of the population and the Indians 50 per cent.

[2] In the early stages the Government provided some financial assistance. The Burns Commission reported that the establishment of the existing credit unions had cost the Government some £F14,600. The Fijians themselves had contributed £F25,485. C.P. No. 1, *Report of the Commission of Enquiry into the Natural Resources and Population Trends of the Colony of Fiji 1959*, 1960, par. 705.

V. D. Stace reported in 1962 that the credit union is 'inter-denominational in its membership and financially self-supporting. Functioning under a special act of the Fijian legislature, the credit union movement is an independent co-operative organisation; nevertheless, it has accepted small government grants since its establishment to assist its development.' South Pacific Commission, Noumea, *Report on Capital Formation Methods and Credit Facilities for Islanders in the South Pacific*, p. 29.

Credit unions were brought to Fiji in late 1953 by Father Marion Ganey, an American Jesuit priest, at the request of the then Governor, Sir R. Garvey. Father Ganey had been working for some years in the British Honduras where he had introduced credit unions to the people.[3] The people in Fiji adopted credit unions with immense enthusiasm. It was not long before Father Ganey was being hailed as the 'champion' and 'saviour' of the Fijians. Some even claimed that credit unions were 'the best thing that ever happened to Fiji'.[4]

Official recognition of the invaluable role of the credit union in Fiji has been frequent. For example, the Governor of Fiji, in 1959, warned the Colony that it could not depend on vast financial assistance from outside for development. 'Real progress of the Colony', he said, 'must depend in the final analysis on the hard work, thriftiness, initiative and enterprise of the individual men and women of Fiji.' He then turned to credit unions as exemplifying these virtues. 'This is the sort of self-help and enterprise that Fiji needs above all else,' he insisted.[5]

Certainly, there was never any doubt in Father Ganey's mind that credit unions would offer the right opportunities for the development of those virtues necessary for economic and social expansion at grass roots level.[6] These virtues have been developed because through credit unions the people have acquired for themselves both physical and immaterial capital.

[3] J. J. Considine, M. M. (Ed.), *The Missionary's Role in Socio-Economic Betterment*, Newman Press, 1961, pp. 210–11.

[4] Reported by Douglas Hyde, the British authority on South-East Asian affairs, in *Catholic Herald*, May 1961.

[5] Reported in *The Fiji Times*, 27 November 1959.

[6] Fr Ganey stated in 1958: 'This question has been repeatedly asked in the Pacific areas, by administrators anxious to help the indigenous people, "What are the types of institutions, appropriate to the different stages of economic development aiming these territories, which will enable the administrations to: first, encourage savings by the local people, second, facilitate the division of credit for the development of production especially by the local people, third, provide opportunities for the local people to gain experience in the methods of economic life by participation?" I believe that the credit union as we know it in this country has come the closest to supplying the correct answer. Other compulsory saving plans have been inaugurated and certainly can be depended on to do much to improve the economic status of the people. Still, the people themselves evidently desire to participate more intimately in managing their economic affairs. The only constructive way to approach the problem is through the techniques of fundamental education, says a distinguished economist. And in credit union education I believe we can offer these techniques to the people of Fiji and the world.' *Report on Credit Unions in Fiji to Joint Board Meeting*, 13 February 1958. See also *The Annual Report of the Credit Union Central Committee of Fiji*, 1955.

Physical Capital Investment through Credit Unions

A survey was conducted in 1954–5 of ten typical credit unions. According to those conducting the survey, the unions chosen were 'neither the best nor the worst and (they) offer a fair cross-section of the activities of the people.'[7] Three of the unions chosen were industrial, one a settlement of Nabua, and the other six were Fijian villages. The industrial credit unions had memberships made up wholly of wage earners.

The majority of loans made by the industrial unions were for provident purposes. Members had regular employment but, because of the high cost of living relative to income, it was only natural that the employees used their unions for provident reasons.[8]

On the other hand, loans provided by village credit unions were mostly for productive purposes—fishing nets, fishing boats, bullocks, wire fencing, sewing machines, carpentry tools.

Immaterial Capital Investment through Credit Unions

Physical capital is important—but useless, unless human capital has also been developed. The principal value of the credit union in Fiji is its capacity for immaterial or educational investment—investment in people. As Professor O. H. K. Spate noted in his report on the Fijian economy, 'the credit unions are making an important contribution to Fijian economic life, and not least in the educational aspect.'[9]

Over the last few years, an increasing number of indigenous people in the South Pacific have discovered that their material and especially spiritual deprivations are not inevitable, and are thus awakening to a new hope for a better life. It is a life in which they want to act for themselves, to stand confidently on their own feet economically, socially and politically.

But the hope is too slow in reaching fulfilment. Social institutions structured for a more stable kinship society are naturally slow to adjust to the new demands for change. Daily, more and more people are facing a personal crisis—a state of frustrated hopes.

[7] *Report Submitted to the Burns Commission of Enquiry*, Credit Union League, Suva, Fiji.

[8] There seems to be evidence, however, that after a period loans were made mostly for productive purposes. This has been the experience of the Carpenter's Employees' Credit Union. J. Collins, S. J., *The Organisation and Operation of Credit Unions in the Philippines, New South Wales and Fiji*, December 1962–January 1963, (cyclostyled) p. 24.

[9] 'The Fijian People: Economic Problems and Prospects', *Council Paper No. 13 of 1959*, par. 369.

Signs of frustration are increasingly evident on the individual and group level, e.g., cargo cults, riots, absenteeism, and crime. Cargo cults in particular are tragic illustrations of misguided attempts at self-determination or self-help. Participants dream of a utopian world in which all present contradictions, injustices and deprivations are wholly removed. It is a world that they will achieve principally through their own efforts. Indeed, to accept hand-outs would be to admit that they are in fact inferior beings, that they are not capable of self-determination.

Credit unions claim to provide opportunities for the people to act for themselves. In fact, 'from the spiritual point of view,' claims Father Ganey, 'there is no other organisation operating at the present time in Fiji which so fulfils the legitimate aspirations of so many people.' Credit unions exist to remove and prevent so much of the frustration characteristic of the peoples in the South Pacific today.

The following analysis, therefore, logically follows two main lines:

(a) credit unions have contributed to the development of the people by removing some causes of frustration;

(b) credit unions have positively invested in people as people.

2. The Removal of Some Causes of Frustration

(a) *Credit Unions Provide Opportunities to Avoid Usurious Interest Rates*

Father Ganey reported in 1954 that the working man's eagerness to have credit unions 'is pathetic': 'Any mention of loan sharks and usury meets with intelligent understanding which could only have been gained through rough experience.' Usury is a world problem. But it is particularly evident where credit facilities are restricted as is the case in most emerging lands. Fiji is no exception.

Detailed knowledge of illegal rates of interest is, naturally enough, difficult to obtain. Sometimes through accident or sheer desperation on the part of the people who are suffering, cases are revealed that effectively uncover the power of the unscrupulous money-lender. It was reported, for example, in 1954 that interest rates calculated at five shillings in the pound per month were being charged and obtained by money-lenders. The interest rate in these circumstances was 300 per cent per annum. One unfortunate man borrowed a sum of ten pounds at the rate of two shillings in the pound a month. The borrower found difficulty in repaying the debt, but he was never pressed for repayment by his creditor. In fact, he was encouraged 'not to worry'. Eventually, he managed to clear himself after twelve years, during which time he paid one hundred and forty-four pounds on his original ten pound loan.[10]

The manager of a large firm in Suva told the writer that he had discovered, in 1964, a money-lender who had obtained the position as paymaster in his firm. His work merely provided the man with an opportunity to carry on his major occupation of money-lending. He would subtract from the workers' pay whatever was owing to him. The manager discovered the situation only when an employee came to him in desperation begging for a loan. He had received a mere seven shillings to support himself and his family over the next week.

In a report to the Burns Commission, the Credit Union League noted that, in 1959, usury 'existed in the Colony in a far more malignant form than was suspected'. 'We are fairly certain', the submission noted, 'that a money-lending couple were able to loan out over £300 in small hurry loans—Friday to Tuesday—at the gate and under the nose of one of our largest credit unions this last weekend. The rate of interest was 3,000 per cent.'[11]

It is inevitable that the power of money-lenders to charge usurious interest rates has weakened since the introduction of credit unions. The unions offer loans at an extremely low interest rate (1 per cent on unpaid balance per month is the maximum). The fact that the astounding sum of £2,016,420 was borrowed from credit unions between the years 1954 and 1965 sufficiently indicates to what extent usurers have had their power weakened or undermined.[12]

Writing to Sir Ronald Garvey, a former Governor of Fiji, Father Ganey commented in 1961 that 'there are still loan men (20 per cent per week) hanging around on pay days at stores and industries in Suva, but we can say that they are fewer in number and their gross take is smaller than ten years ago.'[13]

Employees of the large firm of W. R. Carpenter and Co., Suva, formed a credit union in 1961 with two hundred members and a potential membership of six hundred. Within six months of its foundation, the credit union had assets amounting to £F5,500 and loans had accumulated to £F9,500. Money-lenders had been doing a brisk trade at the exits to this firm for

[10] Reported in *The Fiji Times*, 24 July 1954.
[11] op. cit. See also the Submission of the Colonial Sugar Refining Company to the Sugar Inquiry Commission 1961, as reported in *The Fiji Times*, 6 March 1961.
[12] *The Pacific Islands Monthly*, September 1965, p. 71.
[13] Letter of M. Ganey, S.J. to Sir R. Garvey, 1 June 1961.

years. But the Credit Union League, in its Report to the Registrar of Credit Unions, 1961, significantly noted: 'It was generally conceded that the Credit Union (Employees of Carpenter's) had produced the first effective counter-offensive to the ever growing evil of usury operating around the exits on payday.'[14]

(b) *Improvement in Employer–Employee Relations through Credit Unions*

An American manufacturer stated in 1963 that 'employee credit unions definitely further employee relations'. The management of his company considered the credit union 'one of its valuable assets'.[15]

The basic reasons for this management praise of credit unions may be summarised as follows: (i) Employees take personal responsibility for their financial affairs. Management no longer has to concern itself with a man's personal financial problems. This saves management's time and money. It also prevents the employee from the odious task of having to reveal to management the state of his private affairs. (ii) Financial worries rank high as causes of accidents, absenteeism, poor work. A credit union helps employees solve financial problems. Absenteeism tends to drop and quality of work improves where credit unions exist. (iii) While serving as volunteer directors and officials in credit unions, employees receive first hand experience and insight into business problems that make them appreciate more readily the problems of management. Hence, credit unions help them to become more mature and sympathetic workers.[16]

Representatives of some large firms in the Colony have confirmed these points. One representative of a firm reflected on what the credit union had achieved for his management: 'We do a great deal to encourage the credit union, but we are satisfied that all we do is quite worth while. This union has loaned £F22,000 in its first year. Formerly, all advances were made by me, and I could not possibly have handled anything like one fourth of that amount. Even in trying to handle these advances I am quite sure that I was neglecting many needy cases and falling for the fast arguments of more able talkers.'[17]

His views were strongly supported by the Manager of Bish Ltd, Mr Wood. His firm employs workers from different racial groups. 'I say

[14] Credit Union League file, Suva.

[15] J. F. Golden, president of Western Costume Company, Hollywood. Reprinted by CUNA P.R. Dept. from *Western Apparel Industry*, October 1963.

[16] *Credit Unions* CUNA Form No. M-150, 1961.

[17] Comment recorded by M. Ganey, S.J. in letter to Olaf Spetland, 13 October 1962. The credit union referred to is Carpenter's Employees.

in all frankness,' he said, 'that credit union has relieved me from acting as a loan officer for employee advances.'[18]

Labour turnover can be a costly affair. The editor of *Davui*, the magazine of Carpenter's Employees' Credit Union, noted that credit unions 'by paying fines and late taxes have saved them (the management) the necessity of finding replacements.'[19] The same magazine claimed that the credit union helped to create a happy atmosphere amongst the staff. 'It is bringing the staff together more on common ground,' wrote the editor, 'that is, helping each other and in so doing helping ourselves.'[20] Members of the staff come to see their unity as a bulwark to their common problems.

3. Unions Investment in People as People through Credit

(a) *Education in Saving Money*

If there is to be investment, there must be saving. But if there is to be saving, people must have the will to save. They must know how to save. Thriftiness and initiative are necessary in any economy. But in the emerging countries these virtues tend to be lacking. Apart from the general low income of the majority of the people, there is the prevailing ignorance about the need for and methods of saving.

The South Pacific is no exception to this problem.[21] The late Ratu Sir Lala Sukuna lamented in 1951, when Secretary for Fijian Affairs, that 'Liberality is the law of tradition and to give evidence of thrift or arouse suspicions of miserliness is to sin against the law.'[22] He complained that there was not some method available to teach his people how to save: 'Something . . . was required fully to bring out self-reliance and thrift which in the South Seas are rare qualities in village communities . . . We are still searching for something that will arouse and develop thrift.'[23]

Ratu Sukuna felt that no quick solution could be possible. 'In economic activities as in the sphere of custom, there is a great deal of suspicion and doubt to be overcome.'[24] Consequently, the general lack of confidence in the

[18] Reported in *Na Toso Ni Gauna*, December 1964, p. 4. In 1964, 246 loans were made by Bish Employees' Credit Union, amounting to £F2,058. Membership numbered 85, an increase of 62 in a year.

[19] May 1962, No. 3, pp. 8–9.

[20] ibid. p. 8.

[21] V. D. Stace, *The Pacific Islander and Modern Commerce*, South Pacific Commission, Noumea, 1954, p. 1.

[22] op. cit.

[23] *Council Paper No. 5 of 1953*, par. 4.

[24] ibid.

ability of the Fijian people to save and run their own affairs resulted in strong paternalistic action on the part of the government.[25] If the people would not save freely, then saving would have to be compulsory.

Father Ganey arrived in the Colony in this atmosphere. There was a general scepticism about his proposed efforts to offer the people a chance to save freely and stand on their own feet in money matters.

But there were the optimists also. As the editorial of the major local newspaper noted: 'It is the opinion of more than one observer that the credit union movement may have a profound effect upon the economic development of the Fijian people.'[26] Moreover, it was Ratu Sukuna who saw in credit unions the longed-for opportunity 'to bring out self-reliance and thrift' among the Fijian people.[27] After recognising in credit unions what he was so urgently looking for some months before, Ratu Sukuna placed behind the movement the whole weight of his immense prestige. The trust was fully justified. Within a year of the coming of Father Ganey, credit unions numbered sixty-six. The following are the comparative figures for the first three years of operation:[28]

Date	No. of Unions	No. of Members	Savings	Loans Made since Organisation
31.12.54	66	8,347	£F20,912	£F32,106
31.12.55	139	16,623	£F62,946	£F124,848
31.12.56	187	21,586	£F100,101	£F233,213

Despite the pessimism of the critics, credit unions quickly spread and thousands saved small sums of money each week out of their meagre income. It became clear that credit unions would more than 'counteract some of the harm' of paternalism prevailing in the Colony. Savings have continued to increase. By the end of 1964, the following was the situation:[29]

Date	No. of Unions	No. of Members	Savings	Loans Made since Organisation
31.12.64	288	32,407	£F452,849	£F2,016,420

Little wonder that, in 1959, the Governor singled out credit unions for their role in developing the art of saving, thrift and initiative among the

[25] C. S. Belshaw, *Under the Ivi Tree*, Routledge & Kegan Paul, 1964, p. 218; the *Spate Report*, op. cit. pars. 375–8, 385, 400; and Ratu Sukanu, op. cit.

[26] *The Fiji Times* 30 July 1954.

[27] op. cit. par. 4.

[28] Credit Union League Central Committee, *Report*, 31 December 1956.

[29] *The Pacific Islands Monthly*, op. cit.; Registrar of Credit Unions *Annual Report for Year Ended 31 December 1964*.

citizens of Fiji. Mr P. D. Macdonald, the Colonial Secretary, asserted in 1964 that 'the statistics reveal that credit unions in Fiji are making a real contribution to the solution of one serious problem in Fiji, i.e., the need to inculcate thrift, and the management of money, among the rural population'.[30]

In the first visit to the Credit Union League Office, Suva, in August 1963, the writer asked one Fijian who happened to be waiting for service, what he obtained from joining credit union. He replied first as follows: 'Credit union has taught me, for the first time, to have confidence in money matters. It has taught me to save money, why I should save, how I should save money.' On my visits to the villages in Fiji similar replies were constantly received. The facts and comments speak for themselves.

(b) *Education in Accounting*

Immense care is given by officials to correct accounting procedure. Professor C. Belshaw, an economist, considers that the credit unions have been 'more responsible than any other organ for the recent rapid growth in accounting knowledge' in Fiji.[31] Mr Olaf Spetland, from the International Association of Credit Unions, after an extended visit to Fiji reported:[32] 'I have seen books kept by Fijian cane farmers which are well above the average and would equal much of our first class credit union work elsewhere.'

All credit unions must conduct business according to the exact laws that prevail elsewhere. Father Ganey insisted on this from the very beginning. Hence, he constantly recognised the need to continue to educate officials of credit unions. Consequently, he eventually founded a centre, the Bergengren School, for training officials and providing refresher courses. Space was limited but much successful and thorough work has been done. From time to time short courses are held for larger numbers. For example, in 1964, the League staff assisted at a course conducted for ten days. Forty-two students attended. Forty came from various parts of Fiji and two from Samoa. Sometimes, experts from overseas provide assistance at such courses. Each year an elected representative goes to the international meeting of credit unions in the United States. Contact gained by this travel inevitably assists the educational services of the credit unions in Fiji.

[30] Letter to the Director, Oxford Committee for Famine Relief, 10 June 1964.

[31] R. Firth and B. S. Yamey (Eds.), *Capital, Saving and Credit in Peasant Societies*, George Allen & Unwin, 1965, p. 200.

[32] Cited in the *Report of the Registrar of Credit Unions*, 21 November 1960.

An important contribution to the educational programme was the foundation of a monthly newspaper—*Na Toso Ni Gauna.* During the first six months of 1964 a total of 27,000 were mailed, an increase of 12,000 over the previous six months.

(c) *Education for a Wider Economic and Social Leadership through Credit Unions*

The most notable effects of credit unions in Fiji are not so immediately evident.

A community is a living union of people only if membership draws a person into facing the problems which exist around him. A person must draw strength from the community to try to do something about these problems. Through credit unions people are taught how and why they should save money, and how to solve particular financial problems. But many difficulties remain in the villages in which credit unions exist: obstacles to individual initiative in economic matters such as farming. If credit unions failed to have wider influence in village or national affairs than just the visible saving and lending of money, then it would be right to admonish them for narrowness and even complacency in the face of grave problems.

In actual fact, credit unions, through attainment of their primary ends, have had wider beneficial effects in the village and national life of the Fijian community. The credit union movement has not been the occasion of restricting creativity of individuals or of confirming them in their lack of confidence before the challenges of modern economic demands. On the contrary, in innumerable cases, credit unions have provided individuals with their first opportunities to assume definite initiative in economic and social affairs.

(i) *Development of leadership.* The element of self-confidence is found in both urban and rural credit unions. For example, a president of one union stated spontaneously when asked what he had obtained from membership of his credit union: 'Work on the credit union has given me confidence in myself. Before credit union came to my place, I did not have sufficient confidence to go to the Agricultural Department and ask for advice. I had only eighteen months of education. But as I found I could save and manage money affairs, I gained more confidence. Now I can go to the Agricultural Department and tell them that they are my servants—come and give me advice.'

In these words of a middle-aged man, we have the most notable effect of credit unions—the development of confidence in one's own ability to run one's own affairs, a determination to face up to reality. This point can be appreciated fully only by those who witnessed the tragic lack of confidence that prevailed among so many villagers prior to the arrival of credit unions.[33] Obviously, credit unions have not removed all hesitancy. But their achievement has been, in their short history, tremendous.

Comments in the Spate Report referred to a strong feeling of administrative neglect on the part of the Government. The question session showed that the people were dissatisfied with the impersonal, bureaucratic nature of government departments. In the minds of the people, the actions of the officials in far away Suva showed a basic distrust of the honesty of the people. When loans were applied for from the appropriate department, officials came to investigate the worthiness of the claims. After long delays, the loans might be granted. If the loan was granted, however, it was not made to the farmer directly but to the person or business from whom the object or service was being procured. As one informant noted: 'I have been a cane farmer for six years. I was earning money but not enough to develop my land. I requested a £200 loan from the government. It was granted. But it took eighteen months before the loan was paid.' This meant that the farmer's efforts at self-improvement were held up for eighteen months. Little wonder if people became discouraged. The same speaker contrasted the red tape connected with this loan with the immediate personal, trusting concern of his credit union: 'When the credit union was set up I became a member. My first application was for £200. Two days later I got the £200 and with it I bought twelve cattle. I was helped immediately.'[34]

The hundreds of loans made by credit unions for productive purposes clearly indicate that the immediate service provided a great number of people in Fiji with their first confident steps at investment, and a new life.[35]

[33] This lack of confidence in economic affairs was well expressed in the speech of welcome to Fr Ganey by the people of remote Nuku: 'You who come to us from the great credit union movement must know that in our spiritual and moral life we Fijians, while not perfect, have much to thank God for—but economically we are at a loss. You come bringing an umbrella—an umbrella to protect us. We welcome you—we have awaited your arrival most anxiously . . . We wait for the message of the umbrella.'

[34] For an account of this loan see *Na Toso Ni Gauna*, October–November 1964, p. 1.

[35] See the relevant comments by the Fijian anthropologist, R. Nayacakalou, 'Traditional and Modern Types of Leadership and Economic Development among the Fijians', *The International Social Science Journal*, Vol. 16., No. 2, 1964, p. 268.

This confidence to stand on one's feet in money matters has inevitably overflowed into wider spheres of activity.

(ii) *Removal of cultural obstacles to development through credit unions*

CREDIT UNIONS AND CHIEFLY AUTHORITY. The Nominating Committee of the Carpenter's Employees Credit Union firmly reminded all members to choose officers 'who will do their work thoroughly and willingly'. 'They must be officers', the report continued, 'who can be trusted to look after your savings.' Their advice was followed. But this is not unexpected since the union is an urban one, with membership from different racial groups. The problem is—has the same advice been heeded by credit unions in rural Fiji where the pressure of kinship, liberality and chiefly status are still strong? Credit unions insist on the democratic principle. Only those officers should be elected who have ability. Therefore, chiefs or those of ascribed status who have not the necessary qualifications should not be elected. Co-operatives in Fiji had suffered much in the early years from the failure to insist on the principle of democracy.[36] But credit unions have in fact been little troubled by this problem. Father Ganey insisted, from the very beginning, on the principle of democracy within credit unions.

In discussions, Fijians showed an awareness of a twofold pressure: (1) a pressure, rooted in traditional custom, to give the leadership of the credit union over to those of chiefly status; (2) a pressure to grant chiefs loans without sufficient justification out of fear of their traditional authority.

When questioned about the first pressure, the Credit Union League officials asserted that they could not think of any chief (of whatever status) who had been elected on to the board of directors of any credit union. There may have been one or two cases, they said, but such examples would be too rare to notice immediately.

This in itself is a magnificent achievement. It directly implies that the people have assimilated the basic credit union notion of democratic equality. In the vast majority of cases, they have elected only those officials whom they consider best suited to direct their money affairs. When they have not done so, they gradually realised their mistake, and sought to correct the situation.

As regards the second pressure, informants frequently stated that they would never give way to demands by chiefs for loans simply because they were chiefs. One Buli (a Fijian official in charge of a subdivision of a

[36] *Spate Report*, op. cit. par. 321.

Province) in the Bemana area requested a loan of £300 from his credit union. He was turned down because the committee considered his request unjustifiable. Some admitted that they felt a tension between their loyalty to credit union laws and to their chiefs. 'But', as one asserted, 'we keep our customs out of the credit union.' No doubt in some areas this pressure or tension is felt strongly still.

Credit Union League officials reported that cases had arisen in which chiefs had been threatened with court action by credit union directors for failing to keep up payments on a loan. On the other hand, chiefs with authority over Fijians have become aware of the role of credit unions as a helpful force in the community and of value to themselves. By belonging to credit unions, the people are better able to pay taxes and fulfil their other civic responsibilities.

CREDIT UNION AND KINSHIP OBLIGATIONS. Traditionally, there are numerous kinship obligations and avoidances within the Fijian social structure.[37] It has been asserted that these obligations and avoidances have frequently undermined so many efforts at economic and social improvement among the Fijians.[38] Hence, one would expect that since credit unions are frequently situated in villages away from urban influence, they would have suffered from the same failings. But, from the information gathered, kinship obligations have had only a minimal influence in the operation of credit unions.

CREDIT UNION AND KEREKERE. Kerekere is the practice of 'borrowing' from kinsmen at the will of the borrower. Traditionally, it was a form of social security.[39] By it a man's kin were obliged to see him through material misfortune. It had a distinctive beneficial role in a subsistent economy, for it contributed to social solidarity and helped spread consumption goods more evenly. But, in its traditional sense, kerekere is an obstacle to the integration of Fijians into the now necessary money economy. The Spate Report records that 'kerekere puts a premium on laziness and is often a serious or even disastrous drain on those Fijians who are endeavour-

[37] For an analysis of the kinship structure among the Fijians, see R. Nayacakalou, 'The Fijian System of Kinship and Marriage', *The Journal of the Polynesian Society*, Vol. 64 No. 1, 1955 and Vol. 66 No. 1, 1957.

[38] *Spate Report*, op. cit. pars. 324–31.

[39] M. D. Sahlins, *Moala—Culture and Nature on A Fijian Island*, Ann Arbor, University of Michigan Press 1962, pp. 203–14; *Spate Report*, op. cit. pars. 74–7, 142-5.

ing to accumulate and to invest.' The Government sought to make illegal any kerekere of money or property above the value of five shillings. But the law is practically a dead letter.[40]

Hence, a clear test as to the ability of credit unions to overcome traditional cultural obstacles to development must be the degree according to which it has triumphed over the custom of kerekere. In this matter, credit unions faced a twofold problem: (1) Would Fijians regard the money in credit unions as an object of kerekere? If they did, then they would be extremely slow in repaying loans—if at all. (2) Would Fijians insist that friends and relatives borrow money for them from credit unions by giving false reasons for the loans?

Father Ganey had heard from many quarters that kerekere would be a problem. As early as February 1954, he tested the value of these warnings. He writes on one occasion: 'Last Tuesday I went to three Fijian villages and I put to them . . . "These people in Suva tell me you have a custom called kerekere . . . and that having that custom your people can never manage a credit union for you will not repay loans." '

He records the impressions of the Fijians to this: 'What this particular Fijian, who answered for the village, said was substantially as follows: "We have a custom, kerekere, and we understand the custom . . . We know that when we give something according to kerekere we do not ask for a strict repayment. We are also quite capable of understanding credit union loans, and the repayment obligation and the interest, and we are able to distinguish between the two. We can fulfil our obligations in each and never confuse them in our thinking." '

The confidence was fully justified. Statistics prove the point. The annual report of the Credit Union Central Committee for 1954 stated that, by the end of December of that year, a total of 66 credit unions had been successfully established with a total membership of 8,347. Some 3,215 loans had been made totalling £F32,106. Savings amounted to £F20,396. Despite the huge sums saved and loaned in the first year of operation, the report noted only one instance of irregularity. Matters were rectified promptly

[40] op. cit. pars 142–5.
Professor C. Belshaw does not consider that kerekere is any longer a problem. See *Under the Ivi Tree*, op. cit. p. 211. The Burns Commission Report, however, implied that, though many Fijians condemned the practice, kerekere remained. 'This is certainly one of the most severe handicaps under which the Fijian lives. An energetic and progressive man can be completely ruined by his predatory relatives.' (Op. cit. par. 66.) No doubt areas will differ in the application of the custom. Professor Belshaw's survey was conducted in the Sigatoka valley.

and the credit union did not suffer unduly from its initial setback.[41] The report did not refer to any difficulties about kerekere. Loan repayment was as it should be.

Two village credit unions, chosen at random by the Credit Union League for examination in 1958, had a combined membership of 235. Over a period of time, 100 loans had been made totalling £F865. The average loan was about £F8.10.0. The League reported: 'The average member was repaying his loan promptly and, where there was difficulty in repaying, the committees seemed to be adjusting matters in a manner satisfactory to the borrower.'[42]

The Spate Report, when reviewing co-operatives in Fiji, noted that 'nepotism and speculation were common, although it is fair to say that misappropriation was often not so much a matter of conscious dishonesty as of failure to discriminate between duty to the society and duty to kinship or customary demands: money was needed, money was to hand, and social or family pressure saw that it was used.'[43]

The same report, when speaking of credit unions, significantly records that the unions have not experienced the problems that were being suffered by the co-operatives. If kerekere affected credit unions, it would most surely show itself in the villages. But the village credit unions have an excellent record.[44]

Later, the Burns Commission Report stated that among the credit unions 'there had been comparatively few bad debts, and it is satisfactory to learn that the officials of the unions have no hesitation in taking legal proceedings against delinquent debtors.'[45] The two most recent annual reports of the Registrar of Credit Unions expressed the same confidence.[46]

The conclusion is obvious. The constant rate of repayment by the vast majority of borrowers strongly suggests that the people do not transfer the custom of kerekere to credit union savings.

When questioned about kerekere, members of credit unions showed that they were aware that it could interfere with the organisation of the unions.

[41] op. cit. par. 27.
[42] Submission to the Burns Commission, op. cit.
[43] op. cit. par. 324.
[44] ibid. par. 368.
[45] ibid. par. 704.
[46] The Registrar of Credit Unions reported in the *Annual Report* for year ended 31 December 1964 that 'the percentages which the outstanding loans bear to total assets continue to conform to correct credit union practice.' (Par. 2.)

But they insisted that kerekere was kept out of credit unions. The following are representative of the comments: 'We know kerekere is a problem but we keep it out of the credit union.' 'Kerekere is a problem in economic development but not in the credit union.' 'Kerekere is dying out. We know that the credit union has helped it to die.'

From one point of view, it is understandable that credit unions are an effective barrier to kerekere. Members of the loan committee of a credit union, because of the common bond of village or employment or church membership, are intimately aware of the problems of other members seeking loans. The genuineness of the request for a loan can normally be quickly tested. Moreover, any member would naturally be wary about asking for a loan that is really for a relative lest, if found out, his chances for future loans would be endangered. The role of the common bond, therefore, cannot be overestimated as a counter to kerekere. No doubt there is the odd loan given on false pretences. This would be expected in any such organisation in any part of the world.

A strong impression gathered during the discussions was that Fijians were delighted with the opportunity provided by credit unions to break the custom of kerekere. Credit unions offered them an official and justifiable excuse to refuse pressures of kerekere from relatives and friends.

CULTURAL ADAPTATION THROUGH CREDIT UNIONS. Credit unions have provided one highly successful method of giving new vigour to the Fijian community virtues of liberality and mutual service but now stripped of their cultural hindrances to economic development. For example, kerekere continues to live in the credit union, not in its old customary guise, but adapted to new demands. By saving money, members of a credit union are able to help each other by providing opportunities for others to obtain loans. But members still retain full ownership of their savings.

Father Ganey correctly sensed that kerekere would take on a new life. Speaking of the concept of solidarity characteristic of traditional Fijian life, he said that 'it is quite possible that this priceless and genuine old Fijian element can be reclaimed in its full vigour and be used for service in the modern institution of the credit union.'[47]

Informants frequently said that before credit unions came, they could not trust anyone—even relatives—with their money. There had been too

[47] Credit Union League file (n.d.).

many failures in the past. But now with credit unions 'we trust each other'.[48] The following are comments by members of village credit unions. They aptly illustrate the point: 'Community of thought is the foundation of Fijian life. Credit union is now helping us to live together, to help one another, to live again this community of thought.' 'Before credit union came, I wanted to be alone—but with credit union way of life everyone is a brother. Through belonging to credit union I feel I am doing something for mankind.' 'Before credit union came, I would not have trusted others in the village with my money. This is one of the benefits of credit union. One is now able to trust a member to receive money on our behalf.' 'In some villages it is nearly impossible to get the people to work together. Here in this settlement we see different religions able to work together. I think it is a great thing for Fiji that the people are able to get together to promote economic life, and be able to reduce the poverty among the people.'

4. Conclusion

Credit unions in Fiji are an example of grass roots development. Thousands of people have been taught to save money for the first time.

But the successes of credit unions are far wider reaching than this. Saving—no matter how small—has generated in the people a sense of achievement, a confidence in their own ability to deal with the problems of everyday living themselves. People who for years have been hesitant to take the initiative in economic and social life because they felt others did not trust them to act responsibly, have discovered in credit unions an atmosphere of trust.

It has been said that the 'chief task of education is above all to shape man, to guide the evolving dynamism through which man forms himself as a man.'[49] In this sense, credit unions are educational. Credit unions have provided an atmosphere for self-help. Thousands of people have learned to stand on their own feet, to develop themselves as human beings.

This has been done partly because the philosophy of the credit union is built on the primacy of the person—on the belief that people can

[48] Professor C. Belshaw, in his survey of the Sigatoka Valley, felt that 'it might be argued that the credit unions constitute a rationalisation and control of kerekere, and that their popularity is due to a similarity of function between the two institutions.' R. Firth and B. S. Yamey (Eds.), *Capital, Saving and Credit in Peasant Societies*, Allen & Unwin, 1964, p. 200.

[49] J. Maritain, *Education at the Crossroads*, Yale University Press, 1943, p. 1.

and will act responsibly when stimulated by an atmosphere of trust and respect.

Fundamentally, however, people will be inspired to act for themselves only if they see in their teachers that philosophy as a living reality. The success of credit unions in Fiji must ultimately be due to Father Ganey and to those who worked with him and who now direct the movement. Father Ganey was able to inspire the people to act for themselves because he firmly believed in their potential for self-development. Fijians quickly sensed his fundamental, anti-paternalistic philosophy. They understood credit union philosophy because they witnessed its concrete embodiment in him. Father Ganey once summarised his convictions and approach quite simply:

'To young missionaries who get into this work, I would say that they'll never do very much in this field until they realise that they are not doing the people the favour by going to them; it is the people who do us missionaries the favour by opening the door of their village to us.

'We are not the people's boss; we are their servant. We cannot make the credit union, the co-operative, the new social way of life work; we can only point the way.'[50]

In an emerging land there is a strong temptation for educators to act paternally, to impose from the top an ideal plan for development. But the plan—no matter how objectively correct it is—will most certainly fail and cause suffering to people unless the people feel that they are trusted as human beings. They must feel the need for development. People will feel the need for development only if they feel they are accepted as persons.

When Father Ganey first came to Fiji he spent hours and days explaining credit unions to the people. There was never any attempt to force them on anyone. If after discussions and questions a village still had not felt a need for a credit union, he would never impose it on the people or show impatience. Later, he knew, the village would recognise the need and ask for a credit union. In these circumstances, the credit union was bound to be successful. The free will and intelligence of the people had been acknowledged.

The study of credit union expansion in Fiji fulfils an urgent need. At a period when so much generous aid is being channelled into the underdeveloped world, we need to be reminded through graphic examples just what aid ultimately is for—the development of people as people. We need

[50] Reported in J. J. Considine (Ed.), *The Missionary's Role in Socio-Economic Betterment*, Newman Press, 1960, p. 213.

to be reminded how that aid is to be given, 'that we are not doing the people a favour' by helping them, that 'we are not the people's boss; we are their servant'.[51]

[51] Field work for this paper was conducted during the summer of 1964–5.

Special thanks are due to Father M. Ganey, S.J., to the Credit Union League, Fiji, and to Mr Joane Naisara who acted as interpreter.

5

Credit Unions in Queensland*

by J. Stanford

1. Introduction

Until 1960, the development of credit unions in Queensland had been slow. During the last six years the number and size of credit unions have expanded at an increasing rate. The prospects for further growth are bright.

Queensland credit unions are similar in organisation and operation to credit unions elsewhere and display individual differences. Because there is no special Credit Union Act in Queensland, credit unions operate under the legislative provisions regulating the activities of co-operative societies generally. Consequently, Queensland credit unions possess some distinctive characteristics. For example, they are allowed to trade in goods and to accept money on deposit from non-members. A number of credit unions do trade and while the results of these trading activities have been generally satisfactory some problems have arisen.

Until this study of credit unions was carried out there was very little published information about Queensland credit unions. As credit unions are rapidly becoming a more significant part of the capital market, it would be unfortunate if further research beyond this study were not undertaken.

The Legal Status of Credit Unions in Queensland

Under Queensland legislation, credit unions as such are not recognised. The provisions of The Co-operative Societies Act 1946 to 1962 are general

* The co-operation and assistance of the Registrar of Co-operative Societies and his staff, particularly Mr J. Kilmartin and Mr R. Johnson, which made possible the collection of statistical data on which this paper is based, are gratefully acknowledged. Responsibility for the use of the data and the conclusions drawn rest entirely with me.

[1] A new Co-operative Societies Act, which recognises credit unions as such, received assent in 1968.

and they allow co-operative societies to carry on any business, industry or trade. Dealing in land and the acceptance of money on deposit are also allowed. Societies are allowed to make loans to members for general domestic purposes and business purposes. Consequently the range of activities of societies registered under the provisions of this Act is wide. There are a number of co-operative societies whose main activity is financial intermediation.[2] Not all of these have been regarded, for the purposes of this paper, as credit unions. Only those societies which meet fairly readily the criteria enumerated in the introduction to these essays have been classified as credit unions.

The societies which have been excluded from the classification include a local savings bank, one which makes only housing loans (and is financed by a small life office), two societies which do not make loans to members but to the church to which their members belong and one society financed by an instrumentality of the Netherlands Government.[3]

Formation of a credit union is formally a simple matter. Seven or more persons may form a society after a formation meeting has been held. At the meeting a statement of the objects of the society, its method of finance and the reasons for believing the society will be a success must be presented. A set of rules for the operation of the society must be approved at the meeting. Registration of the society is effected when the rules of the society are certified as conforming to the requirements of the Act and certain prescribed information is forwarded to the Registrar of Co-operative Societies.[4]

2. Analysis of Growth

Membership of Credit Unions

The procedure for gaining membership of a credit union is simple: a prospective member applies for the prescribed number of shares in the credit union. The rules of most credit unions require members to hold at

[2] These societies are included in the statistical section of the Annual Reports of the Registrar of Co-operative Societies as 'Savings and Loan Societies'.

[3] The Netherlands Immigration Board has provided loans to a number of co-operative housing societies in Queensland. These societies lend to former Netherlands citizens. (Details of the amount of loans from this source can be found in the Annual Reports of the Registrar of Co-operative Housing Societies.) The co-operative society mentioned in the text made loans to its members, Dutch immigrants, for household purposes.

[4] Credit unions are also required to register as money-lenders.

least five fully paid shares before full membership rights can bc exercised.[5] The nominal value of shares is usually two dollars and nearly all credit unions make provision for payment of shares by instalments (e.g. 20 cents per share per week). Until the minimum value of shares has been fully subscribed, members are unable to vote, make deposits, apply for loans or receive dividends. Most credit unions charge a small (e.g. 50 cents) application fee to cover administrative costs. Shares in credit unions cannot be legally offered for sale; they must be transferred or repurchased at the discretion of the management of the credit union.

Membership has increased rapidly since 1960 as shown in table 1.

TABLE 1 QUEENSLAND CREDIT UNIONS: GROWTH OF MEMBERSHIP, 1950–66*

Year Ended 30 June	Number of Credit Unions		Number of Members
	Registered	Reporting	
1950	2	2	131
1951	2	2	148
1952	2	1	172 p.e.
1953	2	2	188
1954	3	3	256
1955	3	2	343 p.e.
1956	3	2	374 p.e.
1957	3	3	396
1958	3	3	431
1959	3	3	441
1960	6	6	1129 p.e.
1961	6	6	1324
1962	6	6	1498
1963	9	9	1982
1964	15	13	3203
1965	19	18	4689
1966	23	23	6866
1967	27	26	10,707

Notes: p.e. Partly estimated.

* The above figures understate the number of Queensland residents who are members of credit unions. Some Queensland residents are members of credit unions registered in other states. The number involved could be substantial as the Commonwealth Bank Officers' Association Credit Union, the largest credit union in Australia, and the C.S.I.R.O. Credit Union have Queensland members but are registered in New South Wales.

Source: Statutory Annual Returns of Co-operative Societies.

[5] Average paid-up capital per member is $10 in twelve credit unions; less than $10 in eight; less than $30 in two. The other credit union has a second class of shares, 'withdrawable shares', which are virtually equivalent to deposits, and its accounts do not distinguish between the two types of shares.

The Co-operative Societies Act provides that members of societies must hold at least one share but cannot hold shares of a value in excess of $2,000.

Queensland credit unions are mainly associations of people working for the same employer, organised in the same trade union, etc. The most significant bond of association is that of the same employer and trade union. The largest credit unions in Queensland draw their membership from employees of government departments or instrumentalities. However, as table 2 shows, the range of common bonds of association is large.

TABLE 2 QUEENSLAND CREDIT UNIONS: CLASSIFIED BY BOND OF ASSOCIATION, 1966

Number of Members	Single Employer	Single Employer and Trade Union	Trade Union	Employers' Business Activity	Religious	Social	Self Employed	Total
0–100	1	—	1	1	1	2	1	7
101–200	2	1	—	2	2	—	—	7
201–300	—	1	—	—	—	—	—	1
301–400	—	—	1	—	1	—	—	2
401–500	—	2	1	—	—	—	—	3
501–1,000	—	2	—	—	—	—	—	2
over 1,001	—	1	—	—	—	—	—	1
Total	3	7	3	3	4	2	1	23

Source: Annual Returns; Rules of Co-operative Societies.

Operation of Credit Unions

The operation of a credit union is directed by a committee of management (also called board of directors). The management committee is elected by the members and the rules of credit unions usually provide for retirement by rotation. The most common size of management committees is seven; nine credit unions have a committee of this size while seven credit unions have a committee of nine. Other sizes of committees are twelve (three credit unions); five (two credit unions) and three (two credit unions).

The duties of the committee of management are to appoint officers and staff, decide deposit and loan rates and formulate general management policy. The management committee usually meets fortnightly (in some instances weekly if it considers applications for loans) and members serve without remuneration. Two credit unions, however, pay directors' fees but the amount is nominal.[6]

[6] The Annual Income and Expenditure Statements of four credit unions show the payment of honorariums but it is not possible to determine if this includes payment to directors rather than honorary secretaries or treasurers.

TABLE 3 QUEENSLAND CREDIT UNIONS: RATIO OF OPERATING EXPENSES TO GROSS INCOME BY SIZE OF CREDIT UNION, 1966

Total Funds ($)	Ratio of Expenses to Gross Income (per cent)								
	0–40	41–50	51–60	61–70	71–80	81–90	91–100	Over 100	Total
0–10,000	—	—	—	1	—	—	2	5	8
10,001–20,000	—	1	1	—	1	1	—	2	6
20,001–50,000	1	—	—	1	—	—	—	1	3
50,001–200,000	—	—	—	—	2	1	—	—	3
200,001–500,000	—	—	—	—	—	1	—	1	2
Total	1	1	1	2	3	3	2	9	22

Notes: (a) One credit union, in liquidation, is omitted.
(b) Dividends on share capital are excluded from expenses.
Source: Calculated from Annual Returns.

At least three credit unions have, as well, elected credit committees and supervisory committees.[7] The credit committee examines and approves loan applications; the supervisory committee conducts internal checks and audits of accounting procedures.

Income of Credit Unions

The largest source of income for credit unions is interest received on loans. In 1966, over 96 per cent of income was from this source.[8] Other sources of income are application fees paid by members, interest received on bank deposits, trade discounts and commissions, donations and trading profits.

Expenses of Credit Unions

The major item of expense of credit unions is interest paid on loans which, in 1966, amounted to just over 50 per cent for all credit unions. Other important elements of expenses are postage and stationery, office supplies, accounting and secretarial fees and an increasingly large item

[7] Credit unions have a statutory obligation to report the existence and membership of the management committee only.

[8] The importance of interest as a source of income to credit unions is understated because, in 1966, there was a large number of newly established credit unions whose major source of income was entrance fees. One credit union, the oldest in Queensland, does not charge interest on loans because its members believe lending money at interest is morally wrong. Expenses are covered by an annual poll levy on members. One can sympathise with the reluctance of this credit union to register as a money-lender.

is expenses for credit union activities.[9] The larger credit unions hold loan protection insurance which pays out outstanding loans on the death of a member.

Appraisal of credit union operations is difficult because the usual profit test cannot be applied without qualification owing to the use of volunteer labour. A useful guide, however, *is the ratio of* operating expenses to gross income as shown in table 3.

The number of small credit unions with high expense ratios reflects two influences. Small credit unions tend to be either newly established and thus incur heavy initial expenses at a time when their income is relatively low or they tend to be old and languishing. Larger credit unions tend to have high expense ratios because more of their work is done by paid labour and they acquire their own offices and equipment.

In the early stages of the life of a credit union it may use the facilities of its sponsoring body (e.g. trade union, employer), without cost. A high expense ratio is not necessarily indicative of lower efficiency as, for example, a full-time staff is generally able to provide more convenient service to members.

Earnings rates, the ratio of net earnings to issued capital, for credit unions in 1966 varied over a wide range and reflect the influence of both the expense ratio and gearing ratios.

TABLE 4 QUEENSLAND CREDIT UNIONS: RATIO OF NET EARNINGS TO ISSUED SHARES BY SIZE OF CREDIT UNION, 1966

Total Funds ($)	Ratio of Net Earnings to Issued Shares (per cent)						
	Less than 0	0–10	11–20	21–30	31–40	41–90	Total
0–10,000	5	2	—	—	—	1	8
10,001–20,000	2	1	2	—	1	—	6
20,001–50,000	1	1	—	—	1	—	3
50,001–200,000	—	—	—	1	1	1	3
200,001–500,000	1	—	—	1	—	—	2
Total	9	4	2	2	3	2	22

Notes: (a) One credit union, in liquidation, is excluded.
(b) Net earnings are gross income less operating expenses.
Source: Calculated from Annual Returns.

The allocation of profits is at the discretion of the credit union; the only

[9] Included here are credit union league affiliation fees, expenses for attendance at conferences, expenses for celebration of Credit Union Day on 4 October each year.

TABLE 5 INCOME OF QUEENSLAND CREDIT UNIONS 1950–66 ($'000)

Year	Interest Received Loans (1)	Interest Received Other (2)	Fees Paid by Members (3)	Other (4)	Total (5)	(1)/(5) %	(3)/(5) %	(2) + (4)/(5) %
1950	0·2		0·1		0·4	57·4	39·8	2·8
1951	0·3		0·2	0·1	0·6	55·3	27·6	17·1
1952	0·4	0·1	0·3	0·1	0·9	46·8	29·0	14·2
1953	0·5	0·1	0·3		1·0	52·0	33·1	14·9
1954	0·4	0·1	0·4	0·2	1·1	39·4	32·6	28·0
1955 p.e.	0·5		0·4		0·9	55·9	39·8	4·3
1956 p.e.	0·5		0·2		0·8	64·6	29·0	6·4
1957	0·6		0·4	0·3	1·3	45·8	34·2	20·0
1958	0·7		0·5	0·2	1·5	47·6	35·4	17·0
1959	0·7		0·6	0·2	1·6	46·3	38·9	14·8
1960	2·1		0·8	0·2	3·1	68·2	24·7	7·1
1961	5·6		0·5	0·3	6·6	87·3	8·0	4·7
1962	9·9	0·1	0·4	0·4	10·8	91·6	3·8	4·6
1963	15·5	0·2	0·4	0·6	16·8	92·5	2·6	4·9
1964	32·0	0·3	0·8	0·6	33·7	94·9	2·4	2·7
1965	55·9	0·7	0·9	0·6	58·1	96·2	1·6	2·2
1966	91·6	1·0	1·6	1·0	95·2	96·2	1·7	2·1

Notes: p.e. Partly estimated.
Sum of components may not add to total due to rounding.
Source: Calculated from Annual Returns.

TABLE 6 EXPENDITURE BY QUEENSLAND CREDIT UNIONS, 1950–66 ($'000)

Year	Interest Paid: Deposits (1)	Interest Paid: Other (2)	Wages and Salaries (3)	Accounting and Audit Fees (4)	Directors' Fees (5)	Honorarium (6)	Rent (7)	Other (8)	Surplus (9)	Total (10)	(1)/(10) %	(3)+(4)+(5)+(6)/(10) %	(9)/(10) %	(2)+(7)+(9)/(10) %
1950	0·1							0·1	0·2	0·4				
1951	0·2							0·2	0·2	0·6				
1952	0·3							0·1	0·5	0·9				
1953	0·3							0·3	0·4	1·0				
1954*	0·2							0·3	0·6	1·1				
1955*	0·4							0·3	0·2	0·9				
1956	0·4							0·4	0·2	0·8				
1957	0·5							0·4	0·4	1·3				
1958	0·5							0·5	0·4	1·5				
1959	0·5							0·7	0·4	1·6				
1960	0·5			0·1		0·1		0·7	1·7	3·1	16·1	6·5	54·8	32·6
1961	2·5			0·3	0·2	0·1		1·0	2·5	6·6	37·9	9·1	37·9	15·1
1962	5·3			0·4	0·2	0·1		3·0	1·8	10·8	49·1	6·5	16·7	27·7
1963	10·5		0·2	0·5		0·2	0·2	1·8	2·9	16·8	62·5	5·4	17·3	14·8
1964	21·4	0·1	0·8	1·0	0·3	0·6	0·2	4·3	5·0	33·7	63·5	8·3	14·8	13·4
1965	33·0	0·2	4·3	0·9	0·8	1·9	0·1	6·4	7·9	58·1	56·7	13·9	13·6	15·8
1966	49·9	0·2	9·5	2·0	0·8	2·2	2·4	21·7	6·5	95·2	52·4	15·2	6·8	25·6

Notes: * Partly estimated.
Sum of components may not add to total due to rounding. Dissection of expense categories may not be complete.
Source: Calculated from Annual Returns.

statutory requirement is that five per cent of profits in any year must be allocated to a capital reserve. Dividend rates are at, or slightly below, the rate paid on deposits. One credit union distributes profits to members by way of a rebate on loan interest paid. In 1966, this credit union returned half of loan interest paid. In general, most of profits, after tax has been paid, are retained either as provision for bad debts or as a general reserve.

Problems of Management

To achieve operational efficiency in a credit union requires, in part, the making of a bulk of routine calculations quickly and accurately. Transactions on deposits and loan accounts have to be recorded and interest on loans has to be calculated each month. Use of volunteer labour increases the difficulty of achieving operational efficiency. Credit unions have found a number of ways of overcoming these problems.

Employees of associated bodies, e.g. trade unions, work part-time on credit union business and the services of professional accounting firms are engaged.

One of the most serious problems management of a credit union faces is minimising bad debts. The actual amount of bad debts written off has been small[10] because of the moral pressures exerted on members to meet repayments; the provision of payroll deductions for loan repayments; and the care exercised in granting loans and the provision of loan protection insurance. One of the smaller credit unions has experienced difficulty with persistent bad debts and has instituted legal proceedings against two members.

Supervision of Credit Unions

The Co-operative Societies Act requires that credit union annual accounts are to be audited by a registered public accountant and that two copies of the accounts, together with the auditor's report, are filed with the Registrar. Credit unions are also required to submit a statutory return each year giving details of membership, the management committee, income and expenditure and the balance sheet.

In general, supervision of credit unions is limited to ensuring that the requirements of the Act are complied with. There is no regular supervision designed to ensure the financial stability of credit unions. The reasons for this lack of regular supervision are not hard to find. Credit unions have

[10] Bad debts written off by credit unions in Queensland since 1950 has been less than £3000. Some of these have been ultimately recovered.

TABLE 7A CREDIT UNIONS IN QUEENSLAND, SOURCE OF FUNDS, 1950–66 (2)

Year	Paid-Up Capital		Deposits (b)		Capital and Other General Reserves		Loans from Non-Members		Provision for Bad Debts		Other		TOTAL	
	Amt. ($) '000	%	Amt. ($) '000	%	Amt. ($) '000	%	Amt. ($) '000	%	Amt. ($) '000	%	Amt. ($) '000	%	Amt. ($) '000	%
1950	5·3	48	5·6	50	0·2	2							11·1	100
1951	6·3	40	8·7	55	0·5	3					0·3	2	15·9	100
1952	8·4	40	12·0	57	0·7	3					0·1	—	21·1	100
1953	9·9	42	12·5	53	0·9	5					—	—	23·4	100
1954	10·5	44	12·2	51	1·3	5					—	—	24·0	100
1955p.e.	12·0	49	11·2	46	1·4	5					—	—	24·6	100
1956p.e.	14·0	54	10·2	40	1·5	6					—	—	25·7	100
1957	16·5	61	9·1	33	1·6	6	—	—	—	—	0·4	—	27·5	100
1958	19·2	63	9·1	30	1·8	6	—	—	—	—	0·6	1	30·5	100
1959	22·9	65	8·5	24	1·9	6	2·0	5	—	—	0·1	—	35·4	100
1960	34·0	49	30·0	43	2·5	4	2·0	3	—	—	1·4	1	69·8	100
1961	39·9	37	60·0	57	4·3	4	2·0	2	—	—	2·4	—	108·6	100
1962	44·4	26	116·3	68	5·9	3	2·0	1	—	—	3·2	2	171·8	100
1963	53·2	17	247·7	78	8·9	3	3·0	1	0·2	—	4·1	1	317·1	100
1964	66·4	11	493·9	83	12·7	3	4·5	—	0·4	—	15·8	3	593·6	100
1965	70·2	8	772·4	88	7·0c	1	4·5	—	7·0	1	17·0	2	878·1	100
1966	94·6	7	1141·2	88	18·9	3	6·5	—	6·7	—	21·6	2	1289·6	100

Notes: p.e. Partly estimated.
(a) Figures for 1962 to 1966 exclude funds in respect of trading activities of one credit union.
(b) Deposits include Members Loan Funds, *i.e.* amounts allocated to members from profit but not paid in cash.
(c) Decrease in this item in 1965 was a result of losses incurred by two credit unions.
(d) Sum of components may not add to total because of rounding.

Source: Calculated from Annual Returns.

TABLE 7B QUEENSLAND CREDIT UNIONS, USE OF FUNDS, 1950–66

	Cash		Fixed Deposits with Banks		Advances Outstanding		Loans to other credit unions		Other		Total	
Year	Amt ($) '000	%	Amt. ($) '000	%	Amt. ($) '000	%	Amt. ($) '000	%	Amt. ($) '000	%	Amt. ($) '000	%
1950	4·0	36	—	—	7·1	64	—	—	0·1	—	11·1	100
1951	2·3	15	—	—	13·4	85	—	—	0·1	—	15·9	100
1952	1·2	6	—	—	19·8	94	—	—	0·1	—	21·1	100
1953	5·9	25	—	—	17·3	74	—	—	0·1	—	23·4	100
1954	5·5	23	—	—	18·2	76	—	—	0·3	1	24·0	100
1955 p.e.	4·0	16	—	—	20·2	82	—	—	0·4	2	24·6	100
1956 p.e.	3·2	13	—	—	22·0	—	—	—	0·5	—	25·7	100
1957	1·7	6	—	—	25·2	92	—	—	0·7	2	27·5	100
1958	2.8	9	—	—	27·4	90	—	—	0·3	1	30·5	100
1959	3·0	9	—	—	31·6	90	—	—	0·9	1	35·4	100
1960	5·1	7	—	—	64·2	92	—	—	0·5	1	69·8	100
1961	5·3	5	—	—	102·8	95	—	—	0·5	—	108·6	100
1962	4·6	3	—	—	166·9	97	—	—	0·2	—	171·8	100
1963	21·8	7	—	—	294·2	93	—	—	1·0	—	317·1	100
1964	16·5	3	—	—	560·6	95	11·0	2	5·5	1	593·6	100
1965	31·1	4	—	—	839·2	96	4·0	—	3·7	—	878·1	100
1966	48·8	4	17·0	1	1192·3a	93	5·5	—	26·4	2	1289·6	100

Notes: p.e. Partly estimated.
(a) Cash includes cash on hand and at call with bank.
(b) For 1962 to 1966 figures include funds in respect of trading of one credit union.
Source: Calculated from Annual Returns.

until recently been few in number and small in size and the financial stability of any credit union has never been in doubt.[11] The provisions of the Act were drawn up when credit unions did not exist in Queensland and were designed to deal with the more usual type of co-operative. The Registrar's office is not adequately staffed to undertake regular supervision. Credit unions do not pay any registration fees[12] apart from the money-lender's licence. For a State Government unable to meet all politically important demands on its resources, expansion of staff to supervise credit unions is accorded a very low priority.

Sources of Funds

(a) *Capital and Reserves.* The paid-up capital of credit unions consists of fully subscribed and partially subscribed shares. From the late 1950's, profits of credit unions (gross of dividends on shares) have been liable to taxation. The effect of this is to encourage credit unions to maintain share capital at a low level and to increase the gearing ratio.

TABLE 8 QUEENSLAND CREDIT UNIONS: GEARING RATIO BY SIZE OF CREDIT UNION, 1966

Total Funds ($)	% of Capital to Total Funds				
	0–5	6–10	11–20	21–100	Total
0–10,000	1	–	4	2	7
10,001–20,000	1	3	2	–	6
20,001–50,000	–	–	2	–	2
50,001–200,000	2	1	–	–	3
200,001–500,000	2	–	–	–	2
TOTAL	6	4	8	2	20

Note: Three credit unions are excluded from this classification; two of these are extremely small (total liabilities combined are less than $300). The third, larger but still small, does not distinguish between shares and deposits. Its rules provide for the issue of withdrawable shares (virtually equivalent to members' deposits of other credit unions) and its accounts do not distinguish between the two classes of shares.

Source: Calculated from Annual Returns.

The larger credit unions typically have very low capitalisation ratios. One credit union encouraged members to reduce their share holdings.

(b) *Deposits.* The major source of credit union funds in Queensland is

[11] A credit union is at present in liquidation. It did not fail but rather failed to commence operations. The total funds of this credit union did not exceed $100.

[12] The initial registration fee of $14.70 paid by credit unions is the fee for the barrister who certifies that the credit union's rules meet the requirement of the Act.

deposits. As one of the objectives of the movement is to encourage thrift among members, credit unions encourage regular deposits of any amount above a specified minimum (usually one dollar).

The most attractive feature of deposits with a credit union is the rate of interest paid; in addition there are conveniences stemming from location (e.g. at work after bank hours). The predominant rate is 5 per cent while some credit unions, particularly the larger ones, offer 6 per cent. Queensland credit unions are able to accept deposits from non-members and the largest credit union readily accepts such deposits.[13] An increasing trend is the provision of associate membership (depositing rights only) for relatives of members. In table 7, the source and use of funds statement of Queensland credit unions, the item 'deposits' includes non-member deposits. There is no information available about the average size of deposits;[14] an indication of this is given by the figure obtained by dividing total deposits by total members. The measure shows the 'average deposit' to be fairly low, generally less than $100.

Withdrawal of deposits from credit unions requires formal notice. Below are two typical examples taken from the rules of two of the larger credit unions:

Amount of Withdrawal		*Notice Required*	
Example 1	*Example 2*	*Example 1*	*Example 2*
Less than $10	Less than $200	24 hours	1 week
$11–$20	$201–$600	2 days	1 month
$21–$50	over $1,000	7 days	2 months
$50–$1,500		1 month	
over $1,500		2 months	

An increasing tendency among new credit unions has been for the rules to specify that notice of withdrawal *may* be required.

Employment of Funds

(a) *Advances to members.* The simplest description of credit union loans is small, unsecured, consumer loans. Table 9 shows the maximum loan which credit unions may approve.

Information about the average size of loan granted is not available. How-

13 The 1965 annual report of this credit union noted that 'a large amount of deposits' were held by persons other than members.

14 One credit union noted in its first annual report, 1964, that 10 deposits were in the range of $1,000 to $2,000.

TABLE 9 QUEENSLAND CREDIT UNIONS: MAXIMUM LOANS AS SPECIFIED IN THE RULES OF EACH CREDIT UNION

Maximum Loan $ as permitted by Rules	Credit Unions Registered and Reporting 1966	Credit Unions Registered 1967
500	7	8
600	2	2
700	1	1
800	1	1
1,000	3	5
2,000	3	3
2,500	0	1
Not Stated	6	6
TOTAL	23	27

Note: The Management Committee may restrict the size of loans below the maximum.
Source: Rules of Credit Unions.

ever, in 1962 one credit union reported that of 208 applications received for loans, 43 per cent were for an amount less than $200; 27 per cent for amounts between $201 and $400 and 31 per cent for amounts greater than $401.

One of the basic principles of the credit union movement is that, as members share a common bond of association, the approval of a loan is based on the character of the applicant and formal security is not required. In fact, Queensland credit unions usually require some formal evidence of contracting the debt, e.g. a promissory note, and for a larger loan require some charge on the member's assets or a third party guarantee of repayment. (A bill of sale is usually required in respect of a loan to purchase a motor vehicle.)

The Act provides, inter alia, that credit unions may approve loans for the following purposes:

(i) furniture for homes;
(ii) expenses of removal of household effects;
(iii) purchase of tools, implements, material, stock in trade for any business, trade or industry;
(iv) commencing, acquiring or carrying on any business, trade or industry;
(v) meeting the cost of painting, of effecting additions or repairs to a house;
(vi) paying off a second mortgage;

(vii) meeting expenses of sickness;
(viii) discharge of any financial liability;
(ix) making other loans for any such purpose approved by the members.

The rules of credit unions typically adopt the above list. No comprehensive information is available about the purpose for which loans are, in fact, granted but the 1964 annual report of one credit union disclosed that 134 loans were granted during that year for the following purposes:

Purchase of Furniture and Household Equipment	11%
Improvement to Home	19%
Pay-out of Hire Purchase Contracts	25%
Purchase of Television	5%
Purchase of House and Land	5%
Medical Expenses	2%
Payment of Debt	10%
Purchase of Motor Vehicles	13%
Payment of Car Repair Expenses	7%
Miscellaneous	7%

The number of loans granted for paying out hire purchase contracts is large, probably because this was the first full year of operation of the credit union.

The maximum period of loan is short, usually three years, and no credit union makes loans for a term greater than five years. All loans attract the same rate of interest; the predominant rate is 1 per cent per month. When the demand for loans exceeds available funds, applications are approved on a priority system. For example, the rules of one credit union provide that loan applications are dealt with according to 'the merit of the case, and the urgency of need of the applicant'. Another credit union reported cryptically in 1962 that loan applications were assigned priority on a points system. Where excess demand for loans exists, credit unions typically are reluctant to approve large loans.

(b) *Cash and bank deposits.* Credit unions' needs to maintain substantial cash reserves are few. The flow of cash receipts from deposits and repayment of advances is normally predictable within narrow limits. Deposits are not withdrawable at call; substantial notice is formally required for redemption of larger deposits. The requirements of legal tender are small and as credit unions are eligible to maintain interest-bearing cheque accounts with savings banks, there is a strong incentive to hold little more than petty cash in legal tender. The only information on credit unions' cash position is balance sheet data and if end of June 1966 figures are representative of the average position during the year, credit unions typically maintain a cash to deposit ratio of from $2\frac{1}{2}$ per cent to 5 per cent (see table 7B.

Large cash reserves are a source of embarrassment to credit unions. The interest rate on short-term outlets for funds is lower than their own deposit rate. A recent development in Queensland has been inter-credit union lending. The scale of these operations has been small and informally organised.

Other Activities of Credit Unions

Most credit unions operate a purchasing service which enables members to buy goods at a favourable price and finance the purchase of larger items. Many credit unions offer financial counselling to members but there is no way to judge the extent to which this service is used. An increasing trend among credit unions is their involvement in educational programmes to carry the message of 'credit unionism' and 'co-operation' to potential members of credit unions and to expand the experience of their officers.

The distinctive feature of Queensland credit unions is their activity in trading. This does not mean all credit unions have a trading section; only six or seven have ever traded and only four have traded on a substantial scale relative to their other activities. Two credit unions trade on a sufficient scale to employ staff for this purpose and, for one of these two, trading activity is greater than the normal work of a credit union. Generally the results of trading have ranged from indifferent to good but the experience of one credit union highlights some possible dangers of combining the two activities.

This credit union operates its own shop from rented premises and has made substantial losses in its two years of operation. These losses are largely attributable to two factors: firstly, the gross profit margin on sales has been too low to meet trading expenses. It appears that in attempting to sell below customary price, management has miscalculated the costs of operation. Secondly, withdrawal slips from members' deposits have been accepted in payment of debts incurred in buying goods. The results of this practice have been that the turnover of deposits has been very high with a consequent increase in administrative costs and that some members' accounts have, at times, been overdrawn. The management committee has now levied an activity fee on members. The demand for loans has been unable to be satisfied and this may be, in part, a consequence of the credit union's failure to attract stable deposit funds. In an attempt to expand the trading section, one third of future loans will be allocated to financing sales from the trading section. This brings forward a possible source of conflict between the interests of members of the credit union and those of the credit union, as a distinct entity.

3. Conclusion

Credit Unions and the Consumer

In an economy where the function of financial intermediation has attained a high degree of specialisation, the competition for household savings is intense. Appraisal of claims on different types of financial institutions (and on different institutions of each type) is a complex process. Each financial asset offers a particular monetary return and other services. Associated with each asset is a risk of loss through failure of the institution which issues the claim. The prospective purchaser of a financial claim may not always be fully informed of relevant data on which to base decisions. The advantages of credit union deposits to the consumer are: (a) the high interest return paid, (b) the convenience of acquiring and redeeming deposits, and (c) the estimation of risk.

The interest rate paid on credit union deposits in Queensland has been shown to be generally 5 to 6 per cent, substantially higher than saving bank deposit rates and competitive with deposits with permanent building societies. Permanent building societies in Queensland have been small but recently a number of new societies have commenced operations and old societies have expanded. The impetus for this has been the operation of the Housing Loans Insurance Corporation which insures housing loans against loss through default.

The convenience of credit union deposits depends substantially on whether deposits may be made by direct deduction from wages or salaries. To the extent that a consumer may wish to minimise the number of decisions about portfolio allocation or to 'force' himself to save, the existence of a payroll deduction scheme may constitute, in the eyes of the consumer, a substantial advantage.

Redemption of credit union deposits requires formal notice; this requirement is not likely to be a disadvantage if deposits represent specific 'target' savings or constitute a reserve against general unforeseen contingencies.

On the counts of monetary return and convenience, credit union deposits probably are an attractive asset to consumers. The risk of loss associated with credit union deposits derives from the quality and honesty of management and from general disturbances in the economy as a whole. The consumer is better placed to make some assessment of the activities of management of the credit union, and of the risks associated with loans made, than he is of other financial institutions. As well, the consumer, as a member of the credit union, is able, in principle at least, to influence the activities of the credit union.

Credit union loans offer advantages to the consumer: principally the low interest charge, the absence of a requirement to provide formal evidence of credit-worthiness and the opportunity to consolidate repayment of loans. The disadvantages of credit union loans to the consumer are the limits on the amount which may be borrowed and the de facto restriction on the purpose of loans. Credit union loans in Queensland are generally made for household purposes; the interest rate on loans of this type from most other sources is high. Unsecured personal loans are a field of lending relatively undeveloped in Australia; recent innovations in this area have been made first by some savings banks which offer loans for restricted purposes and then by the trading banks with a full personal unsecured loan service. The potential demand for bank loans is probably large; at this juncture it is difficult to gauge the impact of these innovations.

The Development of Credit Unions in Queensland

The expansion of credit unions in Queensland has accelerated since the beginning of this decade. However, credit unions still occupy a very small place in the capital market: at 30 June 1966 deposits of credit unions represented approximately 0·2 per cent of savings bank deposits in Queensland, and loans of the order of 0·5 per cent of instalment credit balances outstanding.

The inspiration for the establishment of new credit unions has been from (a) 'imitation' effects and (b) autonomous factors. By autonomous factors is meant circumstances peculiar to the group responsible for the establishment of the credit union. Credit unions may also be established by one group because a credit union operated by another group is successful; this is what is referred to here as an 'imitation' effect. Imitation effects have been especially strong since 1959. In particular the successful operation of credit unions by employees of nationally spread organisations in other states (particularly New South Wales) has inspired and encouraged the Queensland employees to emulate this feat. Two local factors have tended to reinforce this influence: (a) the expansion of co-operative housing societies and (b) the formation of a credit union league.

In 1965 a credit union league was formed with the main object of fostering the growth of credit unions by: disseminating information on their organisation and operation; acting as a central co-operative society for component societies; operating as a clearing-house for surplus funds of member societies. At 30 June 1966, ten credit unions had taken up shares in the League; each shareholder is required to contribute annual subscriptions to the League based on their gross interest income.

The League's missionary activities are restricted because it has not yet been able to appoint a full-time organiser but in the short time of its operation the League appears to have done useful work in assisting in the formation of a few societies and in making contact with credit union leagues in other states.

The development of credit unions in Queensland to the present time reflects the growth of five credit unions. The largest five accounted for approximately 82 per cent of total credit union assets in Queensland at the end of June 1966. The significant aspects of these credit unions are that each draws its members from employees of government authorities or instrumentalities (i.e. members are in stable employment) and each operates a payroll deduction scheme.

The Prospects for Growth

Future growth of credit unions depends on the expansion of existing societies and the establishment of new credit unions. The limits on the expansion of existing societies exist in the size of their potential membership and their saving habits. Some credit unions, including one of the largest five, appear to be approaching the maximum of their easily accessible 'market penetration'; for others the scope for expansion is still large. A number of the registered credit unions which have yet to report have a large potential membership.

If the demonstration effects described previously continue to operate, interest in the formation of new credit unions should increase. The formal requirements for registration are simple but the operative constraints on the establishment of new credit unions appear to exist in the enthusiasm and ability of the prospective officials on whose voluntary labour the success of a credit union depends. This factor also inhibits the expansion of credit unions. One credit union, established for twelve years, has expanded very slowly and has enrolled less than 2 per cent of its approximate potential membership. One significant reason for its slow growth is the policy of offering a low (below savings bank deposit) rate on deposits.

Another credit union, mentioned previously as being in liquidation, failed to develop beyond nominal existence.

Issues of Public Policy

As long as credit unions in Queensland remain small in size and few in number, issues of public policy are unlikely to become significant. However, the development of credit unions has reached a stage where some immediate issues are apparent and preliminary consideration of others is required.

Two immediate questions are whether credit unions should trade and whether credit unions should accept deposits from non-members. Credit unions may, under the present provisions of the Act, undertake these activities. Trading in goods may offer advantages to members of credit unions; the argument against allowing credit unions to trade is that by the nature of a credit union the risks associated with making unsecured loans are minimised. Credit unions are not immune from trading risks, and losses from this source could endanger the financial stability of the credit union. The argument against trading is stronger if credit unions trade in goods whose sale is financed by their loans. On the second question, acceptance of loans from non-members, one could argue, is a violation of the co-operative principle on which credit unions are based; and it could possibly lead to a source of instability if these deposits are in the nature of 'hot money'.

A relevant third question is whether there exists a case for active government sponsorship of credit unions. (The obvious analogy is the subsidy of a full-time organiser in New South Wales.) The economic argument for government action rests on the existence of benefits to consumers from membership of credit unions. Given that these benefits exist, it is important to consider credit unions in a wider aspect. The growth of financial institutions has been due, in part, to an ability to avoid concentration of risks. Credit unions, on the other hand, tend to concentrate risks by drawing their membership (and consequently their deposits and loans) from a common group. External disturbances which affect the economic fortunes of specific groups are likely to have serious effects on the stability of a credit union. There does not exist the evidence to demonstrate that the possibility has occurred nor is there any substantial reason to believe that it is likely in the future.

A Credit Union Act

At present, amendments to the Co-operative Societies Act are being formulated for consideration by the State Government. Among these proposed amendments is one which would define a credit union and the activities that it is allowed to undertake. It is thought that the relevant New South Wales Act is being used as a guide. At this juncture there are no official details of the proposals nor any indication of when the amendments will be introduced into Parliament.

6

Credit Unions in New South Wales

by D. G. Flynn, A. C. K. Lo, S. J., and N. Runcie

1. Introduction

The post-1945 period has seen a considerable expansion in the credit union movement in New South Wales. The main influence has been the North American model of credit union operations and, in particular, growth has accelerated since the broadening of the Credit Union National Association (C.U.N.A.) to embrace oversea associations in the late 1950s.[1] Reference to this influence is a recurrent theme in this chapter. Nevertheless, we undertake a broad survey of the earlier history which reveals a more complex pattern.

In table 1A, we set out an analysis of the operating credit unions registered in New South Wales.[2] The credit unions registered at the end of a period represent a net series compiled from registrations at the beginning of the period, plus the new registrations and minus both the liquidations and amalgamations. Thus the number of operating registered credit unions grew from 2 at the end of June 1945 to 279 at the end of June 1967; the latter figure was derived from 304 credit unions which have been registered, with 22 liquidations and 3 amalgamations over the entire post-war period.

The pattern of the development of the credit union movement in New South Wales has evolved principally through the influence of:

(a) the role of the Registrar of Co-operative Societies in implementing government policy and, more recently, the influence of the Credit Union Advisory Committee;

[1] Oversea credit union leagues and associations were admitted to CUNA membership in 1958.

[2] Australia's largest credit union, C.B.O.A. Credit Union Ltd, which operates in the Commonwealth Banking Corporation and the Reserve Bank of Australia, is registered in N.S.W. but operates in all states and embraces bank staff overseas (e.g. London and Papua and New Guinea).

TABLE 1A N.S.W. CREDIT UNIONS: GROWTH AND LIQUIDATIONS, 1945–68

Year ended June	Credit Unions on Register at the Beginning	New Registrations	Liquidations	Amalgamations	Credit Unions on Register at end
1945	0	2	—	—	2
1946	2	8	—	—	10
1947	10	10	—	—	20
1948	20	5	—	—	25
1949	25	3	—	—	28
1950	28	8	2	—	34
1951	34	9	0	—	43
1952	43	5	0	—	48
1953	48	1	1	—	48
1954	48	12	1	—	59
1955	59	14	1	—	72
1956	72	11	1	—	82
1957	82	8	2	—	88
1958	88	12	1	1	98
1959	98	16	1	—	113
1960	113	12	2	—	123
1961	123	7	0	—	130
1962	130	9	2	—	137
1963	137	20	2	2	153
1964	153	29	1	—	181
1965	181	40	1	—	220
1966	220	34	4	—	250
1967	250	29	0	—	279
1968	279	23	0	1	301

Source: Records of N.S.W. Registry of Co-operatives.

(b) the role of the co-operative based credit unions;
(c) the establishment of Universal Credit Union Co-operative Ltd;
(d) the development of the Antigonish movement;
(e) the formation of the N.S.W. Credit Union League Co-operative Ltd and its ties with C.U.N.A;
(f) the economic climate of New South Wales;
(g) the role of the movement's dominant personalities;
(h) the changing emphasis of credit union legislation;
(i) the gradual acceptance by the public of the value of credit unions; and,
(j) the formation of the Association of Southern Credit Unions Ltd.

In New South Wales the most widely accepted concept of a credit union is an association of individuals, formed within a specific bond of association, who pool a portion of their financial reserves and savings and distribute

TABLE 1B N.S.W. OPERATING CREDIT UNIONS: REGISTERED BY TYPE, 1945–68

Year	Building Society	Friendly Society	Parish	Community	Employee					Association and Club	Co-operative	Other	Total
					(a)	(b)	(c)	(d)	Total				
1945	1	—	—	—	—	—	—	—	—	—	1	—	2
1946	6	3	—	—	—	—	—	—	—	—	1	—	10
1947	9	7	1	1	—	—	—	—	—	1	1	—	20
1948	11	8	2	1	—	—	—	—	—	2	1	—	25
1949	13	8	3	1	—	—	—	—	—	2	1	—	28
1950	20	8	2	1	—	1	—	—	1	2	—	—	34
1951	28	8	2	1	—	1	—	—	1	3	—	—	43
1952	29	8	3	2	—	3	—	—	3	3	—	—	48
1953	30	8	3	2	—	2	—	—	2	3	—	—	48
1954	31	9	7	4	—	4	—	1	5	3	—	—	59
1955	33	9	12	6	4	4	—	1	9	3	—	1	72
1956	33	9	20	8	4	4	—	1	9	3	—	1	82
1957	31	9	23	9	4	5	—	2	11	3	—	1	88
1958	30	9	29	10	6	5	—	3	14	4	—	1	98
1959	30	9	35	11	8	9	—	4	21	5	—	1	113
1960	31	9	36	12	10	11	—	5	26	8	—	1	123
1961	31	9	36	13	13	13	—	6	32	8	—	1	130
1962	31	9	36	12	16	17	—	6	39	8	1	1	137
1963	30	7	40	13	16	21	2	13	52	9	1	1	153
1964	29	7	42	13	17	31	5	25	78	10	1	1	181
1965	30	7	43	13	21	37	25	30	113	12	1	1	220
1966	29	6	41	14	25	41	36	41	143	15	1	1	250
1967	29	6	41	14	26	48	42	54	170	16	2	1	279
1968	29	6	41	15	29	49	48	63	189	16	4	1	301

Note: (a) Commonwealth.
(b) State.
(c) Councils.
(d) General (industries in private sector).

Source: Records of N.S.W. Registry of Co-operative Societies.

it to members needing a loan. We distinguish four subsidiary aims:

(a) to increase, by education, the financial expertise of their members;
(b) to increase the material and economic welfare of members;
(c) to offer to members loans which are cheaper than those obtained through other lenders;[3] and,

[3] The 'Antigonish' credit unions in New South Wales have adopted a policy of charging 'market' rates of interest (e.g. 10 per cent flat) and where possible, *making a rebate* to members after providing for administration and services; see *Credit Union Bulletin*, official organ of Credit Union Co-operative Development Ltd, Vol. IV, No. 1, August 1958, p. 4.

(d) to offer to members reasonable rates of interest on deposited funds and, in particular, to encourage regular saving.

Credit unions are guided by altruistic principles. These are expressed in a paternal way as credit unions try to guard their members from the financial hardships which can accompany 'sickness, hard times and distress'. However, it is apparent that credit unions have acquired more ambitious objectives than those associated with a welfare function reminiscent of the friendly society of the last century. In their modern conception credit unions are co-operative instalment credit financiers and, as such, they are competing with a wide range of other financial institutions. With growth, credit unions face new tests of their efficiency.

Nevertheless, this modern conception of a credit union, while it is the essence of some of the larger credit unions, would not be accepted by many in the movement. Moreover, it does not contain an adequate description of the motivation of many leaders in the movement. The credit union philosophy is a statement of belief:

> Credit unionists realise economic well-being is not the ultimate purpose of man's existence. They believe an economic uplift is capable, in many circumstances, of assisting members remove the physical factors which suppress emotional happiness. In being a credit unionist, a member is able to assume an active role in improving his economic position. He is not a passive recipient of financial assistance. He is encouraged to participate in a savings programme. Any change in his economic position is attained without loss of self-respect.

2. Early History

Of all the states in Australia, New South Wales was the first to have a specific Co-operation Act. The 1923 Act was outstanding in its comprehensive and far-sighted provision for all types of co-operative activity, including co-operative credit for rural and urban societies. Whereas, in Canada and the United States, the initial impetus of the credit union movement preceded legislation, New South Wales experience showed that enabling legislation alone would not bring credit unions into existence.

The Commonwealth Parliamentary Enquiry into Small Loans Facilities in Australia[4] showed conclusively that there was a considerable need for small personal loans among the wage-earning class in the twenties and thir-

[4] *Report on Small Loans Facilities*, Commonwealth Parliament, 1938.

ties. This need could have been satisfied on more economic terms than those available, through co-operative credit. However, between 1923 and 1940, there was no co-operative credit development in New South Wales, due perhaps to the restrictive nature of some provisions in the original Act[5] and the related observation that the local co-operative movement was in the tradition of the British movement where the credit union was not an accepted institution. The existing co-operative effort was already taken up in the development of the more orthodox co-operative institutions in dairying, retailing, wholesaling and home building finance. One would not expect a vigorous credit union movement to emerge from the existing co-operative movement until a 'new breed' of co-operators with different aspirations emerged.

An outstanding feature of the co-operative credit movement in New South Wales was the continued and patient advocacy of this type of co-operative by the Registry since the earliest days of the Act despite the lack of response from the established co-operative movement or the trade union movement. Through occasional correspondence with the Russell Sage Foundation and with C.U.N.A., the Registry was kept informed of developments overseas. In a memorandum written in 1946 (and made available by the Registry), Mr A. B. Sheldon, the then Registrar of Co-operative Societies, wrote:

> 'When the Co-operative Act was passed in 1923 in this State, special provisions dealt with the making of personal loans on a co-operative basis under the heading of Urban Credit Societies. . . . Some twenty years ago (1925), a circular pointing out the advantage that might accrue to their employees by the sponsoring of societies of this type was sent by the Registry to some scores of the largest trading concerns in this State. Much to our surprise, the only response was a bare acknowledgment of its receipt from less than a dozen.'

During the depression years of the thirties, the scarcity of saving must have rendered difficult any effort to form co-operative credit societies although, paradoxically, this was a period of great need. However, in 1941 *Smith's Weekly* drew attention to the existence of what, most probably, was the first credit union in New South Wales. In an article entitled 'Co-operative Banking Does Work', *Smith's Weekly* (29 March 1941) referred

[5] For example, the small amount which could be loaned (not to exceed £100), the limited range of purposes, and the limit of a ten mile radius of residence of the registered office of the society; the latter effectively prevented employee-type credit unions which were to prove of great importance later.

to the Amalgamated Sports and Dividing Society of Summer Hill,[6] which was formed in 1937, and observed:

> '... the danger of the small income men falling into the clutches of usurious money-lenders is generally recognised but the extent to which this happens is not appreciated.... Experience of three years has fully convinced Mr L. Herman, the Secretary, of the need for and practicability of workers' financial co-operation. He admits that although he appreciated the necessity of small loans, he had no idea demand was so widespread.... Difficulties of administration, not of demand, of which there is plenty, are providing a handicap to further expansion.'

We shall see that the management problems of the co-operative small loan movement is a recurrent theme.

In the wake of the depression years, the Small Loans Facilities Act was proposed in 1941 to amend the 1923 Act with the hope that some development might result. The Small Loans Facilities Act proposed to:

(a) alter the name of urban credit societies to that of small loan societies;
(b) broaden the purposes for which loans could be granted;
(c) permit loans to be made to members of a particular 'class' or bond of association and not just to the residents of a particular geographical confine as prescribed by the 1923 Act; and,
(d) permit subject to the Register's approval loans in excess of £100.

The Small Loans Act aroused considerable interest from various quarters in the community. The *Sydney Morning Herald* in a special feature article on 27 March 1941 noted:

> 'In Australia, the need for the development of credit facilities for the low and medium wage earner is very apparent. To all intents and purposes the only avenues through which the working people of N.S.W. can secure credit are hire purchase buying, cash orders and money-lenders.... A major purpose in facilitating small loans business by proper bodies at reasonable rates and under government supervision is to save the necessitous and financially ignorant wage earner from exploitation of this kind by three main methods: personal loan departments operated by trading banks; industrial banks; and co-operative credit unions. None has been tried in Australia in such a fashion as to fill the public need.
>
> Australia is very far behind the U.S. and Canada in providing reasonable credit facilities for the big mass of people.'

The 1941 Small Loans Act prompted an upsurge of interest and several

[6] It presumably operated as an unregistered society with trustees.

applications to form credit unions were lodged with the Registry in 1941.[7] However, because of the National Security Regulations (Capital Issues) 1940, an embargo was placed on the formation of small loan societies by the Commonwealth Treasurer on the grounds that savings would be diverted from the government war loans.[8]

3. The Post-war Expansion

(a) *The Take-off Period: 1945 to 1951*

The end of World War Two saw a rapid revival of co-operative activity generally and it also marked the 'take-off period' of credit union development in N.S.W. In 1944 an amending Co-operation Bill was passed in the State Parliament to enable building societies to acquire shares in any other co-operative society, including small loans societies. In the same year the embargo on the formation of small loan societies was lifted by the Federal Treasurer, Mr Chifley. Thus on 15 May 1945, the first *registered* credit union in the State, 'Home Owner's Co-operative Credit Society Ltd', was registered; it was under the same management as a building society, 'Home Building Co-operative Society Ltd'. The 'take-off period' was characterised by the predominance of credit unions sponsored by building societies which, although they were legally constituted as autonomous societies, were operated as financial adjuncts to parent building societies and frequently depended on the parent societies for funds. The link is logical in providing finance for the home owner; however, with few exceptions, these credit unions were essentially lending institutions providing a much needed service. Several friendly societies also sponsored credit unions in this 'take-off period' on a similar basis.

Because of their existing links and pragmatic approach, the building and friendly society credit unions probably could not have been expected to promote credit union development in unfamiliar environments. Thus among the credit unions formed in this 'take-off period', Universal Credit Union Co-operative Ltd (registered September 1946) is regarded as a significant innovation. Kevin Yates, the founder of Universal, had observed North American credit union development during the war; this experience suggested that although credit unions could only exist if there was an

[7] The first application was from B.H.P. employees at Newcastle.

[8] Possible benefits to employee morale were, presumably, weighed against the undesirability of diverting expenditure to consumer durable goods. The potential of credit unions as savings organisations was not realised in this context.

economic demand for their services, the impetus behind the credit union movement's expansion was a sociological one.[9] The nucleus members of Universal seemed to fit the category of 'social activitists'; they were members of a catholic social study group interested in implementing social principles. Thus, in its initial period, Universal was essentially Antigonish inspired and restricted its development programme to the parish-community type of environment. It was the intention of Universal to form other parish credit unions and to form an association of these in due course. This development policy was similar to the one adopted by the Y.C.W. group in Victoria,[10] but Universal's development programme was relatively unsuccessful, although several parish and community credit unions were formed. In 1950 the first employee type credit union was formed (N.S.W. Co-operative Savings and Loans Society); but it was not until 1956 that the first industrial credit union in the private sector was formed (C.S.R. Officers' Association Co-operative Ltd).

The 'take-off period' for co-operative credit development in N.S.W. coincided with the remarkable expansion of instalment credit in Australia in the post-war years.[11] However, co-operative credit development lagged sadly behind the instalment credit boom. Although the majority of co-operators within the building society movement recognised the economic benefits of co-operative credit to the community, only a minority of building societies sponsored small loan societies; and this was partly because the Act did not allow for fees to be paid to directors. However, after a long period of discussion, formal representations were eventually successfully made by the Association of Co-operative Building Societies to amend the Act in 1950. This change involved some reappraisal of the balance between realism and idealism in the Registry and enabled more building societies to form credit unions; but their impact on the overall development of the movement in N.S.W. was not significant.

As early as 1945 the Co-operative Institute of N.S.W. was formed, under the sponsorship of the Registrar (A.B. Sheldon), to promote co-operative activities on all fronts. Three separate attempts were made by the Institute to form an association of small loan societies in 1948, 1950 and 1956; as noted below the last attempt was successful.

[9] Mr Kevin Yates is still an active leader in the credit union, the co-operative and the consumer movements. During the war, Yates visited Antigonish in Nova Scotia while in the R.A.A.F.

[10] See chapter 8 below.

[11] N. Runcie, 'Hire Purchase Institutions', in R. R. Hirst and R. H. Wallace (eds.), *Studies in the Australian Capital Market*, Cheshire, 1964.

In summary, co-operative credit development in the 'take-off period' was slow. This was due to a number of factors: to a lack of voluntary effort and vision except for one or two enthusiasts; to a failure on the part of the small loan societies to work together; and to a lack of imagination in the co-operative movement to exploit the credit union concept in another environment.

(b) *The Drive to Maturity: 1951 to 1957*

This period saw the gradual evolution of the co-operative credit movement away from the existing co-operative movement, to become an autonomous movement in its own right. There were three notable developments in this period as follows: (i) the emergence of the Australian Antigonish movement in 1951, (ii) the emergence of the Anglican credit union movement in 1953, and (iii) the successful formation of the Savings and Loans Co-operative Association in 1956 which became the N.S.W. League two years later.

The development of the Australian Antigonish movement which began with the formation of the Lidcombe credit union in 1951 has perhaps been the most colourful page in the history of co-operative credit development in N.S.W. The Australian Antigonish movement developed primarily as a social reform movement aimed at the ultimate creation of a 'new social order' based on Papal encyclicals and deriving its conceptual framework from the Canadian Antigonish movement. By means of adult education aimed at 'lifting the largest possible number of people to a higher level of life economically and socially', the formation of credit unions was only a first step in the Antigonish programme of reform. Other co-operative services in trading, housing and production were to follow. Because of its admirable but all-embracing reformist zeal, the N.S.W. Antigonish movement tended to dissociate itself from the outside world, including those engaged in other co-operative activities. Although the critics of the Antigonish movement see confusion between its ends and its means, a proper appreciation of the Antigonish credit unions must take account of the overall aims and not just its credit operations in isolation.

The Anglican credit union movement began in 1953 with the formation of St Faith's. West Manly Credit Union Ltd and Clerical Credit Union Ltd were formed in 1954. In the following year, the Anglican credit unions pioneered the first Association in N.S.W. The Associated Credit Unions Ltd was incorporated in June 1955 but it was not successful in the development of credit unions among Anglican parishes. However, members of the

Anglican Association contributed significantly to the formation of the Savings and Loan Association in 1956.[12]

Since its formation in 1945, the N.S.W. Co-operative Institute had provided a link between the small loans societies and other co-operatives in N.S.W. The link, although a tenuous one, nevertheless denoted some continuity between the co-operative credit movement and the co-operative movement in general. In 1956 the Co-operative Institute was instrumental in bringing the co-operative credit movement to form the Savings and Loans Co-operative Association Ltd. Paradoxically, the formation of the Association marked a break between the two movements. Up to 1967 the N.S.W. League had not become a member of the N.S.W. Federation of Co-operatives Ltd which superseded the Institute.

(c) *The Drive for Growth: 1957 to 1967*

With the formation of the Association in 1956 the credit union movement began to take shape and it was in a position to expand in a less haphazard manner. In particular, the visit in 1957 of O. H. Spetland, CUNA Director of the World Extension Department, marked the beginning of a phase of rapid and sustained growth engendered by the stimulating impact of successful overseas experience. The two scholarships offered by CUNA to the Association for Keith Young and Clarrie Murphy[13] to study the industrial credit union movement in the U.S. and Canada in 1958 laid the groundwork for a more imaginative and vigorous development programme in N.S.W. From these, and subsequent scholarships to others, the enormous potential of the industrial environment and the importance of progressive management training for credit union officials through expert training programmes were recognised.

The A.B.C. Staff Association Credit Union was formed in September 1957 and stimulated the movement's interest in the mass media for effective promotional work; in particular, widespread public interest in credit unions resulted from Michael Charlton's interview of Stan Arneil on A.B.C.'s TV programme 'Four Corners' in 1962. It is notable that separate A.B.C. staff credit unions were formed in each state and that this group has been a notable source of energetic promotion.

In this third period, the formation of the Savings and Loans Association,

[12] In particular, Keith Young, who was the secretary of West Manly Anglican and a founding member of the C.S.R. Officers' Association Credit Union, was able to bring the experience of an industrial credit union to the Association. He played a leading role up to 1962.

[13] C. J. Murphy was the first manager of the N.S.W. Credit Union League.

and subsequently the N.S.W. Credit Union League from October 1958, made possible a much closer type of co-operation between the Registry and the credit union movement. However, the existence of the Antigonish groups and the formation of the Southern Association (established 1966) have still involved the Registry in multiple contacts. The three notable developments were the appointment of a Credit Union Advisory Committee by the State government, legislative amendments designed to suit the purposes of the credit unions (which were now more North American oriented) and the appointment of a Credit Union Development Officer in 1964. There is little doubt that the existence of a number of distinct types of credit union has made the devising of the Registry policy an unenviable but exciting task.

In summary, the 'drive for growth' since 1957 has been characterised by the vigorous promotion of employee credit unions by both the Registry and the League; both sponsors realised that a more effective movement would depend on the rapid growth of this type. Further, the movement has attracted sympathetic State government policy reflected in the appointment of a Minister for Co-operative Societies, subsidies for the Credit Union League (e.g. 1966, $3,000) and funds for promotion. The Hon. A. Landa and, more recently, the Hon. S. T. Stephens, have been notable appointments of Ministers who have encouraged the movement.

4. Analysis of the Post-war Expansion

(a) *Credit Union Formation*

Credit union formation in N.S.W. may be analysed (i) by type of credit union; (ii) by type of sponsoring body[14]; (iii) by changes in the rate of formation, and (iv) in relation to changes in personal income. These approaches are not an exhaustive classification but represent an attempt to indicate the kind of research necessary to establish the internal and external forces which have been at work.

In tables 1A and 1B the main types of credit union referred to earlier are distinguished.[15] The dramatic changes in the composition of the movement

[14] A classification of the main sponsoring bodies would be (a) the Registry of Co-operative Societies, (b) the N.S.W. League and the Registry, (c) the Antigonish group, (d) the Southern Association, (e) interstate credit unions, (f) other bodies (e.g. CUNA, CUNA Mutual, the Co-operative Federation).

[15] This classification could be more detailed with advantage: for example, some of

TABLE 1C N.S.W.: CREDIT UNIONS BY TYPE, AS PER CENTUM OF TOTAL, 30 JUNE 1951, 1957, 1967

Year	Building Society	Friendly Society	Parish and Community	Employee	Other	Total
	%	%	%	%	%	%
1951	65·0	18·6	7·0	2·3	7·1	100
1957	35·2	10·2	36·4	12·2	6·0	100
1967	10·4	2·1	19·8	61·0	6·7	100

Source: Analysis of Records of N.S.W. Registry of Co-operative Societies.

are summarised in table 1c. In 1951, the building society credit unions dominated the movement with 65 per cent of the total and were followed by the friendly society groups with 18·6 per cent. However, by 1957 the parish and community credit unions had grown from 7 per cent to become the largest group with 36·4 per cent of operating credit unions. By 1967, the employee type credit unions had become the dominant group with 61 per cent of operating credit unions compared with 12·2 per cent in 1957 and 2·3 per cent in 1951. The above figures are based on the annual tabulations in table 1A. But it is the annual changes, or rather the formation of new credit unions,[16] which emphasise the marked shifts in the direction of the movement.

Changes in the annual rate of credit union formation appear to be a function of four main factors: (i) the type of credit union being promoted and the registration potential for that type of credit union; (ii) the public's image of credit unions and the degree of favourable publicity about credit unions; (iii) the amount of credit union promotion being undertaken; and (iv) a lagged response to changes in personal savings and personal disposable income.

We comment briefly only on the last of these factors. When personal savings declined in N.S.W. by 52·4 per cent in 1952, there was no increase in the number of registered credit unions. Similarly a decline in personal savings of 17·6 per cent in 1954 and 6·9 per cent in 1955 seems to be associated with a decline in the rate of registration to 13·9 per cent in 1956 and

the credit unions in government departments are industrial (e.g. power stations, railways); in the local government or council credit unions there is a case for distinguishing between municipal (urban), shire (country) and county (regional) credit unions.

[16] The annual changes derived from table 1A are new registrations net of liquidations and amalgamations.

6·1 per cent in 1957. Further, a decline in the level of personal savings of 3·4 per cent in 1961 appears to be associated with a low annual increase in credit union registrations of 4·1 per cent in 1961 and 5·5 per cent in 1962. The decline in the rate of credit union formation is not surprising since an initial requirement for forming credit unions is a pool of savings from which loans can be made and an increase in demand for new purchases on the instalment plan. Further, we note a lag in credit union formation from initial meeting to registration which may be six months or longer. Again, the nature of these lags is an aspect of credit union operations on which there is a case for research by the movement.

(b) *Membership Growth*

The membership of reporting credit unions is shown from 1946 to 1967 in table 2. This table demands a measure of comment. The growth of credit

TABLE 2 N.S.W. CREDIT UNIONS: AVERAGE SIZE AND MEMBERSHIP GROWTH, 30 JUNE 1946–67

As at 30 June	No. of Registered Credit Unions	Annual Change %	Reporting Credit Unions		
			No.	Membership	Average Size
1946	10	—	5	193	39
1947	20	100·0	12	932	78
1948	25	25·0	16	2,041	128
1949	28	12·0	20	3,981	200
1950	34	35·7	26	6,032	232
1951	43	13·1	36	8,443	235
1952	48	11·6	40	9,871	247
1953	48	0·0	40	10,792	270
1954	59	22·9	47	11,726	249
1955	72	22·1	64	14,794	231
1956	82	13·9	72	16,220	225
1957	88	6·1	78	20,142	258
1958	98	11·5	89	22,527	253
1959	113	15·5	104	27,171	261
1960	123	8·9	116	31,636	272
1961	130	4·1	124	36,488	294
1962	137	5·5	132	42,619	323
1963	153	14·2	140	53,536	382
1964	181	18·3	169	74,607	442
1965	220	21·5	197	92,199	468
1966	250	13·6	227	111,479	491
1967	279	11·6	260	133,118	512

Source: Analysis of Records of N.S.W. Registry of Co-operatives.

union membership is a more stable growth function than new credit union formation; it is, however, affected by the latter, as credit unions should have at least an initial rapid growth period as they penetrate their market. The growth function also depends on the type of credit union being formed. As shown in table 3 the average size of credit union membership by type

TABLE 3 N.S.W. CREDIT UNIONS: SELECTED AGGREGATES BY TYPES, 30 June 1966

Types of Credit Union	Credit Unions	Members	Share Capital	Reserves	Deposits	Loans to Members	Other Assets	Total Assets
	No.	No.	$'000	$'000	$'000	$'000	$'000	$'000
Commonwealth	25	18415	180·7	105·1	6943·0	5689·2	1641·4	7330·6
State	39	17296	162·8	62·6	5408·4	5285·5	495·8	5781·3
Councils	25	10394	100·4	7·3	2152·0	2220·4	117·9	2338·3
General	35	24219	112·8	36·3	5182·9	5026·0	427·5	5453·5
Total Employment	124	70324	556·7	211·4	19686·4	18221·2	2646·7	20867·9
Associations & Clubs	15	3755	27·0	3·2	321·2	335·4	44·6	380·0
Building Society	26	12501	186·0	167·5	1670·6	2763·2	288·1	3051·3
Community	12	2846	27·6	1·2	366·9	349·1	61·1	410·2
Co-operative Society	1	7893	15·8	21·2	1087·1	743·0	395·1	1138·1
Friendly Society	6	7537	54·2	14·2	1066·1	1237·3	91·9	1329·2
Parish	42	6533	144·7	12·4	420·9	501·5	134·9	636·4
Miscellaneous	1	90	1·3	0·4	—	1·6	0·1	1·7
Total All Credit Unions	227	111479	1013·3	431·5	24619·2	24152·3	3662·5	27814 8

Source: Records of N.S.W. Registry of Co-operative Societies.

varies significantly: in 1966 from 567 for industrial credit unions to 237 and 155 for community and parish credit unions respectively. These influences are also apparent in the growth of the average number of members of reporting credit unions. Thus in 1953, when no new credit unions were registered, the average membership of credit unions increased from 247 in 1952 to 270 in 1953. The average credit union size then declined to 225 in 1956; this would appear to be due to the decline in the relative number of building society credit unions and a relative and absolute expansion of the number of church associated credit unions which are characterised by a comparatively low average membership level.

TABLE 4A N.S.W. CREDIT UNIONS: ANALYSIS OF SOURCES OF FUNDS, 1946–67

Year Ended June	Share Capital		Reserves		Deposits		Other		TOTAL	
	$'000	%	$'000	%	$'000	%	$'000	%	$'000	%
1946	9	79·8	0	0·0	2	14·3	0·2	5·9	11	100·0
1947	35	57·0	1	2·0	24	39·8	0·8	1·2	61	100·0
1948	84	55·9	4	3·0	59	39·4	2	1·7	149	100·0
1949	180	54·7	10	3·1	136	41·3	2	0·9	328	100·0
1950	308	56·6	19	3·6	212	38·8	5	1·0	544	100·0
1951	445	42·8	34	3·2	537	51·6	24	2·4	1,040	100·0
1952	557	48·2	42	3·6	n.a.	—	n.a.	—	1,156	100·0
1953	666	51·5	54	4·1	54	4·3	518	40·1	1,292	100·0
1954	772	53·9	72	5·0	72	5·9	518	36·1	1,434	100·0
1955	1,022	58·3	70	4·0	96	5·5	564	32·2	1,752	100·0
1956	1,246	60·5	82	3·9	168	8·1	564	27·4	2,060	100·0
1957	1,680	63·8	106	4·0	182	6·8	664	25·4	2,636	100·0
1958	1,744	57·5	116	3·9	386	12·7	784	25·9	3,030	100·0
1959	1,222	35·2	108	3·2	1,294	37·3	842	24·3	3,466	100·0
1960	940	22·7	120	2·9	2,202	53·1	886	21·3	5,148	100·0
1961	764	14·8	122	2·3	3,472	67·1	876	15·8	5,174	100·0
1962	780	11·8	120	1·8	4,866	73·9	824	12·5	6,590	100·0
1963	790	8·4	174	1·9	7,524	80·4	876	9·3	9,364	100·0
1964	750	5·0	242	1·6	12,866	86·1	1,084	7·2	14,942	100·0
1965	882	4·2	328	1·5	18,514	87·5	1,469	6·8	21,193	100·0
1966	1013	3·7	431	1·5	24,619	88·4	1,752	6·4	27,815	100·0
1967	1112	3·0	587	1·6	32,935	89·2	2,275	6·2	36,909	100·0

Source: Annual Report, N.S.W. Registry of Co-operatives.

(c) *Sources of Funds*

We set out in table 4A and table 4B our study of the sources and uses of funds of credit unions. We are grateful to the N.S.W. Registrar of Co-operative Societies for assistance in the preparation of these tables.

Until 1958 credit unions in N.S.W. were not taxed. For various reasons it was believed that credit unions were not subject to taxation as in other states. The effect of the ruling is seen in the dramatic change in the sources of funds pattern from 1958 onwards. Since dividends on share capital are not treated as an allowable expense, the members were encouraged to transfer part of their share capital and all future savings to deposits; interest on deposit balances is an allowable taxation deduction. In 1959 the effect of this action was a 30 per cent reduction in share capital and a 235 per cent increase in deposits over the figures for 1958. Share capital as a

TABLE 4B N.S.W. CREDIT UNIONS: ANALYSIS OF USES OF FUNDS, 1946–67

Year Ended June	Outstanding Balances		Other		Total	
	$'000	%	$'000	%	$'000	%
1946	10	87·2	1	12·8	11	100·0
1947	59	97·2	2	2·8	61	100·0
1948	142	95·1	7	4·9	149	100·0
1949	316	96·4	12	3·6	328	100 0
1950	516	94·8	28	5 2	544	100·0
1951	999	96·0	41	4·0	1,040	100·0
1952	1,073	93·0	81	7·0	1,156	100·0
1953	1,206	93·3	86	6·7	1,292	100·0
1954	1,340	93·4	94	6·6	1,434	100·0
1955	1,616	92·3	136	7·7	1,752	100·0
1956	1,922	93·3	138	6·7	2,060	100·0
1957	2,386	90·5	250	9·5	2,636	100·0
1958	2,816	93·0	214	7·0	3,030	100·0
1959	3,242	93·3	224	6·7	3,466	100·0
1960	3,844	92·7	304	7·3	5,148	100·0
1961	4,770	92·2	404	7·8	5,174	100·0
1962	6,039	91·6	551	8·4	6,590	100·0
1963	8,481	90·6	883	9·4	9,364	100·0
1964	13,216	88·4	1,726	11·6	14,942	100·0
1965	18,690	88·1	2,503	11·9	21,193	100·0
1966	24,152	86·8	3,662	13·2	27,815	100·0
1967	31,264	84·7	5,645	15·3	36,909	100·0

Source: Annual Reports, N.S.W. Registry of Co-operatives.

source of funds declined from 57·5 per cent in 1958 to 5·0 per cent in 1964. Deposits as a source of funds increased from 12·7 per cent in 1958 to 86·1 per cent in 1964. The pattern in subsequent credit union formation has been to have a maximum share capital per member of $2 to $10 on which the board generally decides not to pay a dividend. Following a successful appeal by the Revesby Credit Union in 1965[17] credit unions were accepted by the N.S.W. Deputy Commissioner of Taxation as co-operatives for taxation purposes. More recently credit unions in N.S.W. have been forming themselves into purely mutual organisations, following the pattern already established in Victoria,[18] in order to avoid taxation on any surplus arising from transactions among members.

One side effect of the 1958 taxation decision is seen in reserves which have declined from 3·9 per cent in that year to 1·56 per cent in 1966. Although this relative decline is partly due to new credit union formation, credit unions have shown a marked reluctance to accumulate reserves when these must be met from the surplus after taxation.[19]

5. Credit Unions as Instalment Credit Financiers

Credit unions operate, almost universally, on the principle of regular instalment repayment. In the case of employee type credit unions the arrangements are usually made with the employer to effect wage and salary deductions weekly, fortnightly or monthly. For other types of credit union, however, the borrower makes the payment although banker's orders are sometimes used.[20] Thus the main asset of the credit unions, as shown in table 4B, is instalment credit outstanding balances owed by members; this use generally absorbs about 90 per cent of total funds. Some credit unions which have excess funds are able to take up investments including some loans to other co-operatives including the N.S.W. Credit Union League's Central Division. The development of the Central could lead to a greater volume of investments (mainly as short-period deposits) being held.

[17] *Taxpayers' Bulletin* vol. 8, no. 8, March 1965.

[18] See chapter 8 below for a discussion of the mutuality principle.

[19] N. Runcie, 'Credit Union on the Campus—II', *Vestes*, The Australian Universities' Review, Vol. XI, 1968.

[20] In 1967 the N.S.W. State government allowed pay-roll deductions for credit union payments for its employees for the first time. However, prior to this date the practice was widespread in other government instrumentalities.

TABLE 5 SELECTED INSTALMENT CREDIT DEBT IN N.S.W. AND A.C.T., 1959–67

Year Ended June	N.S.W. (INCL. A.C.T.) DEBT				N.S.W. REPORTING CREDIT UNIONS		Ratio (4)/(3)
	H.P. Debt due to Retailers and Finance Companies (1)	Other Instalment Credit Debt due to Retailers and Finance Companies (2)	TOTAL Amount (3)	TOTAL Annual Increase	Amount (4)	Annual Increase	
	$'million	$'million	$'m.	%	$'m.	%	%
1959	347·6	45·6	393·2		3·2		0·81
1960	400·0	58·6	458·6	16·7	3·8	18·7	0·83
1961	402·3	74·3	476·6	3·9	4·8	26·1	1·01
1962	387·8	99·0	476·8	0·0	6·0	25·0	1·25
1963	410·2	100·6	510·8	7·1	8·4	40·0	1·64
1964	441·0	106·3	547·4	7·2	13·2	57·1	2·41
1965	469·1	104·0	573·1	4·7	18·6	41·8	3·25
1966	452·3	107·5	559·8	−2·2	24·1	29·6	4·32
1967	446·4	115·9	562·4	0·0	31·3	29·9	5·57

Sources: (a) *Annual Reports* N.S.W. Registry of Co-operatives.
(b) Commonwealth Statistician, Instalment Credit for Retail Sales (quarterly).

In New South Wales there has been an enormous post-war expansion of instalment credit. In table 5, we show hire purchase and other instalment credit balances outstanding in New South Wales and the Australian Capital Territory. These figures are for goods sold at retail through finance companies and retailers only and exclude personal loans made by finance companies and by banks as well as by credit unions. It is apparent that credit unions, in spite of their rapid growth and the wide range of purposes for which they lend, are a very small proportion of the total instalment credit market.

Credit unions grant loans for a wider range of purposes than most other instalment credit financiers. In a study made of the purposes of credit union loans in 1963 and 1964,[21] the following pattern of advances was revealed for a survey group:

[21] D. G. Flynn, *The Development of Credit Unions in N.S.W.*, unpublished B. Com. thesis, Faculty of Commerce, University of New South Wales, 1966.

TABLE 6 N.S.W. CREDIT UNION LOANS BY PURPOSE, 1967: Percentage Composition of Loans of Selected Credit Unions

Credit Union*	Motor Vehicles: Purchase and Expenses	Furniture and Appliances	Home and Land: Purchase and Expenses (excl. rates)	Debt Consolidation	Medical, Dental Hospital and Funeral	Education	Other
	%	%	%	%	%	%	%
1	47·1	18·4	11·2	9·0	3·2	—	6·8
2	30·6	15·0	32·9	12·7	2·9	—	5·8
3	36·6	18·5	18·0	14·0	1·6	2·1	9·3
4	30·1	9·4	34·3	10·2	1·1	—	14·9
5	38·8	8·3	23·1	12·7	2·1	6·7	14·3
6	23·7	5·8	52·9	5·1	4·6	0·7	7·1
7	27·0	12·3	37·9	8·6	3·3	—	10·8
8	53·9	12·3	14·2	4·5	1·7	1·2	12·2
9	29·3	8·8	34·8	12·1	2·7	0·3	12·1
10	36·4	10·9	36·2	9·1	1·9	1·0	4·4
11	21·3	17·1	23·0	25·0	0·9	—	11·4
12	38·7	15·5	26·0	3·1	2·2	1·7	10·5

*Note:** 1 Summerland Employees Co-op Credit Union.
2 The Lakes Power Station Employees' Credit Union.
3 Macquarie Credit Union Ltd (a county council).
4 A.B.C. Staff Association Credit Union.
5 University of New South Wales Staff Credit Union.
6 Bergengren Credit Union (an industrial company employees).
7 Electricity Commission Employees' Credit Union.
8 C.B.O.A. Credit Union Co-op.
9 Prospect County Council Employees' Credit Union.
10 M.S.B. Credit Union Co-op Ltd.
11 Coalcliff Collieries Employees Credit Union.
12 Irrigation Commission Credit Union Co-op.

(a) the purchase and upkeep of motor vehicles involved between 8·8 per cent (a community credit union) and 45·2 per cent (government department employees) of loans made;

(b) land purchases, housing, renovations and improvements ranged between 22·5 per cent (university staff) and 28·7 per cent (a community credit union);

(c) furniture and appliances financing ranged between 7·7 per cent (university staff) and 20·7 per cent (government department employees);

(d) debt consolidation ranged between 9·2 per cent (a community credit union) and 37·2 per cent (a community credit union).

Further data for a group of credit unions is contained in table 6. This study of lending in 1966-1967 reveals similar diversity in the composition of loans made. The types of loan actually made by credit unions are determined by such factors as (a) the type of credit union; (b) the age of the credit union; (c) the size of the credit union and its maximum loan limit; (d) the rate of growth of the credit union, and (e) the management's promotion policies in the period. Changes in aggregates from year to year for various classes of loans would, no doubt, reveal much greater stability. The maximum loan limit is one factor which requires special note. Originally the maximum permissible loan was fairly restrictive; but in the face of higher incomes, the demand for instalment credit finance in the community and the greater financial stability of some credit unions, these limits have been raised. The Registrar of Co-operative Societies since 1966 has approved loan limits for some credit unions up to $4,000 when secured by a mortgage on real property. Immediately before, the maximum loan limit was $2,000 and in 1964, when the maximum loan limit had only been recently raised from $800, the pattern of limits is as shown in table 7. These provisions have been somewhat more restrictive than those found in other states; the Registrar has discretionary power and considers each case on its merits. Maximum loan repayment periods beyond five years also require permission and conditions have been imposed on credit unions for loans over $2,000 extending up to 7 years and up to 10 years.

One of the interesting features of credit union lending is its policy of non-discriminatory interest rates (i.e. only one rate to all borrowers).[22] In recent years the N.S.W. Credit Union League has progressively raised its recommended 'rate to borrowers' from 5 per cent flat to 1d per £1 per fortnight, to 1 per cent per month.[23] The reasons for these changes are complex but have involved consideration of (a) the need to provide better credit union services to members; (b) a search for a simple viable accounting system which could be applied in all types of credit union; (c) acceptance of an annual rebate to borrowers partly to reduce taxation commitments;

[22] There are several credit unions where there is a higher rate for small loans and a lower rate for loans over $2,000 secured on real property.

[23] 5 per cent per annum is equivalent to an effective rate of 9·32 per cent per annum on a two year contract; 2d per £ per 28 days equals 10·8 per cent per annum compounded four weekly; 1 per cent per month is 12 per cent per annum compounded monthly. When asked, the Registry suggests (1967) 10 per cent per annum on quarterly rests with monthly repayments.

(d) a tendency for an increase in the demand for funds to be associated with an increase in the cost of funds. Credit union loans in N.S.W. generally include a life loan cover effected with an insurance company or carried as a mortality risk from the credit union's own reserves. However, many established credit unions charge rates considerably below these, and one large credit union charges $7\frac{1}{4}$ per cent per annum including a life loan cover; this rate is effectively competitive with the bank overdraft when the life loan cover and fees and charges are taken into account.

6. Credit Unions as Financial Intermediaries

The problem of raising management standards has been one of the fundamental problems in the credit union movement. In N.S.W. a continuous programme of education for directors is undertaken through conferences, schools, monthly chapter meetings and news sheets.[24] The N.S.W. Credit Union League with its CUNA association has been the focus of this activity but other groups such as the Antigonish Credit Union Development Ltd and the Southern Association have been active. However, until there is a survey of the qualifications of credit union directors and an education programme devised which is geared to this need, the movement's education efforts seem likely to bear an ad hoc character and to depend excessively on internal effort.

TABLE 7 MAXIMUM LOAN OFFERED BY 165 N.S.W. CREDIT UNIONS CLASSIFIED BY SIZE, 30 JUNE 1964

Maximum Size of Credit Union's Loan	Frequency	Relative Frequency
$	No.	%
200	2	1·2
400	5	3·2
500	48	29·0
600	32	19·4
700	1	0·6
800	7	4·2
900	4	2·4
1,000	14	8·5
1,200	1	0·6
1,500	3	1·9
2,000	48	29·0

Source: Registry of Co-operatives.

[24] Official organ of the N.S.W. Credit Union League Ltd, *Quest*, Vol. I, No. 1, November 1967 (a sixteen-page newspaper to be published quarterly).

The most striking illustration of the general weakness has been the failure to produce an official manual of credit union operations in spite of the standard nature of their operations and the availability of overseas manuals. This weakness has involved much duplication of effort in the movement especially in the establishment stage. Directors generally give their services free, or for a small remuneration which does not match the economic cost of their services. The directors are generally financial amateurs; but this feature does not make them markedly different from the boards of some public companies and their comparative record is not unfavourable. There have, however, been management 'soft spots' in the movement. In recent years the N.S.W. League has made determined efforts to raise the level of financial expertise of directors. In addition, all credit unions are subject to the possibility of annual inspections by inspectors from the Registry of Co-operative Societies. A credit union, where some deficiencies may exist, would be subject to more frequent inspections. Further, the accounts of most credit unions in N.S.W. are examined by an independent supervisory committee which makes at least an annual report to members.

The size of credit union boards varies enormously and is known to range from three members to at least eleven members, with seven and nine as the common board sizes. In an earlier survey carried out in January 1965, a tendency for the average size of new credit union boards to increase was noted and, under pressure of growth, the number of directors in some of the established credit unions has also shown a tendency to grow. These trends represent attempts to spread the work load and appear to be arrested when the credit union reaches a size which enables it to employ a manager and staff.[25] An early 1967 survey by the N.S.W. Credit Union League showed that at least 45 credit unions in the League employed staff with 46 full-time employees and 46 part-time employees compared with 18 and 39 respectively two years ago.

A classification of N.S.W. credit unions by size reveals a high degree of concentration with a few large credit unions undertaking a high proportion of the business. A survey by the N.S.W. Registrar of Co-operative Societies at June 1964 revealed that the first twenty credit unions, ranked on assets, contained between them:

(a) 11·8 per cent of the reporting credit unions; but
(b) 49·6 per cent of membership;
(c) 47·8 per cent of share capital;

[25] D. G. Flynn, op. cit.

(d) 61·0 per cent of loans made; and,
(f) 57·8 per cent of reserves and unappropriated surplus.

At the same date, 36 Antigonish associated credit unions which represented 21·3 per cent of all reporting credit unions contained 8·5 per cent of total membership and 3·4 per cent of outstanding loan balances. As well, at June 1964, 50 per cent of credit unions possessed membership of between 100 and 199 while some 55·5 per cent possessed outstanding loan balances of less than $20,000. It is believed that this broad picture still applies although there has been some growth generally and a small group of industrial credit unions have grown very rapidly.

There are a number of reasons implicit in the discussion above why a detailed analysis of the cost structure of credit unions must be viewed with reserve. First, the credit unions depend a great deal on voluntary labour and may receive other indirect subsidies such as the use of premises free and, in the case of industrial credit unions, the advantage of pay-roll deductions at little or no charge. Second, and partly in consequence of the first point, the development of costing in the movement has not reached beyond the embryonic stage. Third, the study of costs is probably most easily advanced at this stage of credit union development by financial ratio analysis, but little aggregate data of this kind is available. However, in table 8A and table 8B an aggregate income and expenditure statement compiled by the Registrar of Co-operative Societies is shown. Interest on loans and investment income arising from surplus and liquid funds are the two main items. The former provides over 90 per cent of income. The official statistics of expenditure provide a very limited classification of salaries, wages and directors' fees and all other expenses. The tendency of the salaries and wages to fall rapidly and the other expenses to rise is an apparent paradox; the shift is due to the shift to deposits as a source of credit union funds and this movement also explains the marked decline in the reported surplus.

The credit unions differ in their treatment of reserves from other non-co-operative financial intermediaries mainly in their attitude towards the accumulation of undistributed profits. Credit unions tend to disburse profits in or at the end of the period earned rather than to members in future periods. It would also appear that the desirability of accumulating capital reserves to meet any capital outlay involved in expanding a credit union's activities does not carry as much weight in current thinking as some would like to see.

In N.S.W. the legislation provides for 5 per cent of the difference

TABLE 8A N.S.W.: ANALYSIS OF INCOME OF CREDIT UNIONS, 1953–67

Year Ended June	INCOME					
	INTEREST ON LOANS		OTHER		TOTAL INCOME	
	$'000	%	$'000	%	$'000	%
1953	90·4	95·9	3·8	4·1	94·3	100·0
1954	104·4	96·4	3·9	3·6	108·3	100·0
1955	121·1	95·9	5·1	4·1	126·2	100·0
1956	144·5	95·2	7·2	4·8	151·7	100·0
1957	187·1	94·4	11·0	5·6	198·1	100·0
1958	211·4	94·8	11·5	5·2	222·8	100·0
1959	271·7	95·9	11·5	4·1	283·2	100·0
1960	316·6	97·0	9·7	3·0	326·4	100·0
1961	400·0	96·1	16·0	3·9	416·0	100·0
1962	496·2	96·1	20·0	3·9	516·2	100·0
1963	697·2	95·2	35·4	4·8	732·6	100·0
1964	1033·8	93·5	71·3	6·5	1105·0	100·0
1965	1528·9	93·5	104·7	6·5	1633·7	100·0
1966	2114·1	93·2	153·9	6·8	2268·0	100·0
1967	2820·8	92·0	244·9	8·0	3065·7	100·0

Source: N.S.W. Registry of Co-operative Societies, *Annual Reports*.

TABLE 8B N.S.W.: ANALYSIS OF EXPENDITURE OF CREDIT UNIONS, 1953–67

Year Ended June	EXPENDITURE						SURPLUS AMOUNT AND AS PERCENTAGE OF TOTAL INCOME	
	SALARIES, WAGES AND DIRECTORS' FEES		OTHER		TOTAL EXPENDITURE			
	$'000	%	$'000	%	$'000	%	$'000	%
1953	23·7	41·4	33·6	58·6	57·3	100	36·9	39·1
1954	24·1	42·4	32·7	57·7	56·8	100	51·5	47·5
1955	28·0	36·5	48·8	63·5	76·8	100	49·4	39·2
1956	33·5	36·4	58·2	63·6	91·7	100	60·0	39·5
1957	37·8	33·2	71·1	66·8	114·0	100	84·1	42·4
1958	40·9	33·3	81·8	66·7	122·7	100	100·1	44·9
1959	52·5	24·3	163·2	75·7	215·8	100	67·3	23·7
1960	61·5	22·3	213·2	77·7	274·6	100	51·7	15·8
1961	74·7	20·0	298·0	80·0	372·8	100	43·3	10·4
1962	95·3	20·4	371·6	79·6	466·9	100	49·3	9·5
1963	115·4	17·5	541·2	82·5	656·6	100	76·0	10·3
1964	158·4	15·7	847·8	84·3	1006·2	100	98·8	8·9
1965	219·3	14·6	1280·7	85·4	1500·0	100	133·7	8·2
1966	325·0	15·6	1753·1	84·4	2078·1	100	189.9	9·1
1967	452·5	16·1	2352·2	83·9	2804·7	100	261·0	9·3

Source: N.S.W. Registry of Co-operative Societies, *Annual Reports*.

between the year's surplus and dividends on shares to be placed in a reserve fund up to a limit of 7½ per cent of the net assets of the credit union. This statutory reserve is distinct from other reserves of the credit union.[26]

Since 1958 credit union reserves as shown in table 4A, inclusive of the Statutory Reserve, have declined from 4·1 per cent to 1·5 per cent in 1966. It is possible that the credit union reserves have declined to a level where they may not be sufficient to provide for unforeseen contingencies and losses (such as bad debts), at least in some cases. However, the adequacy of reserves must be assessed against possible contingencies. Here, the record of most industrial (i.e. employee) credit unions is very favourable. In community and parish credit unions the record is less favourable. A study of bad debts written off and arrears over six months in twenty selected credit unions revealed a decline in bad debts and possible bad debts (i.e. loans six months in arrears) of 1·66, 1·24 and 0·96 per cent for the years 1962, 1963 and 1964 respectively.

Again, the survey of twenty credit unions at June 1964 revealed cash (3·5 per cent) and investments (2·8 per cent) of funds. The extent to which a credit union needs to provide for its own liquidity position by holding liquid assets varies. The need for liquidity arises for such reasons as (a) withdrawal of members' shares and deposits and (b) the need to meet seasonal or cyclical fluctuations in the demand for loans. In an attempt to provide a buffer for the liquidity problems of credit unions, the N.S.W. Credit Union League established in 1964 a 'Central' Division. Member credit unions are required to deposit with the 'Central' 5 per cent of their assets on which interest is paid at a rate of 5 per cent per annum (on the monthly minimum balance). Deposits in excess of 5 per cent of total assets are paid at a rate of at least ¼ per cent greater than for bank fixed deposits. In May 1968 it is proposed to raise the deposit rate to 6 per cent. Short-term borrowings from the Central are made at the rate of 7½ per cent per annum on the daily balance. Although credit unions have been restricted in the classes of investment which they have been allowed to undertake, new avenues have been opened up, such as investment with building societies and with the Central which should enable credit unions to perform their savings function more effectively.

[26] In a circular dated 16 July 1965, the Registrar drew attention to the need for adequate reserves. Apart from adequate provision for bad debts, the Registrar advocated a reserve fund of at least 5 per cent of the surplus *before* interest is paid to the depositors to fulfil the original purpose of Section 48 (i) of the Act.

7. Conclusion

In summary, we distinguish the following features:

(a) The Registrar of Co-operative Societies in N.S.W. in implementing government policy has adopted a leading role in fostering and guiding the evolution of credit unions in the State. From time to time policies have been somewhat restrictive and paternal but evidence on the movement's capacity for growth has usually led to their modification. State governments of both political parties have lent a sympathetic ear to the movement's problems. In particular, the evolution of a separate credit union act (which is near completion) and the development of a Credit Union Advisory Council for movement consultation have been welcomed as significant innovations in government relations. But paternalism is contrary to the spirit of independence and self-reliance which it is the purpose of credit unions to stimulate; and so paternalism has not been free of problems.[27]

(b) The main stimulus to the credit union movement and to the N.S.W. Credit Union League has been the 'North American credit union model'. CUNA International Inc. has continued to provide guidance and stimulus. However, the N.S.W. movement is developing local initiative and it has shown signs of maturity through the development of independent credit union newspapers and in the formation of the Australian Federation of Credit Union Leagues (A.F.C.U.L.) and of the South Pacific Association of Credit Union Leagues (S.P.A.C.U.L.).

(c) Stimulus to the N.S.W. credit union movement has also come from the Antigonish group and the Southern Association. The existence of these separate 'leagues' suggests that there are unresolved problems in the development of credit unions in the State.

(d) In our view, the greatest weakness in credit union organisation is the absence of a comprehensive credit union manual, or manuals, which carry the endorsement of either the League or the Registry. The N.S.W. weakness has been a weakness for the movement as a whole in Australia.

(e) The credit union movement remains a comparatively small instalment credit financier. Compared with other financial institutions it has an atomistic structure although a small group of large credit unions do undertake the great bulk of the financing. Nevertheless, the social worth of the movement is not measured in size alone.

[27] An appeal against the Registrar's refusal to register an Antigonish credit union in 1964 was upheld.

7

The History and Development of Credit Unions in the Australian Capital Territory

by J. Ryan

1. Early History: The Innovators

In March and April 1957 the first two credit unions, of the parish type, were registered in Canberra under the new enabling part of the A.C.T. Co-operative Societies Ordinance which was based largely on N.S.W. legislation. The pioneer work was done by Mr F. D. Quinane, who in 1956, as a member of the A.C.T. Advisory Council, became aware of the existence of credit unions in N.S.W., from where he had come to Canberra in 1949. He succeeded in having the legislation passed which enabled credit unions to be registered. The Ordinance is still unamended except for the raising, from January 1967, of the maximum loan limit from $600 to $2000, provided that the excess over $800 is secured. This change had a considerable effect on the rate of growth of the Canberra credit unions.

These twin credit unions, to serve the north side and the south side of Canberra respectively, were formed on the same night at an inaugural meeting convened by Mr Quinane. They soon broadened from Catholic parish credit unions to community credit unions and continued to grow slowly at about the same rate until 1964–65 when the north side group started to outstrip the other, largely because it recruited younger directors and maintained a more venturesome outlook.

Canberra, the seat of the Commonwealth Government, is the only considerable population centre in the A.C.T. which has its own legal and administrative systems quite independent of the State of N.S.W. in which its 900-odd square miles are situated. Canberra's population (in July 1967) was just over 100,000 which is expected to rise to 285,000 by 1980. The large-scale transfer of whole groups of Commonwealth departmental staffs from Melbourne and Sydney in the past ten or twelve years probably explains the noticeable Antigonish flavour of some parts of the credit union movement in Canberra.

None of the four further credit unions formed in the next nine years owed much (if anything) to the two formed in 1957. Each was a quite independent seed, planted and nurtured from outside.

The six credit unions existing at the beginning of 1967 had been registered as follows:

March–April 1957—two parish (later community) credit unions,

May 1959—an employee-type credit union for C.S.I.R.O. staff,

July 1960—one for members of the Commonwealth Public Service clerical organisation,

December 1962—one to serve shareholders of a group of building societies,

May 1965—one employee group to serve Australian National University staff and research scholars.

The credit unions formed since 1957 are discussed below.

The credit union for C.S.I.R.O. staff had as its founder Mr John Gdowski who transferred from Sydney in the early 1950s and in 1959 adopted model rules prepared by the N.S.W.C.U.L. to suit the local laws. Mr Gdowski and his group had remained members of their Sydney credit union until they felt they could form a separate group. This is a process that can be expected to be repeated many times as Canberra's growth continues, for example in the newspaper and broadcasting and TV industries. The other noticeable feature may also be repeated—slow growth due to the fact that members can obtain their larger loans from the 'parent' credit union outside Canberra.

A meeting of the Yass Workmen's Club is given credit for the spark which started the next credit union for financial members of the Canberra branch of the association of Commonwealth public servants. This was for those based on Canberra although it has members living in most countries of the world. Most of the present procedures were introduced by an ex-Queensland credit union member on his transfer to Canberra. With 4,000 potential members, this credit union has every prospect of rapid expansion and is now reviewing its unique procedures. These have proved inadequate to deal with the much greater volumes now following on the availability of $2,000 loans and an increased awareness of the benefits of credit union membership which is percolating through to Canberra residents.

An interesting experiment, of using the credit union idea to serve a group of people primarily interested in building societies, brought into existence the fifth credit union in late 1962. It does not seem so far to have attracted the hoped-for deposits or savings, although there has been steady growth in the balance of outstanding loans. It is perhaps difficult to see how such a unit would easily win the small average savings of an economically diverse membership which is believed to be the weft of a credit union.

In May 1965 the first of the N.S.W. League-fostered credit unions was registered. It was founded by Mr R. W. Parkes (who had seen Mr S. F. Arneil interviewed on TV) with the assistance of a small group of his technical colleagues at the Australian National University. Every assistance was availed of from the League, the adoption of whose standardised procedures enabled a very rapid build-up of membership and service. This is still the only credit union to employ staff, which it has done since February 1966. It offers a sophisticated credit union service to members including withdrawal of savings over the counter, budget savings and financial counselling.

Two further credit unions, bringing the total to eight, were registered in 1967. Both were N.S.W. League-fostered. One, a community credit union in the Woden Valley, was founded by Mr R. W. Parkes whose name has already been mentioned. The other, founded by Sgt (now Inspector) Osborne for the A.C.T. police, was inspired by the Queensland police credit union. It is making good progress.

To complete this rather discursive historical survey, mention must be made of the (unregistered) Association of Credit Unions of the A.C.T., founded in 1965 by Mr F. D. Quinane, in which the Canberra credit unions are loosely knit for the main purpose of law reform. The Association was successful in having the loan limit raised to $2,000 and other suggestions await implementation. The Association is now considering its objects with a view to engaging in League-type, dues-supported activities, which would enable it to affiliate with A.F.C.U.L. It will already have been noted that the Association took no part in the fostering of the credit unions registered in the A.C.T. since it began in 1965.

2. Growth of the A.C.T. Credit Unions

By 1967 there were eight credit unions, a slow growth of six in ten years. Four are of the community type, three are for employees and one is for the members of an (employment) association.

Those founded before 1965 can be grouped together as they are the pioneers, but slow in growth, individual in their approach, and hard to convince of the need for co-operative effort especially involving dues. At least one has now emerged into a new period of rapid expansion, having solved its long-standing problem of dominance by a single idea.

The other group comprised the three League-fostered credit unions formed since 1965. It saw no need for such rugged individualism and wants to expand service to members rapidly with the aid of whatever agencies will help them do this. Whatever the Founding Fathers may think of the idea, these credit unions want to shorten the time that it takes to build up a reasonable service, for which purpose they favour a League 'Central' and as much general and particular promotion as possible, which they see as the League's task. They want to take advantage of all opportunities for promotion.

The growth rate of the next few years should show the effects of the educational and promotional work of C.U.M.I.S. Insurance, the N.S.W. League and the service-minded credit unions. The movement in the A.C.T. could fairly be described as inhibited up till recently but there are signs of a change.

Despite some shortcomings (for example, one credit union would like an arrangement under which loans above $2,000 are possible) there is not an unfavourable legal climate for growth.

The newer credit unions have adopted, initially, the C.U.N.A.-recommended rates of 1 per cent per month on loans and $\frac{1}{2}$ per cent per month for savings. The older credit unions have a wide range of rates and methods of calculation, and some until recently have paid dividends on savings. There is little evidence that the higher apparent rates for loans charged by the newer credit unions are resisted by members nor is it clear that the wide range of interest rates (depending on terms and amount) used by some credit unions has much real effect in attracting savings. Those credit unions with pay-roll deductions are clearly faring better in achieving a high average of savings per member than those without.

The law permits direct lending between credit unions and there is a certain amount of this. Some credit unions are badly affected from time to time by shortage of funds. It is probable that a considerable improvement in the overall picture would follow establishment of a League Central.

Sources and Uses of Funds

There were initially differing practices in dealing with members' shares as some credit unions paid dividends and others did not. Partly because of a desire to minimise income taxation, credit unions have now adopted the

TABLE 1 THE GROWTH OF A.C.T. CREDIT UNIONS

At 30 June	Credit Unions	Members	Loans outstanding to members	Savings and Shares
	No.	No.	$	$
1957	2	n.a.	n.a.	n.a.
1958	2	n.a.	4,410	4,102
1959	3	n.a.	6,410	5,904
1960	4	207	14,016	13,800
1961	4	279	18,690	17,184
1962	5	544	27,690	26,084
1963	5	657	51,310	49,540
1964	5	812	74,098	94,326
1965	6	979	111,954	104,326
1966	6	1,600	183,557	210,087
1967	7	2,286	438,000	442,000

Note: n.a. Not available.

principle of a fixed share holding per member, usually $10 in shares, treated as a refundable deposit (as well, of course, as a useful source of interest-free cash).

All the credit unions accept deposits from people not entitled to borrow and most try to attract such deposits. One credit union distinguishes borrowing and non-borrowing membership and accepts deposits (savings) only from people admitted to this secondary membership. Most credit unions would willingly accept more deposits than they now receive, but it is suspected that on occasions some let seasonal declines in demand for loans influence them to seek to defer deposits.

The available financial data is rather scanty but does suggest that the average saving per credit union member in Canberra is about a quarter of the Australian average. One Canberra credit union (with pay-roll deductions) has succeeded in raising its average to double the general Canberra level so it appears that more could be done in this respect.

Prospects for Expansion

One estimate of the present 'need' for credit unions is over 30, or 4 times the present number. There are good indications that the expansion is under way and that this will be mainly in the employee groups of which the large units transferred to Canberra from other capitals, principally Melbourne, are the chief ones.

League-type promotion in the A.C.T. would result in a rapid doubling and re-doubling of the present number of credit unions, as would the increased prosperity of some of the existing credit unions.

Conditions in Canberra would favour the establishment of a 'service centre' for credit unions not yet able to afford their own office and mechanical accounting. One of the factors inhibiting the growth of some credit unions is accounting and other procedures not capable of handling more volume. Such a centre would solve the problems of many credit unions.

8

Credit Societies in Victoria*

by Andrew C. K. Lo, S.J.

1. Growth of Credit Societies

(a) *Early Development: 1905 to 1940*

The 1938 Report of the Commonwealth Parliamentary inquiry into small loans facilities in Australia noted:

> 'Careful inquiry has shown that, except in Victoria, no organisation exists for the sole purpose of granting small loans on reasonable terms and conditions to members of the general public.'[1]

The historic co-operative credit institution in Victoria was established in 1905 under the Provident Societies Act 1890 as the Co-operative Credit Bank of Victoria.[2] The Credit Bank was founded by a group of civil servants to supply their own credit needs; the institution was modelled on the European people's banks which were introduced to the English-speaking world by the writings of Henry Wolff,[3] a correspondent and friend of Desjardins. The Victorian Credit Bank was successfully established four years before the concept of co-operative credit was introduced into the U.S.A. by Desjardins and it stands out as an interesting page in the history of international co-operative credit development. The Victorian Co-

* The author is grateful to the following for kind assistance and helpful comments on the research project: Mr W. Brodie, the Registrar, and Mr R. Scollard of the Victorian Registry of Co-operative Societies; Mr L. Magree of the Victorian Credit Co-operative Association Ltd; Mr E. Long of the Co-operative Development Society and others.

[1] Commonwealth Parliament, *Report on Small Loans Facilities*, 1938, p. 4.

[2] In 1967 this institution was registered under the Industrial and Provident Societies' Act under a new title: The Co-operative Credit Society of Victoria. In 1966 it had a membership of 1,500, with total assets of $15,000 and loans outstanding amounting to $13,000.

[3] H. Wolff, *People's Bank* (1st Ed.), Longmans Green, London, 1893.

operative Credit Bank had a number of distinctive features. Apart from limited liability with funds raised entirely through share subscription of members, the Credit Bank was an urban institution with a bond of association of members based on occupation.[4] This concept of common bond of association was to become a significant factor in the development of credit unions in North America in the twenties and thirties and in N.S.W. and Victoria in the late fifties and early sixties.

In 1938 T. M. Burke, founder and first manager of the Credit Bank, observed:

> 'The Co-operative Credit Bank has justified all that was prophesied on its establishment, and probably marks the beginning of a function that, if fully utilised, will do great service to the wage-earning community.'[5]

It is interesting to note that, although Australia had a successful working model since 1905, based on an extremely flexible blueprint which was subsequently successfully tested overseas, there was no further co-operative credit development until over thirty-five years later. This absence of development was all the more surprising considering the experience overseas, the undoubted need for small personal loans by the Australian wage-earning class for both providential and consumption purposes,[6] the failure of the banking system to supply the need because of the alleged unprofitability of this form of lending, and the relatively high cost of borrowing from existing sources.[7] The exorbitant rates charged by money-lenders were indicated by various usury limitation bills introduced into state legislatures in the first and second decade of the century (e.g. the N.S.W. Money Lenders' Act 1905).

Perhaps the enormous potential of the Victorian Credit Bank was never well publicised. H. Heaton, writing on co-operation in Australia[8] in 1924 discussed co-operative credit overseas, but failed to examine the local specimen. H. E. Teare in his work on Australian banking[9] in 1926 devoted a special chapter to co-operative credit in Australia, but was unaware of the existence of the Victorian Credit Bank which had in that year well

[4] Raiffeisen advocated limitless liability and People's Banks were established mainly in rural areas with a residential bond. See F. Brauman, *A Man Conquers Poverty*, CUNA, 1963, p. 105.

[5] T. M. Burke, *Co-operative Credit Bank* (a brochure), 1938.

[6] Commonwealth Parliament, *Report on Small Loans Facilities*, p. 3.

[7] ibid, p. 12.

[8] *Commonwealth Year Book of Australia*, Vol. 12, 1924, p. 581.

[9] H. E. Teare, *The History and Theory and Practice of Australian Banking, Currency and Exchange*, Sydney, 1926.

over a thousand members and which had granted over 5,500 loans amounting to over £65,000. Teare noted, however, the preponderance of government aid in agricultural finance and remarked:

> 'as Schulze Delitzsch perceived nearly a century ago, state aid will never wholly help the working classes and the small traders to attain comparative independence.'[10]

Perhaps Professor G. L. Wood correctly interpreted the local situation when he observed in 1937 that Australia was 'a socially advanced community which prefers the technique of state control to that of co-operation.'[11]

(b) *Recent Development: 1940 to 1954*

The current co-operative credit movement in Victoria derived its original impetus from the awakening of 'social consciousness' among groups of Catholic laymen in the thirties and the forties. The Campion movement came into being in 1935, leading to the formation of the National Secretariat for Catholic Action in 1938.[12] The national secretariat initiated general social studies groups among Catholics and included as part of its social programme the promotion of credit unions in Australia. The centre of activities was in Melbourne, but in the forties, members of the Campion movement in N.S.W. contributed to credit union development in Sydney (e.g. nucleus members of the N.S.W. Universal Co-operative Credit Union Ltd formed in 1946). Among the specialised but autonomous groups developed by the national secretariat, there were three which had bearing on credit society development in Victoria: the National Catholic Rural Movement (N.C.R.M.), the National Christian Workers' Movement (N.C.W.M.) and the Young Christian Workers' movement (Y.C.W.). The secretariat requested one of its members, Mr G. F. McDonald, to pioneer co-operative credit development among existing N.C.R.M. groups in country areas and among N.C.W.M. groups in urban areas. A blueprint was produced inspired by the Canadian Antigonish model as expounded by M. Coady and B. Fowler.[13]

[10] H. E. Teare, op. cit. p. 59.

[11] *Horace Plunkett Year Book*, 1937, p. 313.

[12] J. G. Murtagh, *Australia, the Catholic Chapter*, Angus and Robertson, 1959, pp. 177–8, 236; T. L. Suttor, 'Catholicism in Australian Politics since Federation', in H. Mayer (Ed.), *Catholics in the Free Society*, Cheshire, 1961, p. 41; *Australian Encyclopaedia*, Vol. VII, pp. 487–9.

[13] M. Coady, *Masters of their own Destiny*, Harper, New York, 1939; B. Fowler, *The Lord Helps Those*, Vanguard, New York, 1938.

As early as 1941, 'cottage discussions' were initiated by the N.C.R.M. in all country centres where the organisation was active. Mr McDonald recalls engaging in development work in over twenty-five of these centres. Rural parish-based credit societies were formed, for example in Port Fairy in 1943, Cororooke and Dimboola in 1945. Owing to the lack of specific enabling legislation, they were not registered. There would also be difficulties with the National Security Regulations (Capital Issue), if registration was sought, for example, under the Provident Societies Act. There were on record no less than fifteen N.C.R.M. credit societies in existence in Victoria before the Co-operation Act was passed in December 1953.[14] The 13th National Convention of the N.C.R.M. in 1953 resolved that 'N.C.R.M. groups should expand the credit society movement on a grand scale and that a Federation of Credit Societies be formed to ensure the maximum utilisation of the full resources of the societies.' Perhaps the decentralisation policy of the N.C.R.M. and the geographical isolation of the societies militated against the success of the proposed federation.

In urban areas, the efforts of the N.C.W.M. in the forties led to the formation of no less than twelve parish credit societies. The first two N.C.W.M. credit societies were founded in the parishes of Richmond and Oakley respectively in 1943. The N.C.W.M. went into abeyance in the early fifties.

(c) *Current Development: 1954 to 1967*

With the passing of the Co-operation Act in 1953, the impetus for co-operative credit development fell to a vigorous and well-organised Catholic group, the Young Christian Workers (Y.C.W.). The Y.C.W. co-operative movement looked to Antigonish for inspiration.[15] Its approach to co-operative credit has, therefore, been broadly based. The Y.C.W. movement regarded co-operation as 'the expression in the field of economics of a high social ideal'; it saw co-operatives as a means for social reform and regarded credit societies as an integral part of a complex of co-operatives which were designed, not only to improve the standard of living of the worker, but also as a means of providing him with adult education through active participa-

[14] N.C.R.M. pamphlet, *Credit Societies*, p. 15.

[15] For a comprehensive treatment of the Antigonish Movement, see Boavida Coutinho, *Antigonish Movement: Community Development Through Adult Education and Co-operation*, C.I.S.I.C. Institutum Sociologiae Pastoralis, Rome, 1966; Extension Department of St Francis Xavier University, *The Educational and Sociological Reasons for Promotion of Credit Unions*, a résumé of the June 1962 brief to the Canadian Royal Commission on Banking and Finance, Antigonish, Nova Scotia.

tion in economic activities.[16] The ultimate aim was a 'full and abundant life' for the worker.

The Y.C.W. Central Co-operative Credit Society Ltd, which was formed in 1954, was the first society to register under the Act. In 1956, the Y.C.W. Central formed two other parish credit societies, St Gabriel's and St Peter's. From these three societies was formed, in 1957, the Association of Catholic Co-operative Credit Societies Ltd with the aim of pooling resources and of developing credit societies in other Catholic parishes. It is important to note that the Y.C.W. co-operative credit movement as part of an overall co-operative movement, was preceded by successful Y.C.W. co-operative ventures in housing (1945) and in trading (1949). There was no question in Victoria of reliance on funds of the credit societies to finance other co-operative ventures; this was apparently the case with the N.S.W. Antigonish movement, which led subsequently to heated controversies in the early sixties. Also, unlike the early credit unions of N.S.W., which were formed as financial auxiliaries of housing and friendly societies, Y.C.W. Central was formed as an autonomous body with credit society development as one of its specific aims. In this sense, the Y.C.W. Central fulfilled a similar pioneering role to that of the N.S.W. Universal Credit Union. However, the Y.C.W. co-operative credit movement has maintained a close relationship with the Y.C.W. co-operative trading movement; the latter extends its services to all members of parish credit societies. In 1966, 11·5 per cent of the Association's surplus funds was deposited with the Y.C.W. co-operative trading society at 4 per cent and without security.

It is interesting to note that in the early years of formation, the Victorian Y.C.W. co-operative movement and the Antigonish movement in N.S.W. were in contact as both felt they had similar aspirations. In 1957, a Victorian representative was invited to attend the first annual convention of the Australian Antigonish movement in N.S.W.[17] In 1961, Fr John Gallagher and members of the N.S.W. Co-operative Development Ltd attended the annual meeting of the Victorian Association and subsequent discussions were held with a view towards possible future federation.[18] An important difference between the two movements was that whereas the N.S.W.

[16] E. Long, *Helping Each Other Through Co-operatives*, 1961, p. 12. (Australian Catholic Truth Society Pamphlet.)

[17] *Credit Union Bulletin*, official organ of Credit Union Co-operative Development Ltd, N.S.W., Vol. I, No. 1, p. 8, 1957.

[18] *Co-operator*, an official Y.C.W. publication, Vol. I, No. 4, 1961.

Antigonish movement was very much dependent on the dynamic leadership of Fr Gallagher, the Victorian Y.C.W. movement was essentially a lay movement where clerical influence was minimal.

Although the Y.C.W. co-operative movement was Antigonish inspired, the movement has successfully adapted Antigonish concepts to the Australian situation. Firstly, because co-operation was considered to be a 'Christian experiment' for social reform and adult education, there was the tendency in Victoria for the social and religious aspects to predominate over economic considerations in development policies. An important manifestation of this aspect is the low interest rate policy on deposits, pursued by a majority of Victorian credit societies and their somewhat conservative loan policies; this will be discussed later. Secondly, the preoccupation with co-operation as an exclusively Christian and even parish concern, rather than as a community service open to all, resulted in a restrictive development policy at least for the first twelve years; the parish was regarded as both the ideal and the most expedient environment (in theory if not in practice) for co-operative credit development to the perhaps unfortunate exclusion of other equally viable environments such as vocational groupings in places of work. Thirdly, the Antigonish concept of pooling of resources was adopted from the start with the formation of the central association in 1957. This made possible a cohesive and sustained, although otherwise restricted, development programme over ten years, 1957 to 1967. It is most encouraging to note, however, that as a result of the rapid growth of the movement in the first half of the sixties, the period of isolated growth on the part of both the Catholic and non Catholic credit societies in Victoria came to an end in 1966. In 1965, at the instigation of the Latrobe Valley Co-operative movement, with the full collaboration of the Catholic associations, other employee credit socities (notably from the A.B.C. staff and the Campion credit union[19]) steps were successfully taken to replace the Catholic association by a State association. The Victorian Credit Co-operative Association Ltd came into operation in 1966 with a board of twelve directors, of which five represented non-parish credit societies. Fourthly, the tendency for the Victorian movement to develop as a self-contained Catholic movement has resulted in its being relatively insulated from the impetus of the international credit union movement.[20]

[19] This credit union is for employees of the Victorian State Savings Bank.

[20] The 1967 annual meeting of the Victorian Association approved a resolution for Victoria to become affiliated to C.U.N.A. on a trial basis.

2. Analysis of Growth Pattern Since the Act

(a) *The Broad Pattern*

The Victorian Co-operation Act was based on the N.S.W. Act and was passed in 1953 in the wake of the first post-war instalment credit boom. In the face of the new pattern of household consumption, the scope for credit society development was considerable, despite growing competition within the savings and lending markets. The credit society fills in a gap in the personal loan tier and has some comparative advantage over other financial institutions because of its accessibility, availability, personal service, attractive philosophy of self-help and competitive rates for savings and loans.

TABLE 1 VICTORIA: REGISTRATIONS OF CREDIT SOCIETIES, 1954–5 TO 1966–7

Year	Societies on Register at Beginning of Year	New Societies Registered During Year	Societies Dissolved and Registrations Cancelled	Societies on Register at End of Year
	No.	No.	No.	No.
1954–55	—	8	—	8
1955–56	8	6	—	14
1956–57	14	5	1	18
1957–58	18	9	1	26
1958–59	26	5	—	31
1959–60	31	8	—	39
1960–61	39	18	—	57
1961–62	57	16	1	72
1962–63	72	15	1	86
1963–64	86	20	1	105
1964–65	105	22	—	127
1965–66	127	17	—	144
1966–67	144	11	3	152

Source: Registry of Co-operative Societies, *Annual Reports.*

In absolute terms, the share of the Victorian credit societies in the savings and instalment credit market is still relatively unimportant. In 1966, credit societies' savings amounted to \$4·3 million, which was approximately 0·17 per cent of total deposits with Victorian savings banks, while outstanding loans were slightly over 1 per cent of total balances outstanding of instalment credit for retail sales in Victoria. Victorian savings banks' deposits per head of population in 1966 were \$542, whereas deposits per member of credit societies amounted to \$208 only, which is considerably

F*

TABLE 2A VICTORIA: GROWTH OF CREDIT SOCIETIES, 1954–5 TO 1966–7

Year	Registered Societies	Societies Making Returns	Members	Liabilities				Assets		
				Members' Funds		External		Land & Buildings	Other Assets (c)	Total
				Shares	Other (a)	Bank	Other (b)			
	No.	No.	No.	$'000	$'000	$'000	$'000	$'000	$'000	$'000
1954–55	8	6	292	3·0	2·0	—	38·8	—	43·8	43·8
1955–56	14	12	944	59·4	1·6	—	78·0	—	139·0	139·0
1956–57	18	16	1,396	69·4	2·2	—	92·8	—	164·4	164·4
1957–58	26	22	2,009	26·4	2·8	—	193·6	—	222·6	222·6
1958–59	31	28	2,858	47·4	3·8	0·1	219·4	—	270·8	270·8
1959–60	39	34	4,025	42·2	4·2	—	368·2	0·2	414·4	414·6
1960–61	57	46	6,123	59·0	6·6	1·8	605·6	—	673·0	673·0
1961–62	72	67	7,827	79·0	10·6	—	911·4	1·0	1,000·0	1,001·0
1962–63	86	82	10,041	100·2	15·2	0·8	1,414·8	1·6	1,529·4	1,531·0
1963–64	105	102	12,841	128·2	28·6	3·0	2,134·8*a*	4·8	2,289·8	2,294·6*a*
1964–65	127	n.a.	16,727	161·8	46·5	12·5	2,996·1	5·3	3,211·5	3,216·6
1965–66	144	132	20,756	203·0	64·5	25·2	4,138·4	10·9	4,420·1	4,431·0
1966–67	152	149	24,952	242·6	89·3	12·0	5,553·5	29·7	5,867·7	5,897·4

Note: n.a. Not available.

a In 1963–64 deposits were $2,058,976 and loans were $2,010,548.

(a) Members' Funds–Other. This amount comprises statutory and other reserves and any other accumulated surplus after deducting losses on trading.

(b) Other External Liabilities include money received on deposit.

(c) Other Assets comprise current assets, investments and intangible assets such as preliminary expenses.

Source: Registry of Co-operative Societies, *Annual Reports*.

TABLE 2B VICTORIA: GROWTH RATES OF CREDIT SOCIETIES, 1955–6 TO 1966–7

Year	ANNUAL PERCENTAGE INCREASE				
	Societies on Register	Membership	Shares	Deposits (and other non-bank liabilities)	Total Assets
	%	%	%	%	%
1956–57	29	48	17	19	12
1957–58	44	44	−62	108	48
1958–59	19	42	80	13	22
1959–60	26	41	−11	68	45
1960–61	46	52	40	64	63
1961–62	26	28	33	50	49
1962–63	20	24	26	55	53
1963–64	22	28	29	57	50
1964–65	21	30	26	40	40
1965–66	13	24	26	38	38
1966–67	6	20	20	34	33

Source: Registry of Co-operative Societies, *Annual Reports.*

below the savings bank average.[21] North American experience has shown the potentiality of co-operative credit within the savings and personal loans market, and the grounds which have yet to be covered by the Victorian movement.

Assessed on its own terms, the Victorian movement appears to have been remarkably successful since the inception of the Act. Over the 9 years from 1956 to 1964, the annual rate of growth of members and of assets averaged 38 per cent and 50 per cent respectively; see table 2B. Analysis of statistics of 35 of the oldest credit societies[22] over a 6 year period from 1960 to 1965 showed that loans outstanding and deposits increased at annual rates averaging 35 per cent and 38 per cent respectively. For the period 1958 to 1963, total outstanding instalment credit debt for retail sales in Australia grew at annual rates averaging 35 per cent and 38 per cent respectively.

[21] Figures taken from (a) *Banking and Currency Bulletin*, No. 4, 1965–6, pp. 55–6; (b) Victorian Co-operative Registry, *Annual Report*. The savings figure of $208 includes non-member deposits.

[22] These 35 credit societies constitute a complete 'cohort' of Victorian credit societies registered before 30 June 1960. For a more detailed statistical analysis of Victorian credit societies based on these 35 societies, see the author's *The Economics of Victorian Credit Societies, 1954–65*, B.A. (Hon.) thesis, University of Melbourne, 1966.

TABLE 3A VICTORIA: TYPES OF CREDIT SOCIETIES REGISTERED, 1954–5 TO 1965–6*

Year	Parish	Community	Employee	Association & Club	Building Society	Other	All types
1955	1	3	3	0	0	1	8
1956	2	7	3	1	0	1	14
1957	4	8	3	1	1	1	18
1958	9	9	3	3	3	1	28
1959	10	10	3	5	4	1	33
1960	13	10	3	8	6	1	41
1961	22	12	3	12	9	1	59
1962	33	13	3	14	10	1	74
1963	48	13	3	14	10	1	89
1964	60	17	3	18	10	1	109
1965	71	21	3	21	14	1	131
1966	81	25	3	24	14	1	148

**Note:* Table includes societies which have been liquidated.
Source: Registry of Co-operative Societies, *Annual Reports.*

For the period 1958 to 1963, total outstanding instalment credit debt for retail sales in Australia grew at annual rates averaging 10·4 per cent.[23] By 1966, there were 144 credit societies in Victoria with twenty-one thousand members; a total of twenty-nine thousand loans amounting to over eleven million dollars had been made.

The outstanding feature of Victoria's development has been the predominance of parish and community credit societies[24] over other types of societies as shown in table 3A. From 1960 to 1966, parish and community credit societies increased from 56 per cent of the total to 72·7 per cent. Employee credit societies on the other hand dropped for the same period from 20·6 per cent to 15·8 per cent of the total. This trend contrasted with N.S.W. experience: for both states, the period of rapid and sustained development began in 1960 but, from 1959 to 1965, N.S.W. experienced a net increase of 125 credit unions, of which over 81 per cent were employee credit unions. From 1959 to 1966, Victoria saw a net increase of 113 credit societies of which 75 per cent were parish and community types. Several tentative conclusions may be drawn in the light of the comparative experi-

[23] Estimated from N. Runcie, 'Hire Purchase Institutions', in R. R. Hirst and R. H. Wallace (Eds.), *Studies in the Australian Capital Market*, Cheshire, 1964, p. 131.

[24] Parish and community credit societies are grouped in one category for the purposes of analysis because many community credit societies, whose bond of association for members is residential, are in fact parish based, whereas church credit societies whose bond is constituted by a loose definition of 'adherents to parish' often 'turn community' in the long run by switching to a residential bond.

TABLE 3B DISTRIBUTION OF MEMBERS, SHARES, DEPOSITS, LOANS AND TOTAL FUNDS BY TYPES OF SOCIETIES, 30 JUNE 1966

Features of Credit Societies		Parish	Comm-unity	Emp-loyee	Associa-tion and Club	Build-ing Society	Other	All types
Societies with Available Information	No.	67	24	21	13	2	1	128
	%	52·0	18·5	16·2	10·0	1·5	0·8	100
Members	No.	7,381	2,974	7,081	2,959	318	523	21,236
	%	34·8	14·0	33·3	13·9	1·5	2·5	100
Shares	$'000	69	22	66	41	3	5	206
	%	33·5	10·6	32·0	19·9	1·6	2·4	100
Deposits	$'000	918	424	2,026	497	17	38	3,919
	%	23·4	10·8	51·8	12·7	0·4	0·9	100
Loans Outstanding	$'000	923	415	1,995	434	33	48	3,852
	%	24·0	10·8	51·8	11·3	0·9	1·2	100
Total Funds	$'000	1,106	474	2,170	567	34	53	4,408
	%	25·0	10·8	49·2	13·0	0·8	1·2	100

Source: Registry Co-operative Societies, annual statements lodged by societies.

ence of the two states. Firstly, the Victorian movement has shown an 'imbalance' or a lag in the development of employee-type credit societies. Secondly, in view of the remarkable and successful experience of credit union development in the field of employment in N.S.W., the Victorian potential is very considerable. The existence of five well-established and successfully operated employee credit societies in Victoria, with loans outstanding averaging over a quarter of a million dollars, provides a firm basis and an important source of stimulus for the development of similar types of credit societies in Victoria; as members of the newly formed state-wide Association, their contribution to the future development programme will be significant. Thirdly, in so far as successful co-operative credit development in one state will eventually 'spill over' to other states, the success of employee credit unions in N.S.W. would already have set the stage in some ways for rapid development along similar lines for Victoria. There are interesting cases to demonstrate this 'spill over' effect interstate:

for example, A.B.C. staff and the three I.C.I.A.N.Z. credit societies in Victoria were formed through the example and influence of N.S.W. counterparts.

With the restructuring and re-orientation of the Association in 1966 to cover all credit societies in Victoria, a new trend in development may be expected in Victoria. The Association acts primarily as the central bank to members and carries out development, co-ordination and supervisory work, as well as acting as representative for members to the outside world. Members of the Association totalled 96 societies in 1966 and they were grouped into nine regions with regional committees responsible for promotional and educational work in respective areas. The Association also organises conferences and schools for members. It works in close collaboration with the Co-operative Development Society.[25] With the rapid growth of the movement, the role of the Association in the foreseeable future becomes increasingly more important. One of the most important roles of the Association would be to ensure that the quality of management in the movement is commensurate with the rate of growth.

Unlike the N.S.W. Registry, the Victorian Registry does not initiate promotion and publicity of the co-operative movement; perhaps it believes that interest should come from the interested public. Moreover, the Victorian government has not given any subsidy to the Association in this early period as has been the case in N.S.W. However, the restructured Association (now known as the Victorian Credit Co-operative Association Ltd) may warrant governmental assistance to perform its promotional role to ensure that the movement attains a self-sustaining rate of growth.

(b) *Analysis of Credit Societies by Type*

In 1966 the average credit society in Victoria had 164 members with total funds amounting to $34,000 and loans outstanding equal to $30,000; these Victorian averages were slightly less than a third of the corresponding averages in N.S.W. The relatively low Victorian averages were due to the predominance of parish and community credit societies which constituted over 70 per cent of Victorian societies in 1966; as shown in table 3B these societies were generally small in both membership and funds. In 1966, the parish credit society averaged 92 members. The Victorian employee credit societies in 1966 were on average three times the size of parish

[25] The Co-operative Development Society was formed in 1961 by the Y.C.W. to cater for the needs of co-operatives of all types and to aid in education, research, and dissemination of information for all co-operatives.

and community societies in terms of membership, and seven times in terms of funds. In 1966, the employee credit societies had only 16·2 per cent of the total number of societies, but claimed 33·3 per cent of total membership, 49·2 per cent of total funds, and 51·8 per cent of total loans outstanding.

It is interesting to note that in 1966 parish and community credit societies were established in about 30 per cent of Catholic parishes in Victoria and membership of the societies amounted to roughly 15 per cent of the total Catholic population.[26] An analysis of regional distribution of credit societies showed that in 1966 over half of the credit societies were situated in the metropolitan area, with a significant 23·6 per cent situated in country areas.

(c) *Sources of Funds Analysis*

The growth of Victorian credit societies will depend on their ability to attract a supply of funds or savings and, in particular, on how attractive credit society liabilities are relative to liabilities of other financial institutions in the capital market. The ability to attract funds is especially important for growth in the initial stages, although, at a later stage of development, Victorian credit societies have the added portfolio problem of seeking suitable assets at the correct price. The majority of Victorian credit societies are at this stage relatively young. They are facing a situation in the savings market where the degree of competition has increased greatly over the last twenty-five years with the remarkable post-war development of non-bank financial intermediaries such as hire purchase finance companies and building societies.

The Act intends that shares should be the main source of funds for credit societies. However, for tax reasons, the main source of funds has been deposits. N.S.W. credit unions also rely on deposits as the main source of funds, but for a different reason.[27] Well over 90 per cent of credit societies in Victoria operate as mutual societies. Under s. 25 of the Income Tax Law,

[26] Estimated from statistics of *The Official Year Book of the Catholic Church of Australia, New Zealand and Oceania 1966–7*, E. J. Dwyer, Sydney, p. 389.

[27] Credit unions in N.S.W. do not operate as mutual societies although it is currently the intention of the League to request members to adopt the mutuality principle by an alteration of existing rules. Share dividends of credit unions are an allowable deduction under s. 120 of the Income Tax Act, if the credit union is recognised by the tax commissioner as a co-operative concern within the meaning of s. 117. In 1965, a High Court decision ruled that Revesby Credit Union (N.S.W.) qualified under s. 117. In 1966, N.S.W. A.B.C. Staff Credit Union provided another successful test case under s. 117. (See *Taxpayers' Bulletin*, Vol. 8, No. 8, March 1965, pp. 6–8.)

income from loans to members of a mutual society (and this constitutes practically the entire income of credit societies) is not assessable for income tax.[28] Preconditions for the mutuality principle to apply are that: (i) no dividend is paid in the credit society; (ii) any surplus arising may only be distributed to borrowing members; (iii) in the event of winding up, reserves and undistributed surplus go to borrowing members only. With respect to the credit society, (i) and (ii) discriminate against savers. In its application, the mutuality principle also discriminates considerably against savers where the rate of interest on deposits is relatively low, as is the case with the majority of parish and community credit societies (particularly in the event of rising prices). This state of affairs constitutes an inherent source of conflict among credit society members. In the long run, the mutuality principle may place a limitation on the portfolio structure of Victorian credit societies: it may require as high a percentage as possible of their funds to be devoted to members' loans.[29] The almost exclusive reliance on deposits as a source of funds may also affect the adequacy of reserves in credit societies. This will be discussed later. However, the tax benefit resulting from the application of mutuality is very considerable. The paying of an 'equitable' rate of interest on deposit will remove a principal discrimination against savers (as in the case of parish societies). Whereas the Act (s. 38.5) restricts dividend on shares to 5 per cent per annum, there is no such restriction on deposits. The inadequacy of reserves due to the small annual surplus left after deducting interest payments as a cost item may be partly overcome by conservative accounting; through an increase of the accumulated 'interest to mature' on loans outstanding in excess of the amount required.

Analysis of the combined balance sheet of the latest available statistics of 128 reporting societies in 1966 showed in table 3B that deposits constituted 88·9 per cent of total funds whereas share capital amounted to 4·7 per cent. The contribution of banks was negligible. The Association contributed 2·1 per cent of the aggregated member societies' funds.

Credit societies' liabilities may be attractive to members for economic or non-economic reasons or both. For example, deposits with credit societies may be regarded by members of parish societies as a practical way of implementing the Christian precept of helping one's neighbour. Funds may also be deposited with the aim of obtaining credit in the future. Housewives may be attracted by the financial counselling and family budget

[28] N. E. Challoner and J. M. Greenwood, *Income Tax Law and Practice*, Law Book Company, Sydney, 1962, S.25 (209).

[29] Income from investments may be liable to tax.

schemes provided by credit societies.[30] Because of its explicit humanitarian orientation the quality of the services provided by the credit society, especially in terms of financial counselling, must constitute one of its distinguishing features as well as providing the criterion for measuring the excellence of its performance.

A more tangible and economic measurement of the attractiveness of credit society liabilities is the rate paid. Association statistics revealed that the prevailing deposit rate paid by its 72 members in 1966 was 4 to 5 per cent. Only one society, Dnister Ukrainian, paid 6 per cent and then only for deposits in excess of $1,000. 85 per cent of the societies' deposit rates did not differentiate with respect to amount or terms of deposits. Of these, 42 societies paid 4 per cent, 9 paid 4½ per cent and 9 others 5 per cent. 11 societies paid a slightly higher rate for fixed deposits but the terms are not known. The Act (s. 15) provides that one month's notice is required for deposits' withdrawal, although in practice, deposits with credit societies are at call.

Most employee credit societies, which up to 1966 were excluded from membership of the Association, paid 6 per cent on deposits. These appeared to have attracted a much larger volume of funds than members of the Association. Perhaps the availability of pay-roll deduction among employee credit societies facilitated savings in the form of a 'painless extraction'. However, it does appear that economic considerations predominate over non-economic ones with employee credit societies.

It has been the standing policy of the Association to advise newly formed member societies against paying a deposit rate in excess of 4 per cent. This low deposit rate policy appears to stem from an effort to put into practice the Christian orientation of co-operation where savers are expected to be motivated by something more than a purely pecuniary gain; 'investors' will be discouraged from depositing with credit societies. This apparently non-economic orientation has, however, important economic consequences. Firstly, in so far as credit society deposits are interest sensitive, the low rate policy may be a deterrent to growth, especially with reference to increasing competition within the savings market. Secondly, the credit society will reach a smaller number of savers than it would otherwise do. On the other hand, in the absence of empirical findings on the interest sensitivity of credit society deposits, the growth rates of aggregate deposit balances of members of the Association at 35 per cent and 43 per cent per annum for 1965 and

[30] This is a bill paying service for which the households make weekly deposits and are charged an annual fee.

1966 respectively seemed to indicate that the low deposit rate policy was not prohibitive.[31] Perhaps parish and community deposits are less interest sensitive than those in employee credit societies due to non-economic factors. It appears that within the Victorian movement, there are two distinct approaches to co-operative credit: the idealistic and the pragmatic, in some ways reminiscent of the Raiffeisen and Schulze-Delitzsch controversy.[32] It will be interesting to observe the interaction of these two approaches in the next five or ten years of Victorian development.

(d) *Uses of Funds Analysis*

In 1966, as shown in table 3B, 87·5 per cent of total credit society funds was loaned out to members. Employee credit societies loaned out 91·9 per cent of total funds, whereas credit societies sponsored by building societies loaned out 97·1 per cent of their funds, perhaps indicating a comparatively illiquid position in some of the latter cases. The demand for personal loans appears to be relatively lower in the case of parish and community societies. This could be due to the conservative loan policy of a majority of parish and community societies. There is reason to believe that as parish and community societies develop, the demand for loans appears to slacken. The role of the Association as central bank becomes important in this case. The limited scope of credit society activities creates an embarrassing situation for a society experiencing a surplus inflow of funds, especially if such funds are attracted to the society by a relatively high rate of interest. The surplus funds situation often reflects poor management and may be the result of poor portfolio management or the poor quality of services provided by the society concerned (e.g. the long delay in loan approvals) causing members to seek 'near alternative' credit elsewhere. A possible indication of a surplus funds situation experienced by church credit societies in 1966 was the relatively high deposit balance of the Association which subsequently showed a loss for the year's operation, due partly to the inability to re-allocate the funds to other societies. The situation should improve with more employee credit societies seeking membership with the Association. However, the requirement of a deposit of 10 per cent of members' funds as a general condition for borrowing from the Association may be regarded by some members needing funds as relatively prohibitive, causing

[31] Aggregate deposit balance of members of the Association increased from $790,110 in 1964 to $1,066,900 in 1965 and $1,527,119 in 1966.

[32] H. W. Wolff, *People's Bank*, chapter 5 'The Great Co-operative Controversy', London, 1893 (p. 97).

them to seek alternative financial arrangements. The Association pays 4 per cent on deposits and charges 7 per cent on a daily basis.

Credit Society Loans

The scope for lending provided by the Act is restrictive compared to the N.S.W. Act. Victorian societies may only make loans for purposes specified by the Act (s. 14.1). In N.S.W. an amendment was introduced in 1963 to remove a similar restrictive provision in the Act.

Analysis of available information from 128 societies for 1966 indicated that the average size of loans made by societies was $700. There is, however, good reason to believe that this average figure will increase. The loan limit is set at $600, but with approval of the Registrar the limit may be exceeded. Records at the Registry show that most of the societies have a maximum loan limit of $2,000. To date, five societies have a maximum loan limit of $5,000 or over, and of these, one society may lend up to $8,000. Loans in excess of $2,000 are in general secured by mortgage on real property. The current policy of the Registrar is not to approve of loan limits in excess of $3,000. It has been noted that some societies make loans in excess of the maximum limit in the form of investment (s. 54) under the Trustee Act. Often, societies may also overcome loan limits by lending to husband and wife as separate members, although such loans are as a rule secured by mortgage on property.

No survey has been made so far with regard to the types of loans made by credit societies. In general, the majority of loans would be made for purposes of home improvements, purchases of furniture and household durables, consolidation of hire purchase debts, medical and other necessary expenses. Also, little is known of the proportion of loans made by credit societies on first or second mortgages, or the types of security required. With few exceptions, interest on credit society loans does not discriminate with respect to risk or size of loan.

Association statistics showed that, before 1966, over 93 per cent of member societies charged 10 per cent on loans reducing quarterly to give a flat rate of about 6¼ per cent. This rate is further reducible through rebates. In 1966, over 50 societies out of a total of 128 reporting ones gave rebates totalling $18,178.[33] There is also no charge for life loan insurance. In general, the rate of interest charged by parish and community credit societies in Victoria is low compared to the standard 1 per cent per month

[33] See also table 4.

charged by a majority of credit unions in N.S.W. and overseas. Consequently, where the loans outstanding by a credit society are small, its income will also be small and likely to be inadequate relative to the cost required for providing attractive services to members (e.g. by employing a part-time or full-time officer). The dilemma of choosing between low cost credit or attractive services to members at a reasonable cost is one which societies have to face as they grow. This choice is often reducible to one between growth or stagnation. The principle of voluntary effort when applied to a rapidly growing society often means that one group of members (elected officers) is discriminated against within the given society to the detriment of growth. This is not uncommon in parish and community credit societies.

In November 1966, under the new Stamp Act, credit societies became liable to a 1½ per cent tax on their loans outstanding if the rate exceeded 9 per cent. This necessitated a downward adjustment of interest on loans and will have adverse effects on the long-term growth of the societies in Victoria. The credit societies have, however, been exempted from stamp duties on receipts due to representation on the part of the Registry and the Association.

(e) *Bad Debts, Reserves and Liquidity*

A study of bad debt experience of 35 of the older societies over a period of 6 years showed that the societies wrote off on the average 0·13 per cent of loans outstanding.[34] 60 per cent of the societies recorded no bad debts over the six years; but two of the societies, with a relatively loose bond of association, experienced an average write-off of 1·43 per cent and 1·24 per cent respectively. Between 1957 and 1967, there were nine societies liquidated or in process of liquidation; seven of these were community types. Bad debts, however, had not been the cause of liquidation.

The purpose of reserves in the credit society is not to increase stockholders' equities, but to write off bad debts. Accumulation of reserves may be regarded as benefiting future members at the expense of present ones. From this point of view, 'excessive' accumulation of reserves may not be desirable. Further, the allocation of reserves may be taxable. Some societies have adopted conservative accounting methods (by increasing accumulation of interest to mature on loans outstanding) as an indirect way of providing for reserves. The Act itself requires that 5 per cent of annual surplus go into reserves. Analysis shows that statutory reserves as per-

[34] For a more detailed statistical analysis of bad debts see the author's op. cit.

TABLE 4 VICTORIA: FINANCIAL RATIOS OF 35 CREDIT SOCIETIES*, FOR YEARS ENDED 30 JUNE, 1960–65

Year Ended June	All Reserves *a*	Cash and Other Liquid Assets	Bad Debts Written Off	Rebates	Total Gross Income Net of Interest Paid	Total Income Minus Operating Cost *b*
	Total Funds	Total Funds	Loans Outstanding	Net Surplus	Total Funds	Total Funds
	%	%	%	%	%	%
1960	1·45	12·5	0·16	26	4·3	3·0
1961	1·60	9·5	0·15	25	5·7	4·0
1962	1·73	9·0	0·14	24	6·5	4·6
1963	1·71	9·0	0·07	37	6·5	4·3
1964	1·70	8·0	0·13	27	6·8	4·7
1965	1·74	13·7	0·18	34	7·0	4·9
AVERAGE	1·65	10·3	0·13	29	6·1	4·2

Notes: * These 35 credit societies were the only ones in existence in 1960 which still existed in 1965. Of the 35 credit societies, 20 were parish or community types.
a All reserves include the following items: Statutory reserves, general reserves, reserves for bad debts and unappropriated surplus.
b Operating cost includes all cost items with the exception of interest paid on deposits.
Source: Analysis of annual statements of societies lodged with the Registry of Co-operative Societies.

centum of annual surplus averaged 7·6 per cent.[35] However, this gives no indication of the adequacy of reserves since the annual surplus of credit societies is minimised by the heavy reliance on deposits as a source of funds. However, all reserves as a per centum of loans outstanding over a period of 6 years averaged 2·25 per cent. All reserves, in relation to loans outstanding, would be over 17 times greater, therefore, than bad debts written off over the same period.

Liquidity in general refers to the ability of the credit society to meet obligations as they fall due. In Victoria, the Act makes no provision for liquidity and the question is left to the discretion of credit society management. However, very little research has been done on the part of the movement on this aspect of the societies' operations. The external source of liquid-

[35] See author's op. cit.

ity for the societies has to a large extent been stabilised by the formation of the Association which acts as central bank and lender of last resort to member societies and in turn it requires them to deposit up to 10 per cent of their funds with itself. The internal source of liquidity rests with management to ensure (i) a reasonably liquid portfolio and (ii) a flow-of-cash budget adjusted to deposit withdrawals. Analysis of the 35 credit societies over a period of 6 years showed that the ratio of cash and other liquid assets to total funds of these societies averaged 10·3 per cent; see table 4. A further examination of 105 credit societies with available information on deposit withdrawals in 1966 showed that only 16·2 per cent of these had a ratio of total withdrawals for the year to total additional deposits for the year, in excess of one. This factor, together with the relatively quick turnover of credit society loans, indicated a relatively liquid position.

(f) *Management, Income and Expenditure*

The problem of credit society management is closely associated with the problem of growth. For the movement as a whole, there is the general problem of the rate of growth outstripping the supply of properly qualified directors. Since the credit societies are engaged in a highly competitive instalment credit and savings market, the degree of effective penetration of these markets will, in the long run, depend on the quality of credit society management. Increased efforts on the part of the Association will be required to raise the present general level of credit society management. For the individual credit society, the challenge must sooner or later be faced as to whether the management should enter the phase of full-time operation with paid staff, or remain relatively small and continue to operate part time (e.g. after church services on Sundays) and on a voluntary basis. We have already discussed an aspect of this question in relation to the rate of interest charged on loans.

Analysis of 128 credit societies in 1966 showed that 25 per cent paid fees to directors. Of these, one society paid slightly over $1,000 to the directors. 21 societies (i.e. 60 per cent of those which paid directors' fees) paid less than $100. The same analysis showed that 40 per cent of the 128 societies did not pay out any wages or salaries. Of the 60 per cent which paid out wages and salaries, one society paid over $2,000, one over $3,000 and two over $4,000. The average loans outstanding of these four societies was in excess of $250,000.

The above analyses indicated the heavy reliance which the Victorian movement placed on the voluntary efforts of elected officials. While it may be argued that the admirable spirit of the movement requires that directors should operate in a voluntary capacity, there is a definite limit to the size and efficiency of a society based entirely on voluntary effort. This size, however, may be well under the actual potential of a given society. In the case of a parish credit sociey, the potential is very considerably increased if the society decides to extend its services to members of the community rather than just parishioners. Occasionally, the growth attained by a given society is so rapid that the society operates without members realising the injustice done to their elected officers. There is little doubt that imagination and fortitude are required for any society to venture beyond the purely voluntary scale of operation and to embark on a more progressive growth programme to realise the potential of the society, and to extend its services to the greatest number.[36] It is interesting to note that, of the seven parish credit societies registered between 1957 and 1958, four have since extended their scope of operations to become community credit societies.

3. Conclusion

Co-operative credit development in Victoria falls into three distinct phases, with a fourth and exciting phase of development already emerging. In the first phase, the historic Co-operative Credit Bank of Victoria developed in 'splendid isolation'. Since its establishment in 1905 the Credit Bank has continued to operate successfully for over half a century as a working model in Australia, but has failed to induce similar co-operative effort, due perhaps to the absence of organisational backing and continuing apathy in the community.

In the second phase, development work undertaken by the N.C.R.M. and N.C.W.M. in the forties achieved a measure of success and laid the groundwork for further development in the fifties. However, development was hampered in the forties by (a) the lack of specific enabling legislation; (b) geographical isolation of the rural societies developed by the N.C.R.M. which was enhanced by the decentralisation policy of the organisation; (c) the weak organisational framework of the N.C.W.M. which went into abeyance in the fifties; and thus it failed to support further development of the urban parish societies it had promoted.

[36] This issue was discussed by thirty-two representatives from parish credit societies in the first school organised by the Association of Catholic Co-operative Credit Societies; see *The Co-operator*, Vol. 7, No. 5, August 1966.

In the third phase, sustained and rapid development was made possible by three forces: (a) enabling legislation; (b) young and vigorous leadership among Y.C.W. members who were backed by a broadly based and reasonably cohesive organisational framework; and (c) interstate influences. The third phase of development was characterised by a high degree of idealism inspired by the Canadian Antigonish model which had been successfully adapted to Australian conditions within the particular context of the Y.C.W. movement. It showed an idealism which had generated a sustained, although restricted, development pattern.

However, with the restructuring and re-orientation of the Association in 1966, the Victorian movement appears to be moving into a fourth phase of development where a more balanced and fully integrated development pattern may be achieved. Rapid development is to be expected in employee groups; the majority of the older church credit societies are already providing services to the community rather than to parishioners alone. Further, the 'new pattern' Association will be a vehicle for a greater degree of interstate and international influence on the local movement.

The major problems of growth are: (a) the low interest rate policy on deposits and the relatively conservative loan policies of church and community credit societies; (b) the absence of a managerial cadre within the movement to provide the expertise and professional sophistication commensurate with the growing status of the movement, and to cope with the intensifying competition which the movement must face within the finance sector; (c) the stifling effects imposed by the ceiling for exemption from the Stamp Act levy; (d) the failure to exploit the savings as distinct from the lending aspect of co-operative credit which was aggravated by the failure of credit societies to qualify under the Home Savings Grant Act; (e) the failure on the part of one or more credit societies within the movement to see the urgent need for united action to pool resources in terms of funds, experience and aspirations in order to achieve the highest rate of growth possible.

The above problems of growth (with the exception of (c)) devolve mainly from several conflicts inherent in the movement; these conflicts are already being resolved as the movement advances into its fourth phase of development. First, the conflict between idealism and pragmatism as exemplified by the different approach adopted by church and non-church societies to co-operative credit. A balance will have to be achieved between the tendency to regard credit societies as vehicles of social reform, or as nothing more or less than financial intermediaries. Second, the conflict between savers and borrowers manifested by (a) the low interest rate policy on deposits adopted by the majority of church societies, where borrowers are more favoured than savers and (b) the mutuality principle, where once again the suppliers of funds are discriminated against in favour of the users of funds. In both instances, savers are presumably better off materially than borrowers and have, therefore, a moral obligation to help the latter. This not only underlines the credit societies as lending institutions but also reflects a third conflict: between the concept of mutuality more suited to the 19th century Raiffeisen society (where disparity of wealth was common and pronounced) and the concept of self-help which some claim is more suited to the middle-class full-employment Australian society where the individual in the co-operative may be expected, paradoxically, to fend for himself without patronage. Fourth, there is the conflict experienced by church credit societies between remaining small, tightly-knit, self-contained, parish-bound units, and increasing the scale of operation by providing an attractive community service and facing up to the difficulties of switching from a voluntary basis of operation to one where paid staff must be employed. These conflicts which devolve from problems of growth will no doubt be solved as the movement re-orientates itself to achieve the highest rate of growth.

9

A Note on Credit Unions in Tasmania*

by Neil Runcie

1. Introduction

The island State in the Australian Federation probably has not lagged significantly behind the mainland states in its understanding of credit union principles, but it is relatively more limited in its resources. Population is spread widely in Tasmania and, as there is a great shortage of trained leaders, communication is difficult and imposes relatively greater strains on the available talent. Moreover, other social purposes and groups make heavy demands on those able and willing to participate. It may be that the root cause of this difficulty is public education on the need for credit unions.

2. Early History

The earliest groups of credit unions operating in Tasmania were Antigonish inspired and Father Gallagher of the N.S.W. group visited the State and quickly formed five parish-based credit unions in 1958. (The first credit union was Hobart and District Co-operative Society Ltd.) Although only one of these credit unions has been liquidated, the remaining four credit unions have remained small and are isolated. Thus they have had little further direct influence.[1]

The next stage in the development of Tasmanian credit unions did not occur until 1959 when the Public Service Association decided to set up a credit union on the model of that run by the South Australian Public Service Association. The Tasmanian Public Service Savings and Loans

* I am indebted to Mr D. Closs, President, Credit Union League of Tasmania, for most of the information herein.

[1] Some observers have maintained that the primacy of this group has restrained the credit union movement in Tasmania because of, inter alia, their interest rate policies (i.e. 10 per cent flat on loans less a rebate on the completion of the loan).

TABLE 1 TASMANIA: GROWTH OF REPORTING CO-OPERATIVE CREDIT SOCIETIES, 1960–1 TO 1965–6

Particulars	1960–1	1961–2	1962–3	1963–4	1964–5	1965–6
NUMBER OF:						
Societies	7	7	8	12	13	13
Shareholders	902	1,403	1,740	2,715	3,631	4,622
Shares	7,343	9,565	12,248	16,559	21,889	24,502
ANNUAL TRANSACTIONS ($'000)						
Advances to Shareholders	94	201	306	598	1,026	1,102
Advances Repaid	43	94	184	320	630	866
Deposits Made	66	163	252	452	538	928
Deposits Withdrawn	17	60	114	180	180	660

Source: Deputy Commonwealth Statistician, Hobart.

Co-operative Society Ltd is now the largest credit union in the State and operates in approximately fifty departments of the State Government. It had a membership in June 1967 of approximately 3,000, and a membership potential of approximately 5,000. This credit union charges 5 per cent flat on loans and a sliding scale on deposits of 6 per cent per annum up to $2,000, 5 per cent from $2,000 to $4,000 and 4 per cent for amounts over $4,000. The credit union maintains a central office with a staff of five full-time employees.

The third force in the Tasmanian credit union development was the formation of the A.B.C. Staff Association Credit Union, a month after the Public Service group, in December 1959. In June 1967 it had a membership of 328 out of a membership potential of 370. The formation of this credit union was part of an Australia-wide plan for State credit unions in each Australian Broadcasting Commission office. This credit union charges a rate of 1 per cent every 36 days to comply with the ceiling of 10 per cent simple imposed on loans by the Lending of Money Act 1915; deposits received interest at 6 per cent.

3. The League and Legislation

Tasmanian credit unions register under the Industrial Society Co-operation Act 1928. Tasmanian credit unions pay income tax and stamp duty in most cases. There is an apparent need for separate legislation for credit unions and interstate conferences on this need would help to focus the attention of the Tasmanian legislature on the need for reform.

The Credit Union League of Tasmania was formed in 1966 with five member credit unions, and at June 1967 there were 11 members. At this latter date there were four unaffiliated credit unions including three of the Tasmanian Antigonish groups referred to earlier.

Tables 1, 2 and 3 are official statistics from a group of *reporting* credit unions compiled by the Deputy Commonwealth Statistician and serve to illustrate the rapid growth of the movement in Tasmania in spite of the difficulties outlined earlier.

TABLE 2 TASMANIA: SOURCES OF FUNDS OF REPORTING CO-OPERATIVE CREDIT SOCIETIES, 1960–1 TO 1966–7

Year Ended 30 June	Sources of Funds: Share Capital		Deposits		Other*a*		Total	
	$'000	%	$'000	%	$'000	%	$'000	%
1961	15	17·0	70	79·6	3	3·4	88	100·0
1962	15	7·6	172	86·4	12	6·0	199	100·0
1963	19	5·4	311	88·1	23	6·5	353	100·0
1964	25	4·0	582	90·3	37	5·7	644	100·0
1965	30	2·9	941	91·5	57	5·6	1,028	100·0
1966	40	2·8	1,274	90·1	100	7·1	1,414	100·0
1967	78	3·7	1,775	85·0	236	11·3	2,089	100·0

Note: *a* Includes reserves.
Source: As for table 1.

TABLE 3 TASMANIA: USES OF FUNDS OF REPORTING CO-OPERATIVE CREDIT SOCIETIES, 1960–1 TO 1966–7

Year Ended 30 June	Uses of Funds: Outstanding Balances		Other		Total	
	$'000	%	$'000	%	$'000	%
1961	81	92·0	7	8·0	88	100·0
1962	188	94·5	11	5·5	199	100·0
1963	310	87·8	43	12·2	353	100·0
1964	587	91·1	57	8·9	644	100·0
1965	983	95·6	45	4·4	1,028	100·0
1966	1,290	91·2	124	8·8	1,414	100·0
1967	1,889	94·0	200	9·6	2,089	100·0

Source: As for table 1.

10

Credit Unions in South Australia*

by T. P. Fitzgerald

1. Introduction

Credit union development in this State has lagged behind in the Australian pattern. This is particularly evident when comparison is made with the growth in New South Wales and Victoria. The main reasons for this great discrepancy, apart from longer foundation, appear to be threefold:

(1) a near-vacuum of credit union knowledge and techniques;
(2) total lack of particular legislation directed towards credit unions; and,
(3) the introvert and insular attitude of the established industrial credit unions over the years in this State.

For this reason South Australia is vitally interested in the policies and fortunes of the Australian Federation of Credit Union Leagues (A.F.C.U.L.).

The knowledge vacuum must be filled as soon as possible and any education programme must include the following points:

(1) national publicity;
(2) a united approach to the State Government on principles and guidance;
(3) formation of policies, both short and long term, by the S.A. Credit Union League; and,
(4) dissemination of knowledge of credit union techniques through schools and seminars.

This vacuum of knowledge of principles and applied techniques exists at all levels. It has been the most significant cause of credit union slow growth and inertia. Analysing the reasons for this situation one comes up against a complex array of facts and probabilities. Inadequate knowledge is at the

* The author acknowledges assistance from J. A. Rust, a fellow Director of the South Australian Credit Union League; however, the author is solely responsible for the views expressed.

root of the problem. In fact, until the last two or three years, there seems to have been no general awareness that credit union members here are part of a world-wide movement based on clearly defined principles of co-operation. However, the climate is changing and there is now in prospect a real expansion of credit union activity in South Australia.

South Australians are known to be small users of credit, and as one might expect they also have the highest average per capita savings bank deposits in Australia. The total amount of instalment credit provided for retail sales in South Australia for 1966 was \$78·2 million, and the balances outstanding as at 31 December 1966 totalled \$129·1 million. As the total outstanding balances of credit unions in South Australia was \$2–\$3 million at 30 June 1967 it can be seen that there is great potential for credit unions in the field of retail sales alone. The number of shareholders, about 10,000, represents less than 1 per cent of the State population. There is, therefore, great scope for credit unions to develop, but there is much hesitancy and caution in potential members which must be overcome first.

2. Early History

Nevertheless, the credit union movement in South Australia has a comparatively long history and extends back to 1949 (see table 1) when the S.A. Public Service Savings and Loans Society was formed. Until 1958 this society remained the only credit union in South Australia and it is still the largest. The next society to be registered was the Commonwealth (S.A.) Public Service Savings and Loans Society Ltd in June 1958. This group is much smaller than its counterparts in other states. The third credit society formed was Satisfact Society Ltd set up by the teachers' institute to cover the needs of teachers. None of the first three registered credit unions has yet become a member of the S.A. League. The insularity of these groups at this stage is noteworthy.

No survey has been made of the extent to which credit unions operating in Commonwealth instrumentalities interstate are operating in South Australia. It is known that the C.B.O.A. Credit Union, covering employees of the Commonwealth Banking Corporation and the Reserve Bank of Australia, are covered by their credit union registered in Sydney. This sort of centralisation is to be deplored as it does not help the interests of the League in South Australia. In our view, arrangements must be sought to allow local employees to have some measure of control at the State level. We see this development as one which penalises the State leagues and thus the credit union development of the less populous states. This applies particularly to South Australia. This matter must become a task for A.F.C.U.L. We hasten to add that the C.B.O.A. Credit Union is not a member of the New South Wales League and for good reason! The New South Wales League has a policy which demands dues for *all* members of affiliated credit unions. This arrangement does not appeal to Australia-wide credit unions of course. Fortunately, however, not all Commonwealth instrumentalities have adopted complete centralisation. A notable exception is the A.B.C. Staff (S.A.) Savings and Loans Co-operative Society Ltd established in August 1960. This society forms part of a decentralised pattern of credit unions in the Australian Broadcasting Commission throughout Australia.

3. Recent History

Since 1962 credit union formation has shown a steady pattern of growth averaging one or two a year. With the formation of the Credit Union League of South Australia in 1966, it is expected that this rate will be accelerated.

TABLE 1 SOUTH AUSTRALIA: GROWTH OF CREDIT UNIONS, 1949–66

Year ended 30 June	No. on Register	No. Making Returns	Share Capital	Total Assets	Advances
	No.	No.	$'000	$'000	$'000
1949	1	—	n.a.	n.a.	n.a.
1950	1	1	3·2	5 2	4·0
1951	1	1	9·0	12·2	9·8
1952	1	1	19·0	22·2	18·0
1953	1	1	40·6	46·0	38·2
1954	1	1	67·0	73·0	60·8
1955	1	1	90·2	97·2	80·4
1956	1	1	110·2	120·2	102·2
1957	1	1	123·2	147·2	126·2
1958	3	2	144·8	210·2	177·2
1959	3	3	179·6	284·8	244·8
1960	3	3	243·8	401·0	350·4
1961	4	3	320·6	501·0	473·2
1962	4	4	389·8	656·0	600·2
1963	5	5	529·2	896·6	799·8
1964	6	6	705·2	1,299·3	1,144·4
1965	9	9	1,246·1	2,125·6	1,936·6
1966	11	11	1,376·1	2,763·2	2,541·0

Note: n.a. Not available.
Source: Returns filed with the Registrar of Companies, Adelaide.

Credit unions are now operating in the Ukranian community, salaried officers in the gas industry, I.C.I.A.N.Z., within the Social Credit Movement, and in the Roman Catholic parishes. Also, recently, a society of 1,000 members potential has been registered (October 1967) of technicians in divisions of the Post Office, and this group has applied for admission to the League.

The development of parish credit unions (St Bernadette (1964), St Pius X (1965), Good Shepherd (1966)) follows the Victorian pattern and influence. Like the Victorian parish societies, there has been some interest in associated co-operative ventures in other fields. Lending and borrowing policies are similar to those in Victoria. All three societies pay 4 per cent on savings and lend at a standard rate set at 10 per cent per annum reducing quarterly, which is about 6¼ per cent flat. These societies are strictly mutual; they pay no dividends on shares and make rebates only to borrowers. On this basis they have achieved taxation concessions and only pay tax on earnings earned outside the society (i.e., bank interest only at present).

OPERATIONS OF CREDIT UNIONS IN SOUTH AUSTRALIA

At June 1967 there were 12 credit unions which were of the following types:

Parish credit unions	3
Industrial credit unions	7
National groups	1
Community	Nil
Other	1
	12

All of these report difficulty in obtaining adequate manpower to do the necessary work, and this appears to result from insufficient education of members. Frequently, one or two directors who are dedicated workers carry the load virtually unaided; many directors merely fill the board positions without any real appreciation of credit union principles. The most urgent need is for credit unions, with the assistance of the League, to embark upon a systematic and sustained education programme. Most of the early credit unions charge a 'flat' rate of interest on loans, whereas the more recent ones prefer an interest rate adjusted monthly or quarterly. The flat rates vary from 3¾ per cent to 5 per cent, whilst the adjustable rates vary from 2½ per cent per quarter to 1 per cent per month.

In respect of deposits, too, there is a marked difference in approach between the old and the new credit unions. The earlier ones tend to pay higher rates on deposits, from 5 per cent to 6 per cent calculated monthly, whilst the later ones pay lower rates, usually 4 per cent, whilst allocating greater amounts to reserves. It is the general intention of the recent credit unions to spend more on education in preference to increasing the rates on deposits.

As noted above, some credit unions in South Australia have discovered the value of being true mutual co-operatives and to achieve this status no dividend may be paid on shares. The principal benefit is that taxation is chargeable only on income from outside the membership, such as bank interest; taxation is, therefore, negligible. Those credit unions, however, that continue to pay dividends on shares, are taxable on their total profits, which makes considerable inroads into members' funds, and is the main reason why adequate reserves have not been built up.

Sources and Uses of Funds

With only one exception, all funds are derived from members by way of share capital, entrance fees, deposits and retained profits. The one industrial society still receiving assistance from employers intends to sever this link. Entrance fees are usually charged at either 10 cents or 50 cents, but in some cases no fee is charged. The total amounts involved do not make a significant contribution to members' funds. Reserves appear to have been neglected in most cases, but there is a growing realisation of the need for adequate reserves. Those credit unions paying full taxation felt that it was desirable to reduce profits by increasing the interest on deposits, rather than build up reserves, as the allocation to reserves would have to be made from profits which would attract taxation. The adoption of the mutuality principle would overcome this situation and encourage the accumulation of adequate reserves.

Most credit unions accept deposits from non-shareholders, but these are not significant except in the case of parish societies, where there are 282 shareholders and 222 other depositors. These other 'depositors' are usually members of the family of the shareholder, and there has been no concerted attempt to seek deposits from other sources. Although it is the aim of the S.A. Credit Union League to provide a central banking service for its members this has not yet been put into effect. In fact, there seems to be no great demand for this service up to 1967. However, this situation could change.

4. Our Aims and Problems

All societies in South Australia are registered under the Industrial and Provident Societies Act, 1923–58. This registration is necessary because of the absence of any specific credit union legislation in South Australia. Under the Playford Government administration, which lasted approximately 30 years, such legislation was not considered. This is surprising in view of:

(1) the obviously great social benefits to all citizens, and

(2) the great strides in other states during this period. However, the movement's inherent weakness of organisation did contribute to a lack of approach to the government-of-the-day.

Significantly, there were no credit societies in the country areas at the end of 1967 and, more important still, no liaison between city and country interests. In the hill districts surrounding Adelaide there are approximately seven co-operative societies. These are centred mainly on and around fruit and vegetable growers; their main functions appear to be:

(1) provision of adequate cold storage facilities, and

(2) supply of materials and equipment, for growers' use by means of a co-operative store.

Here, again, they have no association beyond a common membership in the Cold Stores Association of South Australia. What is needed to give the necessary interaction between all these isolated interests is some form of common bond of association. This could be supplied by two means:

(1) through the formation of a Co-operative Institute or Association, or

(2) some link through the already formed Credit Union League of South Australia.

Over and above this we feel that what is really needed in the long term is a Registrar of Co-operative Societies. This official would have some responsibilities for advice, supervision and promotion activities in the co-operative sphere.

All of these facts show and underline the weaknesses of the movement in this state. Highlighting this insularity, lack of cohesion and effort in general are the parish credit societies. These are significant in three main respects:

(1) recent development (e.g., the oldest society would be less than 5 years old in mid-1967);

(2) confined to the Catholic church parishes at the moment; and,

(3) their probable development towards 'open' community type societies.

They are, of necessity, fairly weak at the moment. Also, it appears they have realistically assessed the situation now existing and are pressing for the following:

(1) all societies to become members of the League in South Australia for the very good reasons of unity, strength and education;
(2) an active campaign to foster the true spirit of co-operation within industrial societies; and,
(3) a determination that all citizens shall be given the opportunities inherent in true credit society principles.

5. The League and the Future

The problems and policies of the League are the focal point of discussion in the next stage of development of the movement in South Australia. It is important, in our view, for the movement in each state and in Australia as a whole to produce long-range plans for growth. These must be realistic in the light of resources and must be subject to constant review.

In the South Australian League we have given thought to such matters as:

(1) the need for separate credit union and co-operative legislation in South Australia;
(2) the need for a promotional grant from the State Government similar to that in New South Wales and Queensland;
(3) the need for further assistance from other Leagues, the Australian Federation and CUNA;
(4) the need to increase League membership from among the existing credit unions;
(5) the vital need for good clear direction and communication at the federal level; and,
(6) the provision of schools and seminars at a state level as an urgent measure.

Some aspects of the problem have been mentioned already in the C.B.O.A. case; in part this latter credit union's policies involve a conflict between centralised efficiency and decentralised democracy. Some form of local league membership may help to reconcile the dilemma. Further, it is interesting to note that the near-insularity of some other public service credit unions (referred to earlier) must be modified by change. First, there will be the formation of other public service credit unions (e.g. the P.M.G. Department) which will become members of the League. Second, there is the factor of outside challenge. In South Australia these influences have not been apparent in the form of, for example, stamp duty on agreements. It is only by unity before the event that these challenges can be successfully met. Recognition of this aspect may not be long delayed. Insularity and co-operative enterprise are a contradiction in concept and philosophy.

Because the League at its present embryonic stage of development is unable, by itself, to provide services which assist with promotion and attract members, the formation of the A.F.C.U.L. has been vital. It is now hoped to provide Australian and CUNA promotional material exclusively through the League. Again, the associated development of Cumis Insurance will be a significant aid.

The legislation in South Australia does not lay down maximum loan limits, although the rules of individual societies may do so (e.g. Commonwealth Public Service Society $400). However, another influence here is the maximum amount under Life Loan Protection; insurance from one main company is $3,000 and this is an effective ceiling for most lending.

The 'master plan' for S.A. League development has involved our setting up three committees:

(1) publicity (for the public);
(2) services (for existing credit unions);
(3) promotion (for new credit unions).

The tasks of the League would, however, be greatly assisted by governmental recognition of the movement through the establishment of a Registry of Co-operative Societies (with similar functions to those in New South Wales) and a separate Credit Union Act perhaps based on the New South Wales model legislation when it becomes available.

In summary, further thinking and discussion has produced these thoughts:

(1) confirmation of South Australia's place as the cinderella state in the movement;
(2) conviction that we must, in future, be represented at all A.F.C.U.L. meetings, schools, and seminars;
(3) also, we must provide schools at the state level ourselves;
(4) a conviction also that the image projected by CUNA up to date in Australia is confused and not well defined; and,
(5) the need for a full-time Secretary of A.F.C.U.L. as soon as it is possible.

There is little doubt that the credit union movement in South Australia will expand in the next few years but much hard work is in store for the few willing workers. Undoubtedly the greatest problem, the lack of sufficient workers, can only be overcome by more effective education.

The League is planning action to increase membership as well as services to members. It hopes to report a substantial increase in membership by 1969 and expects that this will be achieved by formation of new credit unions. Much groundwork is necessary in 1968 and dramatic results are not expected until the League is strong enough to provide a full-time field officer. Unfortunately, this does not appear to be likely for some time unless there is outside assistance.

11

The History and Development of Credit Unions in Western Australia

by Rodney G. Smith

1. Introduction

During the ten years before 1904, Western Australia experienced an industrial boom due to the rapid increase in gold production. The finding of the precious metal produced a sudden inflow of population to the Colony and the expansion of trade that followed inspired many English investors with confidence in the future prospects of the Colony. In 1901 Western Australia became a State in the Commonwealth and, by 1903, it had taken on the image of a thriving, expanding state.

All arrivals to the country were quickly welcomed into the ranks of the friendly societies that had been formed by the English, Scottish and Irish migrants who had introduced this social activity in their new land. Because of a keen demand in certain quarters for an Act to govern the growing activities of co-operative societies, the Government produced a Bill in 1901 known as the 'Industrial and Provident Societies Bill', but because it excited a good deal of hostility among parliament members the Bill ultimately lapsed.

In 1903, the then Premier of the new State, the Hon. Walter James, reintroduced the Bill with a new title, the 'Co-operative and Provident Societies Bill'. In presenting the Bill the Premier said, 'There is nothing dangerous in this Bill; on the contrary, it is a very just measure of reform, necessary to enable societies formed with an object of which we all approve to carry on their business'. The Bill was founded on an Imperial Act of 1893 which in its turn was founded on Acts which had prevailed from earlier times. The object of the Bill was to allow people of limited capital, and in some cases limited in number, the advantages and privileges of the Companies Act without placing upon them some of the more irksome processes and expensive proceedings which have to be gone through to comply with the Act.

It is very doubtful that the term 'credit union' had been known when the Bill was introduced, although one of the objects of the Bill was to encourage thrift and promote prosperity among persons who were, perhaps from want of funds, excluded from embarking on larger ventures. The Bill also sought to afford the utmost protection to shareholders of a society and to secure the proper supervision of the accounts of any society which might be formed in accordance with its provisions.

On 19 August 1903 the Bill was adopted and remained in its original text until minor amendments were made in 1947. Fifty-seven years after the Act became law, the first credit union in Western Australia was registered under this Act. Until this time credit unions had been known to very few people in the State.

2. Formation of the First Credit Union

Federal industrial unions with branches in Western Australia were, without doubt, the prominent influence for the beginning of credit unions in the State. The main influence was the A.B.C. Staff Association in New South Wales. The Western Australian branch had been kept aware of the activities of the credit union in New South Wales and was interested to watch how this 'new idea' was going to develop. By 1960 it became very evident that the credit union was a success and two members of the New South Wales branch credit union, Stan Arneil and Hugh Duffy, travelled westward to encourage the West Australians to start their own credit union.

The two 'visitors from the East' found little difficulty in convincing their fellow employees that a credit union could be established for the convenience of staff members of the Australian Broadcasting Commission in Western Australia. Armed with all the necessary literature including a sample copy of rules, the visitors assisted in the formation of the first credit union in Western Australia. The local Association branch was anxious to assist as it was evident that starting a credit union within the membership of the staff association was an excellent medium for attracting new members to the Association, a feature which has remained true to this day. In the middle of 1960, the Registrar of Friendly Societies had received notification that the Governor had approved the rules of the A.B.C. Staff (Western Australia) Association Credit Union as a co-operative society within the meaning of the Act and registered the first credit union in Western Australia.

The Registrar of Friendly Societies

The Registrar of Friendly Societies in Western Australia is responsible for the administration of the Act and for ensuring that all registered societies conduct their activities within the ambit of the Act. Each credit union is required to submit an annual return to the Registrar, showing details of its membership movements, with a copy of the profit and loss account and balance sheet to the close of business on 30 June each year. This statistical data is collated in a report to the Chief Secretary on the proceedings for the financial year of friendly societies and co-operative and provident societies.

3. Growth of Credit Unions in Western Australia

In his report for 1966 (the last report available at time of writing) the registrar of Friendly Societies reported, 'The operations of credit unions continue to expand and as at 30 June 1966 loans had passed $2·5 millions, investment by members totalled $2,394,826, representing approximately $260 saved per member.' Since their inception in 1960, there have been more credit unions registered under the Act than any other type of consumer society. It is therefore interesting to note below the details of the rapid growth of credit unions in Western Australia.

The main details of credit union growth 1960/61 to 1966/67 are set out in tables 1 and 2.

In the *Daily News* (Perth's evening newspaper) of 3 December 1964 an article on the business page featured the growth of credit unions in Western Australia, and reported:

> 'The office was modern, efficient. Machines whirred, processing the hundreds of accounts handled each day. This was a credit union . . . one of the fastest growing babies of Western Australia's financial world.'

The reporter was commenting on his impressions of the largest credit union in Western Australia, the C.S.A. Credit Union which draws its membership from members of the Civil Service Association. The C.S.A. Credit Union had its beginning in 1960 and was formed within the confines of two government departments housed in the same building. Less than three years after its formation, the credit union grew to demand full-time staff. At this stage of its growth, the Civil Service Association took on the responsibility of staffing the credit union and decided to open membership of it to all members of the Association throughout the State.

By 1964 another credit union was beginning to feel the problems related

TABLE 1 WESTERN AUSTRALIA: GROWTH OF CREDIT UNIONS 1960–1 TO 1966–7

Year	Societies on Register at beginning of Year	New Societies Registered during Year	Societies Dissolved or Registration Cancelled	Societies on Register at end of Year
	No.	No.	No.	No.
1960–61	—	4	—	4
1961–62	4	2	—	6
1962–63	6	2	—	8
1963–64	8	3	—	11
1964–65	11	3	—	14
1965–66	14	2	—	16
1966–67	16	3	—	19

Source: Registry of Friendly Societies, W.A.

TABLE 2 WESTERN AUSTRALIA: GROWTH OF REPORTING CREDIT UNIONS, 1960–1 TO 1966–7

Year	Societies making returns	Members	Borrowers during year	Loans made during year
	No.	No.	No.	$
1960–61	3	348	n.a.	n.a.
1961–62	6	894	n.a.	n.a.
1962–63	8	2,436	n.a.	n.a.
1963–64	11	3,841	n.a.	n.a.
1964–65	13	7,687	5,616	1,000,366
1965–66	15	9,257	3,721	2,071,906
1966–67	19	11,900	n.a.	n.a.

Note: n.a. Not available.
Source: Registry of Friendly Societies, W.A.

to growth. This was the Administrative and Clerical Officers' Credit Society which was formed in 1961 and takes its membership from within the membership of the Administrative and Clerical Officers' Association throughout Australia. The directors of this society were confronted with the decision of whether to restrain the growth of the society owing to the volume of work, or employ a full-time secretary and to increase membership and so to justify the need for full-time staff. Although the credit union did not call on any other credit union for experience in this matter, their decision was progressive. As a result the first full-time secretary in a Western Australian credit union was appointed in August 1965.

G*

TABLE 3 SOURCES AND USES OF FUNDS OF WESTERN AUSTRALIAN REPORTING CREDIT UNIONS

Year Ended 30 June	Sources of Funds										Uses of Funds					
	Share Capital		Reserves		Deposits		Other		Total		Loans to Members		Other		Total	
	Amt. $	%	Amt. $	%	Amt. $	%	Amt. $	%	Amt. $	%	Amt. $	%	Amt. $	%	Amt. $	%
	'000		'000		'000		'000		'000		'000		'000		'000	
1961	3	9·4	—	—	27	84·4	2	6·2	32	100·0	28	87·5	4	12·5	32	100·0
1962	7	8·0	1	1·0	77	87·5	3	3·4	88	100·0	80	90·9	8	9·1	88	100·0
1963	20	6·0	5	1·5	291	88·2	14	4·3	330	100·0	309	93·6	21	6·4	330	100·0
1964	31	4·0	9	1·1	734	92·3	21	2·6	795	100·0	774	97·3	21	2·7	795	100·0
1965	54	3·2	20	1·1	1,581	93·7	34	2·0	1,689	100·0	1,598	94·6	91	5·4	1,689	100·0
1966	63	2·5	57	2·2	2,394	93·3	52	2·0	2,566	100·0	2,501	97·4	65	2·6	2,566	100·0
1967	86	2·3	121	3·3	3,430	92·7	63	1·7	3,700	100·0	3,572	96·5	128	3·5	3,700	100.0

Sources and Uses of Funds

One of the most important objects of the credit union is to keep before the members the need for saving. Without this important source of funds the credit union could not exist. Similarly, having received the funds, it is just as important to lend the money as quickly as possible. The following statistics show how credit unions in Western Australia have received their funds and used them in loans to members and purchasing the necessary requirements for the administration of the society.

4. Organisation of Western Australian Credit Unions

In the early stages of credit union development in Western Australia, the credit unions had a strong leaning toward the American pattern of organisation and structure. It now appears that the credit unions are developing a system of administration peculiar to their own needs. This condition can probably be attributed to the wide field of activities in which the Act allows them to engage and also to the absence of American influence in the training of credit union leaders.

The operations of the credit union are entrusted to the board of directors who are appointed by the membership at the annual general meeting. All credit unions to date specify that an annual general meeting must be held, although the Act does not specifically call on them to do so. At each annual general meeting the directors retire in rotation and, unless advised by the retiring director to the contrary, they are automatically re-elected to the position of director if unopposed. Many credit union directors receive an honorarium for their services; in most instances the sum is only nominal to cover out-of-pocket expenses. However, in some credit unions, the sum paid is several hundred dollars, and in some credit unions the chairman of the board may receive up to $200 extra.

As in other credit unions, the board meets to consider such matters as policy, administration, and delegation of duties; however, unlike American and most other Australian credit unions, it is common practice in Western Australia for loan applications to be considered at the full board meeting. In general, Western Australian credit unions have not adopted the practice of a loans committee as distinct from board members.

In most credit unions throughout the world, it is the accepted practice to have a supervisory committee, or an audit committee as it is sometimes called. Very few credit unions in Western Australia have a committee, although most have an internal auditor; the other credit unions leave the audit to the hired auditor who examines the accounts once a year. Perhaps the reason for this variation from the usual practice is that the Act only requires an audit to be conducted at least once every year and the audit can be conducted by two members of the credit union if the board wishes.

The Act stipulates that the society must appoint a secretary. The secretary is responsible to the board of directors for the administration of the credit union. The term 'secretary' should not be confused with the duties of 'secretary' in credit unions in other countries. The secretary of the credit union in Western Australia is the chief administrative officer and can be compared with the credit union manager in other Australian states and countries throughout the world.

By June 1967 there was still only one full-time secretary employed by credit unions in Western Australia; however, as the societies develop and expand, there will no doubt be many more credit unions which will find it necessary to convert from self-help to full-time paid staff.

The accepted practice of appointing a treasurer by the credit union movement in the Eastern states has had its influence on the credit unions in Western Australia. Most credit unions in the State have appointed a treasurer, although the Co-operative & Provident Societies Act does not require that they do so. The treasurer's principal duties are mainly confined to the accounting needs of the society; however in some credit unions he is also classified as a director and is given full voting rights on board decisions.

The community credit union which has proved to be very successful in other states of Australia and countries around the world has yet to be organised in Western Australia. There appears to be a lack of interest in starting a credit union of this nature in Western Australia. As the credit union movement is still only a relatively new movement in the State, any enthusiasm shown to organise a community credit union is often dampened by people who are not aware of the movement and who look upon the suggestion with scepticism.

Several attempts have been made to organise a parish credit union in Western Australia and in this field once again, the move has failed. As credit unions become more and more popular, the parish and community credit unions will take their place with the other credit unions formed by industrial and employee groups.

The credit union has experienced little difficulty in expanding after becoming organised and registered. All credit unions with the exception of one, draw membership from employee or industrial unions, and this homogeneous arrangement has made for rapid growth for some credit unions.

Because the members share the same interests, whether it be working for the same employer or being members of the same association or union, they develop a distinct pride for the credit union and this pride is reflected to others who have not joined. Experience shows that it is not too long before the non-member feels he is missing out on something and joins the credit union. Perhaps this explains why many credit unions in Western Australia have nearly 100 per cent membership. Of course, there will always be the member who will only join for what he can get and not for what he can contribute to the credit union; this is inevitable.

Development of the League

As credit unions progressed in Western Australia, it became very evident that the whole movement in the State should become more consolidated. Many directors had little or no experience in managing a credit union, or like organisation, and the need for management training became more and more urgent as the movement progressed. For these and other reasons the Credit Union League of Western Australia was formed in 1966.

Early in 1963, movements were made to form a representative body for credit unions in Western Australia and, in December of that year, the Credit Union Research and Advisory Council was formed. The Council was a voluntary body, made up of representatives from different credit unions who met together to discuss problems facing the movement and to exchange ideas and know-how on the many issues involved in running a credit union. The meetings of the Council were of tremendous benefit to those who attended. The Council did not concentrate on starting more credit unions although any group which was interested received assistance. On several occasions the Council realised other benefits of formation apart from their being just a 'get-together for credit unions'. One occasion was a State-wide, but unsuccessful, effort for credit unions to become approved societies for the holding of members' deposits in the Commonwealth Home Savings Grant scheme.

In November 1965, the majority of credit unions were represented at a meeting to hear Mr C. Compton, of Cuna Mutual Insurance Society of the U.S.A., speak on the need to form a league in Western Australia. Mr S. Arneil was also invited to speak on the advantages of a league. For the first time in the history of credit unions in Western Australia the opportunity arose to meet and discuss the international scene.

In June 1966, the League was registered and since its formation much work has been done to accomplish its purpose. Several weekend schools and seminars have been held to train directors and officers. A loan protection fund for members has been arranged and a Central fund has been organised. A special effort to relieve the State stamp duty imposition on receipts and cheques was negotiated.

The Work Ahead

In June 1967 there were 17 registered credit unions in Western Australia; 14 of these were formed in the first five years, which indicates that there has been a sudden decrease in the number of credit unions being formed. Although there are nearly 12,000 credit union members in Western Australia, this still represents only 1·4 per cent of the total population. These facts prove that credit unions have only 'scratched the surface' for the people in the State. There remain many thousands of persons yet who are not serviced by a credit union and there is much work yet to be done to project the credit union philosophy to the Western Australian public. Many people have not heard the term 'credit union' and are forced to other financial houses for assistance and are compelled to pay higher interest rates.

Personal loans are much publicised on television and in newspapers by banks and finance companies, yet one impression is that when you try to avail yourself of these services, you are turned away for lack of security, or you may be considered a credit risk. The average family man finds it difficult to obtain bank overdraft facilities on the basis of his honesty alone. If he does obtain an overdraft he is often so 'tied up' that he would find it difficult to shop around for further credit.

With the advent of credit unions to Western Australia has come the opportunity to fill the gap for the credit needs of the family man, youth, working girl and mother. The Western Australian has become so accustomed to the restrictions placed upon him by other credit outlets, that he is often left amazed when the credit union advances a loan on the basis of his character alone.

5. Conclusion

Within a short time, credit unions in Western Australia have made many remarkable changes for their members, in relieving debts, obtaining homes, furniture, cars and many other useful and enjoyable assets; but above all the credit union has proved a reliable and convenient method encouraging the habit of saving.

The time will come when credit unions will be an accepted way of life in Western Australia. This will bring career opportunities for men and women employees in credit unions and staff industrial awards will one day come into existence as the industry increases. It is reported that in the future, money as we know it now, may simply be electrons flashing down wires or invisible patterns of molecules on computer tape. If the predictions are true, credit unions in Western Australia must be prepared and will need to adapt their services to meet the needs of their members.

In a world today where selfishness is displayed in all walks of life, the men and women who give of their talents, time and energy, to help bring better living conditions are scarce. These men and women are prepared to adopt and put into practice the credit union slogan: 'Not for profit, not for charity, but for service'.

12

Credit Unions in New Zealand

by C. Smith

1. Early History

It may be shown that New Zealand credit union development has actually proceeded through four stages:

(a) the money clubs;
(b) friendly societies extending to their members credit union facilities;
(c) the formation of 'independent' credit unions; and,
(d) League formation and the foundation of a New Zealand Credit Union Movement.

The earliest New Zealand legislative reference authorising 'co-operation for the accumulation of small savings and for obtaining temporary advances on easy terms' is in 1884.[1] The purpose of the authorisation was to extend the facilities of the Friendly Societies Act, 1882, to enable societies formed for this purpose to register under the Act. Again in 1911, the authorisation was repeated,[2] apparently to clarify the previous authority, as the 1882 Act had been superseded by the Friendly Societies Act, 1909.

It is interesting to note that the New Zealand law has a precedent in the English Friendly Societies Acts where similar provisions appear: thus on 23 April 1903 (in substitution of that of 16 May 1876) there is an authority to 'create funds by monthly or other subscriptions to be lent out to, or invested for, the members of a society, or for their benefit pursuant to Friendly Societies Act, 1986.' Even earlier, on 23 March 1877 (modified in 1883) in England authority was granted, 'to promote thrift among labouring classes by affording them the opportunity of depositing their savings and receiving the interest on the same'.

However, the earliest actual development in New Zealand was of co-

[1] *The Gazette*, No. 67, 5 June 1884, p. 919.
[2] *The Gazette*, No. 44, 25 May 1911, p. 1754.

operative money clubs which may be traced back to the English Loan Societies Act, 1840 (which is still operative in England). In New Zealand, 7 August 1885 was the date of registration of the Sydneyham and Suburban Co-operative Money Club followed by the Ivy of Linewood Co-operative Money Club on 1 December 1891; the latter organisation cancelled its registration as recently as 1944. It is known that eight money clubs had been registered by 1919 of which four had cancelled their registration.

The Friendly Societies

In February 1943 CUNA received a letter from L. J. Retallick, District Secretary of the Ancient Order of Foresters' Friendly Society, acknowledging information received from CUNA and advising that the Triennial Conference at Wanganui had decided to form a credit union. It was registered under the enabling provisions of the Friendly Societies Act in August 1943.[3]

The Manchester Unity Independent Order of Oddfellows moved more quickly and their credit union was the first in New Zealand. It was registered in May 1943 and at the end of the first year it had a membership of 493 with assets of $N.Z.7,619; the total lodge membership at that time was approximately 25,000.[4] There are now nine separate district credit unions of this lodge with total credit union funds at 31 December 1966 of $N.Z. 3,806,536 and members' loans of $N.Z.2,435,348; the balance of the funds is advanced for investment.

It should be noted that the New Zealand friendly societies in their own right have accumulated substantial 'small loan' funds under Section 55 of the Friendly Societies Act amounting to nearly $N.Z.6,000,000. The societies have approached the government, from time to time, for a lifting of the savings limit to $1,000, then to $1,500 and subsequently to $2,000 (the present limit). However, the unsecured loan limit remains in law at $100.

The First CUNA Affiliate: A Parish Credit Union

The next significant development was in June 1955 when parishioners of St Mary's Catholic parish met at the instigation of Thomas C. Mitchell. Literature and information had been obtained from CUNA and from

[3] It is of interest to note comments by Mr Bergengren on the C.U.N.A. file copy.

[4] Early reports on this development are contained in *The Credit Union Bridge*, October 1943 and May 1944; Mr J. L. Stewart, the Secretary of the sponsoring lodge, kept in touch with the world movement.

Father Marion Ganey in Fiji. The charter meeting to form St Mary's Parish Credit Union was held in July 1955 and in August 1963 the name was changed to St Mary's (Hamilton) Credit Union as there were now five parishes within the original boundaries. This credit union was the first New Zealand credit union to affiliate with CUNA in November 1958.

In most social movements one enthusiast is necessary to provide the initial drive and enthusiasm. The beginnings of credit unions elsewhere show this. It was Tom Mitchell's enthusiasm and desire to share the credit union ideal with as many potential groups as possible which led to a two-day conference in November 1958. This meeting was widely publicised and reported.

Next, two Maori investment societies were formed in 1959 and, although annual seminars were held, progress was slow.[5] In March 1961 St Joseph's (Matata) Credit Union was formed to serve a Catholic parish on the east coast of New Zealand in the Bay of Plenty and the St Joseph's (Wellington) Credit Union was formed to serve a Catholic parish in Wellington. The latter credit union was registered under the Industrial and Provident Societies Act.

The New Zealand Credit Union League

In November 1961, Father Ganey arrived in New Zealand on the invitation of the St Mary's (Hamilton) Credit Union. There were two direct results of his visit. First, the formation of the New Zealand Credit Union League was effected. Second, there was advice that the loan charge should be 1 per cent per month on the unpaid balance. The operating rate at the time was almost half that recommended. The view was accepted that the increased income was necessary to provide for services to members. Initially two credit unions joined the League (St Mary's (Hamilton) and St Joseph (Matata)) and there has been steady growth as shown in table 1. T. J. Barber became the first League chairman and the writer became managing director; we both continue actively in these positions.

From 1963 to 1965, as the table shows, progress was slow. However, this was a period in which rules were redrafted and conferences held. In particular in 1965, following attendance by the writer at a CUNA

[5] For a discussion of savings and credit in a Maori community see Joan Metge, 'Rural Local Savings Associations (Maori Komiti) in New Zealand's Far North' in R. Firth and B. S. Yamey (Eds.), *Capital, Saving and Credit in Peasant Societies*, Allen & Unwin, 1964.

TABLE 1 GROWTH OF N.Z. CREDIT UNION LEAGUE

Year 30 September	No. of Credit Union Members
1962	2
1963	6
1964	9
1965	9
1966	12
1967	24

Mutual School in Sydney, a two-day school was held in Hamilton with tutors C. C. Compton and S. F. Arneil. CUNA Mutual obtained a licence to operate in New Zealand on October 1966 with the first contracts effective from 1 January 1967. CUNA International Inc. voted to accept the New Zealand League affiliation in November 1967; this development had been the subject of a request from New Zealand for several years.

On 30 September 1967, the 24 credit unions affiliated with the League had 4,396 members, assets of $N.Z.493,078 and outstanding loans to members of $N.Z.425,552. In the previous year the corresponding figures were 2,816, $N.Z.309,418 and $275,354 respectively. Outside of the friendly societies group of credit unions, which have not joined the League, twenty-four of the twenty-seven active credit unions in New Zealand are League members. At 30 September 1967 eight credit unions serve on a religious bond basis (Catholic), ten are community credit unions and eight are industrial credit unions.

2. Structure and Growth Prospects

Structure

The structure of New Zealand credit unions closely follows the U.S.A. pattern. The credit unions do not attract taxation but dividends to members are taxable in the hands of the recipient. All contributions are treated as shares with no specified capital contribution other than the $2 for a share required to be paid to qualify as a voting member. Bank borrowing is available but is used to provide liquidity to level out peaks in cash flows. Provision is made for accepting deposits but the League recommends that the credit unions refrain from using this facility unless a change in tax structure requires a change. An entrance fee is generally charged, but it does not exceed 50 cents per member.

Ten per cent of the *gross* income is generally allocated as a reserve for delinquent loans and the maximum interest rate of 1 per cent per month, which is specified in the rules, is inclusive of the costs of making the loan. These costs, mainly legal, are often substantial as every loan over $100 must be secured by law.

Dividends range from 3 per cent to 4½ per cent per annum (mostly 4 per cent) and are calculated on the minimum monthly level in the member's account. By way of comparison, call money in New Zealand Government institutions (e.g. Post Office Savings Bank) is 3 per cent per annum at call and 4½ per cent per annum where the term is twelve months.

Growth Prospects

There are a number of limitations on growth. First, although it is believed that there is no shortage of leadership, education or enthusiasm in the movement, there was an initial shortage of funds to provide the impetus to growth. The technical 'know-how' gained during Father Ganey's visit in 1961 shortened the embryonic stage and enabled a self-sustaining level of activity to be reached more quickly. A second concerns the absence of suitable enabling legislation. Without a Credit Union Act a wide variance in standards of acceptable performance could emerge, but all new credit unions have, in practice, closely followed League recommendations. A third limiting factor could be that the Public Service Investment Society has operated a savings and loan service for civil servant members since 1928 as part of its activities. Membership of the latter society has grown from 4,500 in 1947, to 18,698 in 1957, and to 59,817 at 31 March 1967. Some of the spectacular growth of the latter years was due, in part, to the extension of facilities to groups other than government employees (e.g. municipal employees). At 31 March 1967 the members' savings in this organisation exceeded $N.Z.5,750,000; it also operates a co-operative trading department and is organised on a country-wide basis. The Public Service Investment Society is registered under the Industrial and Provident Societies Act. It is in this field of government employees that some spectacular development has come in other countries. A fourth possible limiting factor arises from the nature of the New Zealand economy itself. Here there are two notable features. First, the economy has been based on rural rather than manufacturing development; and this limits the scope for industrial credit unions. Second, tight monetary controls have tended to curb the availability of instalment credit compared, for example, with Australia. Hence the impetus to debt consolidation through credit unions may not have been as strong as across the Tasman. The shortage of cars arising from the New Zealand balance of payments is a unique feature limiting the demand for instalment credit.

Nevertheless, the New Zealand credit union movement has many advantages. In contrast to Australia, one League unites the credit unions and only one government reduces the volume of organisational contact necessary in that direction. But far more significant is the 'CUNA Mutual' League assistance programme which will start in 1968. Within three years this could lead to a self-supporting movement of 150 credit unions. Over ten years a target of 250,000 members and funds in excess of $N.Z.25,000,000 may not be an unrealistic target.

In conclusion, over the past eighty years New Zealand has a history of successful co-operatives with some sections of the movement becoming large and significant. We are confident that the credit union movement with its philosophy and its expansion ideals will be accepted by a rapidly increasing number of New Zealand people in the next decade.

Part III Prospects for Growth

13

Australian Credit Unions—Where are they Going?

by S. F. Arneil

It is important for the credit union movement to be able to see itself as a whole in Australia, in Fiji and in New Zealand at the present time. This is because the separate credit unions and the leagues need to combine to pool their resources and knowledge for expansion, protection and services. There have been two recent organisational developments aimed at these objectives; first, the formation of The Australian Federation of Credit Union Leagues (A.F.C.U.L.) in May 1966, and second, the formation of The South Pacific Association of Credit Union Leagues in November 1967. Credit unions believe in self-help and the formation of these associations is intended for mutual assistance.

From the beginnings of growth in the early post-war years in New South Wales and Victoria, the movement has spread to other States, and has been assisted since the late 1950s by the stimulus of Cuna International (formerly the Credit Union National Association) and later by Cuna Mutual Insurance Society and its affiliate, the Cumis Insurance Society. In New Zealand the origins are also recent; but they were influenced by developments in Fiji. The source of development in our neighbours in Fiji was different: it arose from an invitation to Father Marion Ganey from the former Fijian Governor, Sir Ronald Garvey, to come from British Honduras in 1953. Thus the success of Fijian Credit Unions springs from Father Ganey's earlier successful efforts in the Caribbean. In spite of earlier contacts with the N.S.W. League the need for A.F.C.U.L. to cement those international links in the region is obvious.

A.F.C.U.L. has been stimulated by restrictive legislation in some States and an overall legislative pattern which is inconsistent and inept. If there is inter-State co-ordination for Company Law, why is there not for credit unions ? The Federation policy is to seek a separate Act for credit unions in all the States and Territories: a good deal of thought has been given in the movement in New South Wales to proposed 'model legislation' which it is hoped will guide the other States.

The various New South Wales Ministers, from both sides of the political fence, are to be congratulated on their long-standing vision in attempts to provide suitable legislation. However, the framing of suitable legislation in Australia for credit unions is difficult because of the lack of understanding of this new force in society. The present State Co-operation Acts and other impinging Acts in Australia are dominated by 'building societies' thinking, and in this field it is the material security which is paramount as against the substitution of character, as part security in the credit union case. The Federation will probably deal with these legal difficulties, State by State and promote the introduction of Federal Credit Union Law in Australia. The United States analogy is before us: parallel State and Federal legislation has evolved a legal framework for credit unions in the United States which has facilitated their growth in the context of a great Federation. Further research into the legislative provisions is necessary to produce a model adapted to the Australian environment.[1]

There is an urgent need for machinery to facilitate the transfer of surplus funds from credit union to credit union and from one State to another, and even internationally; the Australian economy is one and there are common interests in all regions. There are different patterns of development revealed in each of the States in this book. One long-range aim of the Federation is to ensure that the same range of credit union facilities is available to all communities in Australia. An example of the new facilities now available is Cumis Insurance Society (Inc.), which was formed in the United States in 1960 and was registered in every Australian State and in the Australian Capital Territory in 1967–8. Its insurance package provides protection in one policy against any damage to a credit union by dishonesty or 'Act of God' (e.g. fire). It is expected that Cuna Mutual Insurance Society will provide life loan cover for borrowers and life savings insurance for deposits (e.g. double savings on death), as well as normal life covers for credit union members and their families, and superannuation cover for credit union employees.[2]

[1] Cuna International Inc., *Comparative Digest of Credit Union Acts*, 1966 edition.

[2] On the relations between Cuna International Inc., Cuna Mutual Insurance Society and Cumis Insurance Society see J. Dublin, *Credit Unions, Theory and Practice*, Wayne State University Press, 1966.

Final application for registration of 'Cuna Mutual' was lodged in early September 1965 and some delay has occurred, although these facilities are already available in New Zealand, Fiji and Western Samoa. In contrast to the position in the early 1960s, there are now a number of insurance companies willing and anxious to undertake various types of insurance for credit unions.

An illustration of the need for the Australian Federation of Credit Union Leagues, and a stimulus to the formation of the Federation, was provided by the controversy over Home Savings grants. The policy of the Federal Government, in spite of submissions by individual State Leagues, was to accord only 'temporary status' (which expired in 1967); the Leagues and the Federation regard this treatment as inconsistent and discriminatory. However, the Minister's view was that the primary function of a credit union was not housing finance, although credit unions could assist in getting people into homes. The 'deposit gap' is only one facet of this problem in the view of the Federation.[3]

As shown in the statement of objects of A.F.C.U.L. (see Appendix A) the development of sound management practices is given top priority. The N.S.W. League took the initiative in 1965 in inviting Cuna Mutual Insurance Society to establish the first annual residential training school in Australia. This school is attended by students from all States in Australia and from the Pacific, and it includes Government officials from various State Co-operative Departments as well as permanent employees in the movement. The schools, which are known as 'the Newport Schools', are a permanent feature. All costs additional to the income from student fees are borne by Cuna Mutual Insurance Society as a practical gesture to assist a young credit union movement. The Federation, which now acts as co-sponsor of the Newport Schools is conscious of the need of schools in all States and at the local level. It will encourage such schools and assist in the training of local lecturers.

The initial object of the South Pacific Association is to enlarge the Bergengren School at Suva to accommodate students from any area of the Pacific. Following the establishment of the first Newport School by Cuna Mutual, similar schools have been held by that organisation in New Zealand and in Fiji. Cuna International have also generously supported the Australian and New Zealand credit union movement by sending lecturers to visit all States for both night and weekend schools.

[3] See the Australian Federation of Credit Union Leagues, *Credit Unions: The case for their inclusion for the purposes of the benefits of the Act* (*Home Savings Grant Act, 1966*).

Education is a 'grass roots' matter and communication to the member will be greatly facilitated by the new New South Wales Credit Union newspaper, *Quest*. Another task for A.F.C.U.L. may be to facilitate *Quest*'s distribution to the other States, perhaps as an example of what can be achieved.

The development of management techniques in the movement will proceed with increasing professionalism. The standardisation of accounting procedures is already well advanced in New South Wales but the full potential has not yet been realised in this computer age. The development of new services will require continuous review: for example, credit union credit cards, 'lines of credit' up to a prearranged amount, accounts payment services, instant and emergency loans, instant withdrawal facilities, 'low cost' education loans.

One of the most exciting advances in management has been mooted by A.F.C.U.L. It envisages the production of a standardised E.D.P. programme suitable for all credit unions in Australia which belong to a credit union league. It is suggested that even new credit unions should avail themselves of the programme and at one stroke reduce the clerical work load to a fraction of its present state and increase the information available to the credit union directors.

In all of these areas of management and promotion the United States and Canadian credit unions have made progress, and the movement in the South-West Pacific region has access to this and other experience through Cuna International and Cuna Mutual Insurance Society.

As in the United States, A.F.C.U.L. might also be expected to lend support to other consumer organisations and to sponsor 'Truth-in-Lending' legislation. The leagues and the individual credit unions are usually at some pains to point out to borrowing members the effective rates of interest actually charged on their own lending arrangements. But there is room for improvement here, as the 'best practice' is not always followed, and there is no substitute for continuous educational effort to encourage borrowers to measure carefully costs and benefits.

The policies of the A.F.C.U.L. must also recognise the environmental position within the South Pacific, and the close proximity to Asia. This is a challenge and a responsibility. For example, one of the primary objectives of the South Pacific Association of Credit Union Leagues is to sponsor leader training in credit union techniques at the Bergengren School in Fiji. The 'family system' in a community poses special problems and credit union organisation gives new opportunities. Some Australian groups (e.g. Torres Strait Islanders) may benefit from attendance at the School.

It would appear that the bitter controversy and misunderstanding between the credit union movement and the banks in the U.S.A. will be avoided in this region. In the early 1960s the rising success of the credit unions in the personal lending field contributed to a change in bank thinking here. Changes in established practice were introduced by banks, with material security in instalment loans ostensibly being reduced to a minimum, or even eliminated. Banks may have been jealous of this amateur encroachment on their own domains! However, the banks have found that credit union accounts are valuable, and they are frequently more stable than many others. There is no doubt, however, that the Australian credit union movement, and some other financiers, will face increasing competition in instalment credit operations from the banking system in the next decade. However, moves to impose restrictions on credit unions similar to those already imposed on banks will tend to defeat the whole social purpose of the movement. The credit union movement has already taken steps to underwrite its own liquidity through the formation of Centrals in Victoria and New South Wales; and the transfer of funds exists, to a lesser extent, in some other States. Further, a stabilisation fund is proposed for New South Wales. These developments could become Australia-wide through the Federation. There is no doubt that self-help of this kind will be more effective than liquidity ratios if most credit unions can be induced to join a league unless, of course, these ratios are proposed for all financial intermediaries as part of a general monetary control.[4]

The rather confused position regarding the taxation of credit unions in Australia and the effect of the taxation imposed on some credit unions since the late 1950s has had some adverse consequences. Members have been reluctant to pay the Taxation Commissioner out of their surplus. Hence the policy of 'minimising' the surplus has led to more limited reserves than might otherwise have been accumulated. It is a tribute to credit union management that deficiencies on liquidation in credit unions run by mem-

[4] For a discussion of liquidity ratios see N. Runcie, 'Some Thoughts on Protecting Depositors', *Credit*, Quarterly Review of the Finance Houses Association, London, April 1960. The author is critical of this proposal in connection with the operation of U.K. finance companies. But similar ratios are not proposed for Australian finance companies. Is this proposal, then, discriminatory action against credit unions? It may be that co-operatives are particularly exposed; but there is a big difference in the rate of the cash return flow between building societies and credit unions. It may be that additional protection to that required for small depositors in private sector companies is needed. But the evidence should be brought forward.

bers are almost unknown in the movement in Australia so far. The development of heavy stamp duties by State Governments is a burden which the credit unions share with other enterprises in Australia; some aspects of this development are causing concern, and some measures (for example, the discriminatory Victorian stamp duties for loans carrying interest at more than 9 per cent effective and the Tasmanian $1\frac{1}{2}$ per cent stamp duty on the amount advanced above $200) vitally affect credit union operations. By way of contrast the West Australia Government abolished stamp duties on credit union receipts in 1967.

A.F.C.U.L. and its constituent Leagues are concerned to suggest *guidelines* for credit union operations for three main reasons. First, these policies guide the formation of new credit unions and assist the directors who may not have had previous credit union experience. Second, these policies give an image of the credit union movement in the community and effectively embody its ethical code. Third, the policies are designed to achieve maximum growth of the movement as a whole.

The interest rates recommended are 5 per cent on deposits and 1 per cent per month on loans; and a portion of any surplus may be rebated to borrowers. Credit union experience is that borrowings are not greatly affected by the *initial* level of the borrowing charge up to this point; 1 per cent has the advantage of simplicity and ease of understanding to the borrower and is most convenient for clerical operations. Criticism of this policy comes from 'low rate' credit unions and from 'high rate' credit unions. The interest rate policy may lack flexibility and allowance for the situation of the individual credit union; it may be framed to cover the weaker parish and community credit unions rather than the stronger industrial credit unions; but it does possess simplicity until research and experience accumulate and there is a larger and more sophisticated movement.

Although there are many interests in common with the rest of the co-operative movement there are some sources of apparent conflict (e.g. over liquidity ratios). In the event, the credit union movement has chosen the path of separate development on two main grounds: first, that specialisation in debt financing and the encouragement of savings are in the interests of the growth of the movement; and second, that conflicts of interest may arise between the credit union members as such and the other co-operative activities. It is unlikely that the policies of the main Leagues will be modified in the near future on these issues; but it is also apparent that these attitudes reflect the present stage of development of the credit union movement.

In summary, the organisation of the credit union movement has taken on shape with the recent formation of the Leagues and the Associations. Policies are still being developed, but the ultimate aims are embodied in the nature of the movement. It is paradoxical that measures which have threatened its existence and growth have provided a stimulus and 'a reason for existence'. For the movement is essentially a democratic type of movement which has international affiliations. It could be a political force, but, apart from conventional lobbying, it has shown no such inclination. At every stage of its development growth has been hampered by a shortage of trained leaders. This training is one of the benefits to society of the movement. But, at home and abroad, the main aim of the movement is economic well-being. There is no doubt that the credit unions can make a significant contribution through the encouragement of savings and the development of sound personal loan plans; in both the prospects of expansion are a challenge in all the countries in the South-West Pacific.

Appendix A

EXTRACT FROM THE CONSTITUTION OF THE AUSTRALIAN FEDERATION OF CREDIT UNION LEAGUES (1966)

4. Objects

(a) To maintain the present high standard of credit union organisation, operation and supervision.
(b) To publicise the credit union movement and maintain such publicity organs as may be necessary and incidental thereto.
(c) To promote the organisation of credit unions both by direct effort and in co-operation with other agencies having similar purposes.
(d) To encourage and assist in the organisation of city and district chapters of credit unions and of credit union leagues.
(e) To establish and maintain such central agencies as may from time to time be deemed necessary to the effective operation of this Federation and its objectives.
(f) To receive by gift or will, money or other property and to distribute it as may be deemed best for the objectives of this Federation and to do any and all other things necessary and proper in connection with or incidental to any of the foregoing and not inconsistent with the laws of the land and without pecuniary profit to anyone.
(g) To adopt rules and regulations amongst the members of the Federation for the conduct of its affairs and the affairs of its constituent members in conformity with its purposes and spirit of the Federation as herein set forth.
(h) To do or perform any one or more of the acts or things herein set forth within the various States and Territories of the Commonwealth of Australia.
(i) The enumeration of specific objects or powers shall not be deemed to limit or restrict, in any manner, the general powers of the Federation and the enjoyment and exercise thereof.

(j) To make approaches to the Commonwealth Government and/or the State Governments, and/or any outside bodies for the general welfare and benefit of the credit union movement in Australia.

(k) To seek to bring about a separate District of CUNA International Incorporated, embracing Australia, New Zealand, Fiji and Indonesia, Malaysia and the British areas of Borneo, together with all islands and island groups south of 10°N. latitude and bounded by 95°E. longitude in the west and the International Date Line in the east but excluding any portion of the Philippines situated therein.

14

Conclusion: Some Tentative Findings

by Neil Runcie

1. Growth of the Credit Union Movement in the South-West Pacific

The credit union movement in the South-West Pacific region has the opportunity both to develop a useful financial service in the area and to play a role in relationship to neighbouring areas, including notably South-East Asia. The idealism of the movement and the underlying philosophy of self-help is well suited to the training of social leaders; but full advantage will not be obtained unless a sense of social leadership is combined with the development of managerial skills. While credit union leaders are aware of these opportunities the movement remains small and limited by the scarcity of managerial talent. This is the essence of the opportunities for growth which form the theme of this concluding chapter. This survey attempts to provide some tentative findings.

A critique of credit union development in the South-West Pacific would require more knowledge and appraisal than is available from the studies in this volume. Several areas of activity (e.g. Western Samoa) have been omitted pending further research; while more extensive studies of credit unions in New South Wales and Victoria have been initiated. Nevertheless, we have made a start in this volume with providing guide-posts to assist current thought about credit unions, both within and outside the movement in the region. Management technique in credit unions in this region of the world is unsophisticated. For example, few credit unions have developed measures of their market potential in money terms for either 'savings' or 'loans' and probably none has carried out surveys of the financial needs of its members. The challenge of immediate need in all the territories of the region has preoccupied available talent. The establishment period of the credit union movement in the region, which this survey examines, has been characterised by doing: the planning of development has been essentially pragmatic, but surprisingly rapid growth has been achieved recently.[1]

The number of registered operating credit unions in Australia in the post-war period is summarised in table 1. These statistics are provisional and will be clarified by further research. For example, it should be noted that a number of unregistered societies have operated and, in particular, in Victoria there were at least 15 such societies in existence in 1954.[2] However, the dominance of the New South Wales credit union movement in Australia up to 1960 is apparent. It is only in the early 1960s that an Australia-wide credit union movement emerged and the New South Wales portion of registered credit unions declined from 70 per cent in 1960 to 54 per cent in 1966. The successful formation of A.F.C.U.L. in 1966 marks the end of the establishment period although weakness of the movement in some states may be an early restraint on the emergence of a new phase of operations.

The dominance of the New South Wales credit unions in the establishment period is further revealed in the membership of reporting credit unions in table 2. These statistics do not include the members of 'non-reporting' credit unions which are those which lag in sending annual returns to the authorities; and, in general, we believe these omissions to be of the newer and of the smaller credit unions and, in the aggregate, their omission represents a minor understatement. Thus, in 1961 the N.S.W. members were 77 per cent of the Australian aggregate while in 1966 the corresponding percentage had fallen to 67 per cent. A similar pattern is revealed in table 3 which relates to advances.

The number of operating credit unions in Fiji has exceeded the number operating in New South Wales almost from the inception of the Fijian development. The impressive growth of community credit unions in the island group is summarised in table 4. However, since 1958, credit union membership in N.S.W. has outstripped that in Fiji and, of course, the financial resources of the N.S.W. credit unions were much greater.

Further, the growth of saving clubs and of savings and loan societies in Papua and New Guinea is not less impressive. In fact this two-tiered devel-

[1] The period up to 1967–8 appears comparable to the 'establishment period' up to 1934–5 in the U.S.A. where the organisation of CUNA and the Federal Credit Union Act both became effective in 1934.

[2] These societies were presumably using the legal form of an association with trustees; it is believed that most of these societies have subsequently registered.

TABLE 1 AUSTRALIA: REGISTERED OPERATING CREDIT UNIONS, 1945–67

Years Ended June	Queensland	N.S.W.	Victoria	Tasmania	South Australia	Western Australia	A.C.T.	Total
1945	—	2	1	—	—	—	—	3
1946	—	10	1	—	—	—	—	11
1947	—	20	1	—	—	—	—	21
1948	—	25	1	—	—	—	—	26
1949	—	28	1	—	1	—	—	30
1950	2	34	1	—	1	—	—	38
1951	2	43	1	—	1	—	—	47
1952	2	48	1	—	1	—	—	52
1953	2	48	1	—	1	—	—	52
1954	3	59	1 prov.	—	1	—	—	64
1955	3	72	8	—	1	—	—	84
1956	3	82	14	—	1	—	—	100
1957	3	88	18	—	1	—	2	112
1958	3	98	26	4 prov.	3	—	2	136
1959	3	113	31	4 prov.	3	—	3	157
1960	6	123	39	4 prov.	3	—	4	179
1961	6	130	57	7	4	4	4	212
1962	6	137	72	7	4	6	5	237
1963	9	153	86	8	4	8	5	273
1964	15	181	105	12	6	11	5	335
1965	19	220	127	13	9	14	6	398
1966	23	250	144	13	10	16	6	462
1967	27	279	152	16	11	17	7	509

Notes: prov. Provisional.

TABLE 2 AUSTRALIA: MEMBERSHIP OF REPORTING CREDIT UNIONS, 1945–67

Years Ended June	Queensland	N.S.W.	Victoria	Tasmania	South Australia	Western Australia	A.C.T.	Total
1945	—	n.a.	n.a.	—	—	—	—	n.a.
1946	—	193	n.a.	—	—	—	—	n.a.
1947	—	932	n.a.	—	—	—	—	n.a.
1948	—	2,041	n.a.	—	—	—	—	n.a.
1949	—	3,981	n.a.	—	n.a.	—	—	n.a.
1950	131	6,032	n.a.	—	126	—	—	n.a.
1951	148	8,443	n.a.	—	234	—	—	n.a.
1952	172e.	9,871	n.a.	—	310	—	—	n.a.
1953	188	10,792	n.a.	—	469	—	—	n.a.
1954	256	11,726	n.a.	n.a.	603	—	—	n.a.
1955	343e.	14,794	292	n.a.	710	—	—	n.a.
1956	374e.	16,220	944	n.a.	806	—	—	n.a.
1957	396	20,142	1,396	n.a.	918	—	n.a.	n.a.
1958	431	22,527	2,009	n.a.	1,069	—	n.a.	n.a.
1959	441	27,171	2,858	n.a.	1,241	—	n.a.	n.a.
1960	1,129e.	31,636	4,025	n.a.	1,476	—	207	n.a.
1961	1,324	36,488	6,123	902	(2,000)e.	348	279	47,464
1962	1,498	42,619	7,827	1,403	(2,700)e.	894	544	67,485
1963	1,982	53,536	10,041	1,740	(3,450)e.	2,436	657	73,842
1964	3,203	74,607	12,841	2,715	(5,200)e.	3,841	812	103,219
1965	4,689	92,199	16,727	3,631	(6,300)e.	7,687	979	132,212
1966	6,866	111,479	20,756	4,622	(8,100)e.	9,257	1,600	162,680
1967	10,707	133,118	24,952	4,838	99,15	11,900	2,286	196,960

Notes: e. Estimated.
n.a. Not available.

TABLE 3 AUSTRALIA: CREDIT UNION ADVANCES OUTSTANDING, 1945–67 ($'000) (For Reporting Credit Unions)

Year Ended June	Queensland	N.S.W.	A.C.T.	Victoria *a*	Tasmania	South Australia	Western Australia	Australia
1945	—	n.a.	—	n.a.	—	—	—	n.a.
1946	—	10	—	n.a.	—	—	—	10e.
1947	—	59	—	n.a.	—	—	—	59e.
1948	—	142	—	n.a.	—	—	—	142e.
1949	—	316	—	n.a.	—	n.a.	—	316e.
1950	7	516	—	n.a.	—	4	—	527e.
1951	13	999	—	n.a.	—	10	—	1,022e.
1952	20	1,073	—	n.a.	—	18	—	1,111e.
1953	17	1,206	—	n.a.	—	38	—	1,271e.
1954	18	1,340	—	n.a.	n.a.	61	—	1,439e.
1955	20	1,616	—	43	n.a.	80	—	1,759e.
1956	22	1,922	—	139	n.a.	102	—	2,185e.
1957	25	2,386	n.a.	164	n.a.	126	—	2,701e.
1958	27	2,816	4	223	n.a.	177	—	3,247e.
1959	32	3,242	6	271	n.a.	245	—	3,796e.
1960	64	3,844	14	414	n.a.	350	—	4,686e.
1961	103	4,770	19	673	81	473	28	6,147
1962	167	6,039	28	1,000	188	600	80	8,102
1963	294	8,481	51	1,529	310	800	309	11,774
1964	561	13,216	74	2,290	587	1,144	774	18,646
1965	839	18,690	112	3,212	983	1,936	1,598	27,370
1966	1,192	24,152	184	4,420	1,290	2,541	2,501	36,280
1967	1,400e.	31,264	438	5,868	1,889	2,800e.	3,572	47,231e.

Notes: *a* Victorian series includes all assets other than land and buildings and involves some slight overstatement.
n.a. Not available.
e. Estimated.

TABLE 4 GROWTH OF CREDIT UNIONS IN FIJI, 1954–67

Year Ended 31 December	Credit Unions	Membership	Savings	Outstanding Loans	Reserves	Total Assets
	No.	Nc.	£F	£F	£F	£F
1954	66	8,347	20,912	16,328	766	22,396
1955	139	16,623	62,946	56,710	2,283	67,910
1956	187	22,446	103,174	97,658	3,814	112,816
1957	220	23,858	128,151	122,211	5,075	138,932
1958	231	24,143	137,495	130,622	6,284	150,409
1959	240	24,244	160,232	151,680	7,449	173,567
1960	252	25,239	195,345	188,617	8,832	215,344
1961	262	26,934	241,027	234,906	11,464	268,688
1962	274	28,970	310,815	308,681	13,118	342,529
1963	286	30,320	371,138	365,251	15,151	418,064
1964	288	32,407	452,849	437,386	17,114	504,150
1965	299	32,392	511,949	502,440	16,503	581,278
1966	303	32,596	534,596	539,202	17,142	613,973
1967	307	33,465	591,566	590,852	21,673	678,199

Note: £1F. — $2·5 Aust. (1954–66)
Source: Fiji Credit Union League.

opment in the area has been both better planned and more experimental in approach than elsewhere. Given the less developed financial system in Fiji and in Papua and New Guinea, the contribution of credit unions appears relatively more significant than in Australia and New Zealand. However, at this stage, a detailed economic appraisal of the contribution of credit unions in these areas is not undertaken pending further research beyond that carried out for this survey.

In part, the aim of this survey was to record some of the contemporary history of the movement. It revealed in Australia one very early credit union formation by international standards. The Co-operative Credit Bank of Victoria was formed in 1905 (before the first credit union in the U.S.A.) and it registered under the Victorian Provident Societies Act 1890 to supply the credit needs of a group of civil servants; this institution had the essential bond of association for lending purposes which distinguishes credit unions. The same society continues to operate under the 1953 Victorian Co-operation Act as The Co-operative Credit Society of Victoria. At a much later stage, in New South Wales, an unregistered credit union appears to have operated for several years prior to World War Two in a Sydney suburb. But these isolated 'happenings' were not responsible for the emergence of a credit union movement. It is surprising that this early local initiative and example was not more influential. In the event, imitation and stimulus from abroad were to prove far more important in establishing the credit union movement in Australia.

Not surprisingly, the New Zealand survey revealed greater continuity with the English co-operative tradition than elsewhere in the region. The evolution of the modern credit union through friendly societies, and the earlier existence of money clubs, perhaps reflects greater dependence on English legislation and a more active general co-operative movement. Nevertheless, as in Australia, the emergence of a movement as such derives from the North American model and the stimulus and direct interest of CUNA International, Inc. and its affiliates. Without the latter support, and support from Fiji and Australia, the New Zealand movement would have been even more limited in scope and achievement.

2. The Concept of the Credit Union

Six main views of the concept of a credit union arising from this survey are distinguished below. Credit unions are variously seen as:

(a) small co-operative banks;

(b) co-operative welfare organisations;
(c) small loans and savings organisations to relieve financial hardship;
(d) part of the consumer co-operative movement;
(e) staff welfare organisations; and,
(f) co-operative instalment credit financiers.

These views are an analytic device to trace the evolution of the concept of a credit union in the region context; several subsidiary classifications are developed which have important relevance to the Australian discussions. But it is believed that the various concepts have wider applicability.

The concept of a credit union as a small co-operative bank immediately places credit unions in both an historical and a modern context. On the one hand credit unions are linked with the nineteenth century development of people's banks, and, on the other hand, they are struggling in the third quarter of the twentieth century to evolve more along the lines of the modern bank.

Historically, the notion of a credit union owes much to Robert Owen and the co-operative movement in England and its European counterparts, and to the Schulze-Delitszch and to the Raiffeisen societies in Germany. The writings emanating from these sources influenced Desjardins when he came to establish the first Canadian credit union, Caisse Populaire de Levis, in 1900. From these origins, West Germany and Quebec possess two of the most powerful co-operative financial systems in western countries.[3] The development of credit unions in the less developed economies, such as Papua and New Guinea, is in line with this conception of a small co-operative banking movement, as was the Co-operative Credit Bank of Victoria in 1905.

However, the mid-twentieth century challenge to the development of credit unions as a co-operative banking movement comes from other pressures. From the economic point of view the modern bank exists to:

(a) mobilise a portion of the community's savings and make it available to producers and to consumers;
(b) provide the community with its most convenient means of payment; and,
(c) create credit subject to official supervision.

Credit union banking development arises from all three functions and calls for further comment. First, credit unions mobilise savings, and the existence

[3] For a brief history of the movement see J. Dublin, *Credit Unions: Theory and Practice*, chapter 9, Wayne State University Press, 1966.

of credit unions with surplus funds has led to the emergence of credit union Centrals with machinery for transferring funds to other credit unions in need of funds and to other types of co-operative. Further, success in fund raising, as well as in the granting of loans, has led to pressure to widen the range of purposes for which credit unions may lend. Second, the move towards a chequeless society, computerised accounting and the scope for local and universal credit union credit cards offers scope, not only for the further development of credit union account payment services, but for the development of the essential banking function (viz. providing a means of payment). Third, the growth of credit unions along these lines must bring them into closer contact with, and supervision by, governmental authorities.[4] Further, the ability of credit unions to create credit will be enhanced by developments along the lines envisaged in the second comment above.

The second view of credit unions, as co-operative welfare organisations or as extensions of same, is partly linked with the English friendly society development, and is the view taken by some legislators of the nature of the movement. In line with the philanthropic movement, some of the earliest credit unions were formed by friendly societies in Australia and New Zealand. The emphasis on the desirability of unpaid voluntary directors partly springs from this source of the conception of the movement. The severe limitations which earlier legislators (e.g. in N.S.W.) placed on the purposes and the maximum loan was probably influenced by this view.

Yet another variation of the welfare concept of a credit union springs from church participation (especially by Roman Catholic clerics) in support of the movement. The welfare concept of a credit union in this context partly explains the smallness and motivating spirit behind some of the parish credit unions. However, this view of the nature of a credit union does not explain the widespread evolution from parish to community credit unions, and the expansionist philosophy of the Antigonish movement especially as expounded by Father Gallagher in N.S.W. It does not explain the pioneering development of community credit unions on Fiji by Father Ganey.

The third concept of a credit union, as a small loans and savings organisation to relieve financial hardship, is deeply rooted in the historical origins of the movement. It was poverty which stimulated the formation of

[4] In the U.S.A., Senator Patman has suggested that credit unions be given the right to operate chequeable deposit accounts; see J. Dublin, op. cit., p. 195.

a new institution by Raiffeisen in Germany (1864, at Heddesdorf) and by Desjardins in Quebec (1900, at Levis). Similarly, philanthropist Edward A. Filene was so impressed with co-operative savings and loans societies among the poor farmers of India that he supported the formation of the first U.S.A. credit union in Massachusetts in 1908 to overcome poverty. He subsequently became the outstanding benefactor of the movement. The difference, compared with the welfare concept, is the emphasis on self-help as the essence of the movement. The evolution of the Raiffeisen societies in Germany turned on this point when the wealthy backers of the movement lost interest. The concept of regular savings, or at least a savings plan, belongs to this self-help philosophy which has become a feature of the movement.

The fourth view of credit unions, as part of the consumer co-operative movement, is more complex and it consists of two main streams of thought. First, there are the credit unions which have been formed following the establishment of a retail co-operative and which remain either directly or indirectly linked with the retailing venture. Secondly, there is the Antigonish co-operative development which sees the credit union as the central part of a general co-operative development aimed at improving the education and welfare of members.

A paradox in co-operative development of credit facilities has been the lack of interest of retailing co-operatives, with a few exceptions, in credit unions. Where co-operative retailers provide banking and credit facilities for members this lack of interest is not surprising and helps to explain the near-absence of credit unions in the United Kingdom, where perhaps a fifth of the population belongs to a retail co-operative. But the credit union movement, in turn, has evinced a desire to avoid initiative in forming retail and other co-operatives, except in the insurance field and in Antigonish-inspired credit unions. The apparent inconsistency in credit union behaviour is explained by the credit union view that effort is best concentrated on the specialised functions of funds raising and lending. Again, although some housing co-operatives have formed credit unions there has been little reverse initiative. The credit union movement tends, perhaps wisely, to be preoccupied with its specialist function.

The fifth view of credit unions, as staff welfare organisations, helps to explain the rapid growth of the industrial or employee credit unions. These credit unions are based on a single employer who sees such advantages from the credit union as staff attraction and retention, the elimination of staff welfare funds, the encouragement of staff initiative and a restraint on strike action. Many employer-based credit unions receive either direct or indirect assistance, such as pay-roll deductions, at no charge for regular savings and loan repayments, the use of premises at little or a nominal charge, employer indulgence for staff time spent on credit union work. Although some employer representation on credit union boards is occasionally to be found either directly or indirectly, this feature negates the essential self-help feature of credit unions. Such credit unions are generally not interested in the movement as a whole.

The initiative in the formation of industrial credit unions in Australia has been almost wholly from employees who have contemplated the costs and benefits of co-operative instalment credit including the provision of attractive deposit facilities and the convenience of credit union loans. Nevertheless, highly competitive instalment credit financing exists from private enterprise and, although there are and were notable high cost areas (e.g. some second mortgage financing), there has been at least less publicity for loan shark activities than in many other countries. Thus, generally, industrial credit unions have been able to develop as semi-independent institutions with limited and passive employer patronage.

The sixth view of a credit union is as a co-operative instalment credit financier. The growth of the demand for instalment credit facilities has been very rapid in the post-war years in most advanced western countries. The boom in the demand for consumer durable goods, and for motor cars in particular, has opened up new financing opportunities. Paradoxically, the demand for instalment credit facilities is directly, and not inversely, related to the income level (subject to some qualifications). In the Australian instalment credit boom of the post-war years credit unions have lagged; they represent only a minor portion of the total volume of financing. Nevertheless, motor car and other consumer durable financing have come to occupy a significant portion of the total credit union lending.

Again, at least two views of the desired pattern of lending development are to be found. On the one hand there is the narrow view of the range of purposes for which credit unions should be allowed to lend; and, on the other hand, there is a broad view. The narrow view wishes to assign a function to credit unions as a particular type of instalment credit financier (i.e. for certain types of loan only); while the broad view sees credit unions evolving into new forms of lending as fund raising permits along the lines of a co-operative bank. In Australia, the controversy over credit union recognition as a savings institution for the Commonwealth Government's home savings grants is an illustration of one facet of this controversy.

Jack Dublin in his review of credit union development in the U.S.A. has put the issue in these terms:[5]

'In winning the day for a Federal Credit Union Act, the credit union movement lost a major battle.

'Instead of laying the foundations for development of a co-operative people's banking system, the movement began to build on a narrow, small-loan framework.

'Rules and regulations now govern every conceivable aspect of federal credit union management. Page upon page of instructions keep elected officials and employees well inside the small-loan limitations, and warning signals are quickly raised if a credit union ventures to make a loan that approaches the legal limits.

'In 1964, at the initiative of the bureau, the Federal Credit Union Act was amended to give federal credit unions the right to invest in other federal co-operative agencies and other corporations wholly owned by the government. This was the first substantial expansion of investment powers for federal credit unions since 1937, and it could make the next step easier in moving towards a credit union-owned, movement-controlled federal co-operative agency which could combine the functions of central banking and share protection, using the interlending experience of central credit unions and the techniques of stabilisation programmes in credit union rescue operations.'

With a background of experience of credit union development in an underdeveloped economy (i.e. Tanzania), Dublin argues that U.S. credit unions have been placed in a strait-jacket and advocates a broader approach. He states:[6]

'It is difficult to say exactly what shape the co-operatives of any country will take. The possibilities for different types of co-operatives are practically limitless. Why shouldn't credit unions be the financial centre of other co-operatives owned by their members? Why shouldn't there be a credit union available to accept investments from other corporations—or make loans to them?'

The various main concepts of a credit union outlined above are distinguished for two main reasons: first, to outline some of the main operating ideas found in and about the credit union movement; and second, to suggest by comparison some of the limitations implicit in each approach. The variety of significant concepts found reflects the establishment phase

[5] op. cit., pp. 154–5, 158.
[6] ibid., pp. 51–2.

of the credit union movement in the South-West Pacific; but other possible types of credit union organisation may develop. Nevertheless, the concepts outlined above appear to be the most significant.

3. Opportunities for Growth

The first part of this chapter advanced the view that the credit union movement in the South-West Pacific region had, after a long period of struggle in the post-war years, just completed the establishment phase of its operations in the second half of the 1960s. In the second part it was argued that various operating concepts of a credit union could be distinguished and that each had played a part in the development of thought about credit unions. Pending further research this later discussion was based mainly on Australian experience and thus really only constitutes a set of hypotheses about the movement in the region. The concluding part identifies some of the controversial issues about the development of the movement.

(a) *Credit Unions as Small Inefficient Organisations*

There are some who take the view that credit unions are small inefficient organisations. Yet, in the market economy, the test of their efficiency is their ability to survive and to grow in the face of severe competition from much larger financial institutions. The critics point to subsidised elements and unfair competitive advantages possessed by credit unions in the form of, for example:

(i) voluntary labour;
(ii) 'no charge' payroll deductions;
(iii) nominal charges for the use of premises;
(iv) government subsidies for promotion; and,
(v) taxation advantages.[7]

Are credit unions such inefficient organisations that they could not exist without these 'subsidies'? In the absence of competition it is fairly clear that credit unions could raise their charges significantly without greatly affecting demand; that is, the demand for their services tends to be 'price inelastic'. The impact of competition varies significantly between economies; but highly competitive rates exist from the banking system and from some large finance companies in some economies (e.g. in Australia) for some classes of business. The particular package of services differs between

[7] For a critical account of these advantages see R. T. Patterson, *The Tax Exemption of Co-operatives* (2nd ed.), University Publishers, New York, 1961.

financiers and there is imperfect knowledge and mobility between markets by credit users. Thus, although credit unions could raise their charges by a margin in most economies, they are not profit-maximising institutions and the existence of these 'subsidies' does not necessarily represent an inability to meet the 'test of the market'. The 'subsidies' are, in part, benefits of the bond of association which also imposes costs in the form of a limited market. Thus the bond of association, rather than credit union inefficiency, tends to impose an atomistic structure on the credit union movement. Moreover, there are social benefits arising from the credit union movement, for example, in the form of 'leader training', important 'lender of last resort' facilities for some classes of borrower, and desirable effects on 'debtor morality' which the market test does not measure.

(b) *The Link with CUNA International, Inc. and its Affiliates*

From the point of view of the movement in the South-West Pacific, the link with CUNA International, Inc., and its affiliates, has brought enormous advantages and some disadvantages. On the one hand, it has brought a humanist tradition combined with an internationalism which has particular appeal to the present stage of Australian and New Zealand development; it has brought an interest in management education which is part of the dynamic U.S.A. economy. Moreover, with the enormous scope for social experiment in the United States and access to oversea experience, it has a fund of specialised knowledge. On the other hand, the CUNA link has tended to cut the local credit union movements off from other co-operatives; it has brought a sense of autonomy associated with self-interest. Up to a point, the development of credit union self-interest has fostered the growth of the movement by minimising diversion of effort; but the other side of the coin has been some intolerance towards other types of co-operative, and some lack of inventiveness in fostering social experiment of a local nature.

(c) *The Role of the Government Regulatory Agency*

The role of the government regulatory agency in the U.S.A. has been critically reviewed by Jack Dublin and referred to earlier. It could be maintained that the agency of the N.S.W. State Government is the most developed regulatory agency in the region, and that perhaps it too combines both promotion and paternalism. The long history of legislative change in this state is the story of an attempt to produce viable enabling legislation and the state's movement towards a separate credit union act is a milestone in credit union development in the Antipodes. In simple matters, such as consistency between the model rules, the regulations and the statutory provisions, and details such as the complexity of the formation procedure, the Australian legislation reveals a shortage of skilled personnel (and of their available time) in the regulatory agencies. A similar deficiency exists in the absence of an official manual of credit union operations; but this does not necessarily reflect indifference. In the N.S.W. case it is surprising that the Registry has not prepared a manual on operations. However, there has been a conscious attempt to encourage the N.S.W. League to develop management services and training (via a financial grant). Also by retaining a tight rein on credit union formation through registration and by inspections of registered credit unions, the N.S.W. Registry has been attempting to ensure a sufficiently high management standard in the movement. Nevertheless, a 'full service' concept of the Registry's role would require the preparation of a manual of operations.[8]

(d) *The Interest Rate Dilemma*

There is an interest rate dilemma in the movement. This arises for a number of reasons. First, because the various credit union leagues have felt that it is desirable to have a policy (e.g. 1 per cent per month on loans and 5 per cent on deposits/shares) as a guide to new credit unions and as a means of projecting the image of the credit union movement in the community. Acceptance of these guide-lines by leagues has emerged, partly on advice from CUNA, to provide a margin for the services necessary for the growth of the movement. This policy does not recognise the diversity of the movement (e.g. between employer and community credit unions and even within these groups); nor does it recognise that the maximum growth of a credit union, and greatest member satisfaction, might be achieved by more diversity in the range of rates to suit individual situations. Here, there appears to be a case for a more flexible statement of league policy. Such a statement need not necessarily conflict with league opposition to 'high cost' credit unions which are considered to be in conflict with the idealism of the movement.

Second, the more fundamental aspect of the interest rate dilemma is the inevitable conflict in credit union operations between the interests of the borrowers and of the lenders. The reconciliation of this conflict is not easy.

[8] The League, or even the Registry, could probably have such a manual prepared on a contract basis by a large accounting firm if internal resources do not permit the necessary staff allocation.

A sufficiently high interest rate may be necessary to attract funds for expansion which is ultimately in the interests of a wider range of borrowers. What is a 'sufficiently high interest rate' will depend on the sensitivity of lenders to the interest rate paid, which will vary according to the credit union's situation (e.g. between parish and industrial credit unions), including desired growth rate and other factors. Further, one might expect some change in interest rate policy with the age and degree of market penetration of the credit union.

A third aspect of the interest rate dilemma arises from the lending policy of the credit union: if it minimises its lending risks it may be able to pay a higher deposit rate or charge a lower rate on lending. But 'low risk' credit unions are criticised for negating credit union philosophy.

The fourth aspect of the interest rate dilemma concerns the problems that arise when excess funds emerge in the credit union because one set of possible adjustments concern the interest rates charged on borrowing and on lending operations.

A fifth aspect of the interest rate dilemma arises from the single-rate principle which applies the same lending rate to all borrowers. This principle is generally but not universally accepted, and means that charges are not related to risks (e.g. differences in security offered) or costs (e.g. differences between small and large loans) or purpose (e.g. education loans might be thought socially desirable compared with some other borrowing).

Although there is a case for uniformity in interest rate policies, a case at least equally strong can be made for diversity in the movement, and over time. The solution to the 'interest rate dilemma' is the most critical test of the perspicacity of the individual credit union board. It raises a whole range of issues connected with funds management and all too frequently credit union boards are not aware of the range of alternative solutions.

(e) *The Emergence of Excess Funds*

The emergence of credit unions with excess funds in significant numbers is a major influence on the evolution of the credit union. One could argue that this is not a problem, as an objective of the credit union movement is to encourage savings. However, this represents a new problem in funds management, for excess funds must now be invested, because of their volume, at a rate equal to, or preferably greater than, the rate of interest paid on deposits, for otherwise the borrowing member is penalised. Thus, a greater emphasis on credit unions as savings institutions has involved pressure to widen the range of credit union investment opportunities; for example, it has led to the development of Centrals to facilitate the transfer of funds from surplus to deficit credit unions. Other influences which have enhanced credit unions as savings institutions are the development of life savings insurance for depositors and the emergence of credit union stabilisation funds.

Excess funds raise other problems in funds management besides the prima facie need for a widening of available investment opportunities. Funds may not be permanently in excess and the management of the credit union might decide that it is better not to take temporary action; for example, an extreme illustration might be to change interest rates for short-term reasons. Further, the nature of the problem posed by excess funds can be shown to depend on the stage of development of the credit union.

In the intermediate period, solutions to the excess funds problem may involve managerial problems and techniques in greater depth than when cash inflow and approved loan applications are matched. Examination of the following aspects is suggested:

(i) analysis of the cash inflow and projections for future accounting periods;
(ii) estimates of the 'market potential' for the credit union in both deposits and loans;
(iii) the devising of new loan plans to attract some of the market potential;
(iv) effects of different interest rates for various classes of lender (e.g. for over $10,000 and for non-member depositors);
(v) effects of the curtailment of deposit facilities;
(vi) investment risks and interest rates available on possible investments outside the credit union; and,
(vii) effects of various possible downward adjustments of deposit and of lending rates.

Of course, even prior examination of these issues may still not prevent excess funds from emerging, as not all factors affecting the flow of funds are within management's control.

The existence of attractive investment opportunities and of 'controls' considerably eases the problem but raises delicate problems of income allocation between depositors and borrowers. Further, there are costs in handling excess funds and risks of various kinds which suggest that, in the long run, the credit union should seek a positive net return from these funds. Otherwise the credit union has no future as a savings institution.

(f) *The Need for Reserves*

Why do credit unions need reserves?

First, where taxation of the surplus exists, the effect has been to shift the sources of funds pattern to a high capital gearing ratio (capital: total funds); thus, these credit unions are much more exposed than most other types of corporation to liquidation through losses. Reserves are a cushion against these risks; for example, if shareholders' funds are only 2 per cent of total funds and bad debts of more than 2 per cent of total funds are experienced, the credit union is exposed to liquidation and members may not be able to recover 100 per cent of their funds. Second, where credit unions carry their own mortality risks, there are the same possibilities of a bunching of losses which doubly expose the credit union to liquidation. Third, costs of operation rise in the process of liquidation and it would be prudent for the contingencies reserve to recognise this risk. Fourth, not all types of contingency can be defined in advance (e.g. retrospective stamp duty or other taxation) and reserves are partly for adverse uncertainties as distinct from known risks. Fifth, most corporations regard reserves as a survival fund. It is a provision for the future paid for by the present and past members, to ensure survival and growth which benefits some and perhaps most present members. For example, survival is the problem in the face of the unknown impact of the intensification of bank competition in the instalment credit area at rates highly competitive with those of credit unions; and growth, by new services to members, is an opportunity which may involve the risks of experiment. Sixth, the building up of reserves relieves the pressure on the credit committee; it enables a more venturesome policy and the acceptance of marginal risks in accordance with credit union philosophy. Seventh, because of the onerous nature of the obligations of credit union directors, the existence of small reserves may act as a brake on the willingness of professional people to serve in the movement.

There may be dangers in conventional wisdom of the kind outlined above. The pragmatic challenge of the credit union movement to sacred truths in received management doctrine is refreshing but not always penetrating. There may be a case for deficit financing over one or even two years, for example:

(i) in the establishment phase of a credit union, and

(ii) where it is planned to provide new services aimed at giving higher market penetration.

Although reserves may exist for (ii) they will generally not exist for (i) and, in this case, directors must be confident that the deficit will not adversely affect confidence in the credit union and its long-run growth.

Tardy recognition of bad debts and inaccurate methods of income deferral are special problems[9] which call for the attention of leagues and regulatory agencies, as well as the supervisory committees. It is the reserves other than these special provisions, which have been our concern above.

The alleged need to build up reserves, in the present for the future, means that present members are being asked to pay for future benefits; and these benefits are not necessarily in the form of a cash distribution to exactly the same group of members. Thus, it is frequently argued that future members should pay for future benefits. With the growth limits imposed on the credit union by its bond of association and the protection of its market by the same means, the credit union may be less in need of reserves than most commercial corporations. But this does not mean that they do not need *some* reserves for the reasons outlined above.

(g) *Democracy and the Principles of Consumers' Co-operation*

In an International Labour Office study, a co-operative is defined as:[10]

> 'An association of persons, usually of limited means, who have voluntarily joined together to achieve a common economic end through the formation of a democratically controlled business organisation, making equitable contributions to the capital required and accepting a fair share of the risks and benefits of the undertaking.'

This concept is further elaborated in what are known as 'the co-operative principles':[11]

(i) membership of the society must be fully voluntary and, within certain limits, open to everyone;
(ii) all members must have an equal voice;
(iii) all members make a roughly equal contribution to the capital of the society;
(iv) interest on shares is restricted and low;
(v) 'surplus' is distributed in proportion to the business done; and,
(vi) a co-operative must be owned and controlled by those who use it.

The emphasis in these views is on a democratic organisation for economic purposes. In general the democratic form is embodied in open membership,

[9] N. Runcie, 'The Measurement of Unearned Income: a General Theory', *Australian Economic Papers*, June–December 1964.
[10] *Co-operative Management and Administration*, I.L.O., 1960, p. 5.
[11] ibid. p. 7.

each member having one vote only, education of all members in co-operative thinking, and neutrality in race, religion and politics. The distinct economic features are embodied in limited interest on capital, patronage refunds (e.g. on purchases in a retail co-operative), selling for cash at 'fair market prices' and efforts to expand constantly.

While credit union philosophy embraces all of these principles, there are a number of features which call for special comment. First, the concept of a democratic organisation has a number of distinctive credit union features connected with its committee system. The supervisory committee is independent of the board of the credit union and is elected at annual meetings to report to members at the next annual meeting, or as required, on the management of the credit union. Most credit unions have supervisory committees and their operation is part of the built-in democracy of the credit union movement. Some supervisory committees adopt a narrow view of their function as account checkers; whereas a wider view, as auditors of the overall operation, is more in accord with democratic control. Moreover, a paid auditor is usually required to furnish a report and attest to the accuracy of the accounts. The main risk is that the supervisory committee will take up too much of the board's time and for this reason they are sometimes not elected till the first annual general meeting or sometimes later. However, there is no doubt that the supervisory committee may perform a useful role for the board, as well as for members, although it is sometimes a source of conflict and dissipation of energy which may not be in members' interests.

A similar practice, of electing the credit committee of the credit union at annual meetings, is more controversial and a large number of credit unions do not follow this practice; they make the credit committee a committee of the board. A compromise is sometimes followed with a mixture of board members and members elected direct to the credit committee by members. It is claimed on the one hand, for example by Mr Arneil, that the separately elected committee at the annual meeting relieves pressures on directors and preserves democratic control. On the other hand the writer believes that credit policy, interest rate policy and funds management are intimately related and that the board's control is undermined unless the credit committee's policies are firmly under its control. Expanding the size of the board helps to spread the directors' load; and membership of the credit committee for a period is a highly educative experience for any director. Too many elected committees enhance the possibility of conflict.

The co-operative principle of neutrality in race, religion and politics has rested rather heavily on the parish credit unions, although they may preserve this feature in their internal organisation. In consequence there has been a marked tendency for parish credit unions to convert to community credit unions and give all members of an area covered by a parish the benefits of membership. Sometimes a religious group breeds an intolerant attitude towards the ideas of others and vice versa: this sort of fervour ill becomes a philanthropic movement in an ecumenical age.

In co-operative and credit union literature the word 'education' is probably the one most misused. It most frequently means promotion of the business of the credit union or other co-operative. Nevertheless in the credit union area there is scope for consumer 'education', and financial counselling is probably the most important feature. Similarly, and somewhat paradoxically, in retail co-operatives there is a strong principle of encouraging cash payments; on the United Kingdom scene Margaret Digby comments:[12]

> 'Consumers' co-operatives, in their earlier years, did much to check the evil of credit trading by taking a stern line with their members and insisting on cash payments.'

Although these Victorian attitudes towards the use of credit have been substantially modified, they constitute some historical explanation of the tendency for credit unions to draw apart from the rest of the co-operative movement. The gap has been slow to heal, with adverse consequences on both sides.[13]

The education for directors is more ambitious. It involves more than the supply of information and it is aimed at improving management techniques. The appointment of a Director of Research at CUNA International Inc. is a progressive move in this direction. At the regional level, the Bergengren School in Fiji, which is supported by the South Pacific Association of Credit Union Leagues, and the residential and other schools organised by the New South Wales League are examples of attempts to meet the problem of education for management responsibilities. However, as these efforts and the efforts of chapter meetings tend to demonstrate, an excessive desire for autonomy seems to have inhibited the seeking of assistance from universities and other educational institutions. These forms of 'in-breeding' reflect a desire to insulate the credit union movement from

[12] M. Digby, *The World Co-operative Movement* (2nd ed.), Hutchinson University Library, 1960, p. 92.

[13] It is interesting to note Margaret Digby's criticism of the U.K. co-operative movement for its lack of support of credit unions, op. cit.

criticism which may serve to stimulate its efficiency but undermine 'the faith'.

Perhaps one of the significant advances has been the extensive development of financial ratios by Dr W. Polner of CUNA International Inc. The standardised nature of credit union operations makes the movement particularly suitable for managerial research along these lines. But more detailed research may reveal a variety of norms and ranges of operational efficiency. Again, for example, at what stage in growth should credit unions employ full-time staff? A few credit unions have pioneered the application of computers to their operations, but much research remains to be done both at the individual and the aggregative level to improve the quality of management. Nevertheless the education of directors has both democratic and economic features in the application of the principles of consumers' co-operation.

Finally, it is suggested that the application of co-operative principles requires us to see credit union evolution in Australia and New Zealand at present as a co-operative association of households, formed within a specific bond of association, which pools a portion of member households' savings and allocates the major portion of such savings as loans. Although the members of credit unions are individuals they are essentially concerned with the needs of households and certain recent extensions of membership have recognised this feature. The threefold aim remains their concern (i) to increase the efficiency of the individual household's management of surplus funds, (ii) to increase its ability to borrow funds and (iii) by these and other means to increase the household's welfare. Thus, although our survey reveals that credit unions are specialist financial institutions, their ultimate objectives are concerned with the improvement of consumer welfare in the broadest sense by the application of the principles of consumers' co-operation. On the other hand in both Fiji and Papua and New Guinea the credit unions are much more concerned to finance members' productive activities. This is to say, in both advanced and less advanced economies, credit unions 'teach people about money'.

Select Bibliography

1. Savings and Loan Societies in Papua and New Guinea

(a) *Books, Pamphlets, Articles, Theses*

Bailey, A. A., 'Credit Unions Down Under', *The Credit Union Magazine*, June 1965.

Collins, F. J., 'Savings and Lending Through Co-operation', *Australian Territories*, October 1966.

Coombs, H. C., 'Pennies and Politics—Reserve Bank in Papua–New Guinea', *New Guinea*, Vol. 1, No. 2., June–July 1965.

Elvery, A. W., 'Savings and Loan Societies in the Territory of Papua and New Guinea', *Australian Territories*, March 1962.

International Bank for Reconstruction and Development, *The Economic Development of the Territory of Papua and New Guinea*, John Hopkins Press, Baltimore, 1965.

Phillips, M. J., 'Savings and Loan Societies in Papua and New Guinea', *South Pacific Bulletin*, Vol. 14, No. 1, January 1964.

'Savings and Loan Societies—A Progress Report', *Australian Territories*, January 1965.

'The Introduction of Savings and Loan Societies in Papua–New Guinea', *Proceedings, Regional Technical Meeting on Economic Development and Capital Formation*, South Pacific Commission, Noumea, 12–22 March 1962.

(b) *Official Publications*

Registry of Savings and Loan Societies, *Annual Report of the Registrar*, 1962–1966/7.

What is a Savings and Loan Society? (in English, Pidgin English, Police Motu and Tolai Language).

Savings Clubs (in English, Pidgin English, Police Motu and Tolai language).
Reserve Bank of Australia, *Annual Reports*, 1960–7.
Savings and Loan Societies, *Ordinance* 1961–6.
Savings and Loan Societies, *Regulations*, 1962–3.
Savings and Loan Societies, *Standard Rules*.

2. Credit Unions in Other Pacific Territories

Belshaw, C. S., 'Institutions for Capital Formation and Distribution among Fijians', in *Capital, Savings and Credit in Peasant Societies*, Allen and Unwin, London, 1964. (Ed. Firth, R. W. and Yamey, B. S.)
Under the Ivi Tree—Society and economic growth in rural Fiji, Routledge and Kegan Paul, London, 1964.
Boyan, R. H., 'Savings and Investment (including Co-operatives and Loan Societies)', *Training Course on Incentives to Economic Development*, South Pacific Commission, Noumea, September 1965.
'What kind of Credit Society?', *Co-operatives Booklet No. 1*, South Pacific Commission, Noumea.
Burns, A. et al., *Report of the Commission of Enquiry into the Natural Resources and Population Trends of the Colony of Fiji*, Council Paper No. 1 of 1960, Government of Fiji.
Credit Union National Association, 'Credit Unions in the South Pacific', *The Credit Union Magazine*, April 1965.
Pitaduna Stainer, 'Savings and Loans Societies and the Western District Association in the Western Solomons', *Co-operatives Newsletter*, South Pacific Commission, Noumea, July 1965.
Spate, O. H. K., *The Fijian People: Economic Problems and Prospects*, Council Paper No. 13 of 1959, Government Press, Suva.
Stace, V. D., 'Co-operatives in relation to Capital Formation and Credit' *Proceedings*, Second Technical Meeting on Co-operatives, South Pacific Commission, Noumea, April 1961.

3. Credit Unions Elsewhere

Boyle, G., *The Poor Man's Prayer*, Helicon, Baltimore, 1962.
Braumann, F., *A Man Conquers Poverty*, CUNA, 1963.
Canadian Royal Commission on Banking and Finance (Porter Commission), *Report*, Queen's Printer, Ottawa, 1964.

Croteau, J. T., *The Economics of the Credit Union*, Wayne State University Press, 1963.

CUNA International Inc, *International Credit Union Yearbook* (annual), Madison, Wisconsin.

CUNA International Inc, *The Credit Union Magazine*, Madison, Wisconsin.

Dublin, J., *Credit Unions: Theory and Practice*, Wayne State University Press, 1966.

Mercure, G., *Credit Unions and Caisses Populaires*, Working Paper prepared for the Royal Commission on Banking and Finance, Queen's Printer, Ottawa, 1962.

Polner, W., *Operating Ratios, 1963*, CUNA International Inc, Madison, Wisconsin, 1965.

Dividends Paid by Credit Unions in the United States and Canada at the End of 1963, CUNA International Inc, Madison, Wisconsin, 1964.

Credit Union Officials in the South Pacific

Australia

The South Pacific Association of Credit Union Leagues

S. F. Arneil, President
The South Pacific Association of Credit Union Leagues
The Corso
Manly, N.S.W., Australia

Australian Federation of Credit Union Leagues

S. F. Arneil, President
Australian Federation of Credit Union Leagues
Thc Corso
Manly, N.S.W., Australia

Queensland

H. M. Marsh, Secretary
Queensland Co-operative Credit Union League
P.O. Box 79, Kedron
Brisbane, Queensland, Australia

New South Wales

L. J. Robinson, General Manager
N.S.W. Credit Union League
17 Burwood Road
Burwood, Sydney, N.S.W., Australia

Victoria

L. F. Magree, Secretary
Victorian Credit Co-operative Association Limited
Lombard House
157 A'Beckett Street
Melbourne, Victoria, Australia

Tasmania

D. Closs, President
Credit Union League of Tasmania
121 Collins Street
Hobart, Tasmania, Australia

South Australia

T. P. Fitzgerald, President
Credit Union League of South Australia
c/o P.O. Box 51
Greenacres, South Australia, Australia

Western Australia

R. Waite, President
Western Australia Co-operative Society Limited
Box H 524, G.P.O.
Perth, Western Australia, Australia

Australian Capital Territory

R. W. Parkes, President
Association of Credit Unions of the Australian Capital Territory
c/o 81 Archebald Street
Lyneha, Australian Capital Territory, Australia.

New Zealand

Colin Smith, Manager
New Zealand Credit Union League
Whitehall House
109 Collingwood Street
Hamilton, New Zealand
Post to: P.O. Box 585
Hamilton, New Zealand

Fiji

Joane Naisana, Managing Director
Fiji Credit Union League
P.O. Box 74, Pratt Street
Suva, Fiji Islands

Western Samoa

Sio Aukusitino, Managing Director
Western Samoa Credit Union League
P.O. Box 218 Lalovaea, Apia
Western Samoa

Papua and New Guinea

Papua and New Guinea Federation of Savings and Loan Societies Limited
P.O. Box 208
Rabaul
Territories of Papua and New Guinea
Daniel To Rot, President
Soapa Lusiata, Vice-President
Francis Molet, Secretary

Eastern Highlands League of Savings and Loan Societies Limited
P.O. Box 144
Goroka
Territories of Papua and New Guinea
Soso Subi, President

Ruipo, Vice-President
Stephen Golituwe, Manager

Gazelle League of Savings and Loan Societies Limited
P.O. Box 466
Rabaul
Territories of Papua and New Guinea
Meriba To Makala, President
Francis To Keret, Vice-President
Johnson Karangap, Manager

Registry of Savings and Loan Societies
Second Street
Lae
Territories of Papua and New Guinea
N. J. Mathews, Registrar
M. J. Samuel, Deputy Registrar